From the Island's Edge

From the Island's Edge

A Sitka Reader

Edited by Carolyn Servid

GRAYWOLF PRESS

Publication of this volume is made possible in part by a grant provided by the Minnesota State Arts Board through an appropriation by the Minnesota State Legislature, and by a grant from the National Endowment for the Arts. Significant additional support has been provided by the Andrew W. Mellon Foundation, the Lila Wallace–Reader's Digest Fund, the McKnight Foundation, and other generous contributions from foundations, corporations, and individuals. Graywolf Press is a member agency of United Arts, Saint Paul. To these organizations and individuals who make our work possible, we offer heartfelt thanks.

Published by Graywolf Press
2402 University Avenue, Suite 203
Saint Paul, Minnesota 55114
All rights reserved.

Printed in the United States of America.

ISBN 1-55597-213-6

9 8 7 6 5 4 3 2

Second Printing, 1995

From the Island's Edge : A Sitka Reader / edited by Carolyn Servid.
    p.   cm.
   ISBN 1-55597-213-6 (pbk.)
    1. Nature—Literary collections.   2. American literature—20th century.
I. Servid, Carolyn.
PS509.N3R44   1994
810.8'036—dc20   93-41089
                                         CIP

Acknowledgments

Although many of the contributions to this anthology appear for the first time in this volume, others have been previously published. We thank authors as well as publishers for their permission to reprint, and are pleased to acknowledge their cooperation.

John Luther Adams. "Resonance of Place (Confessions of an Out-of-Town Composer)" initially appeared in *Chorus!*, October 1992. A longer version with musical notations appeared in *North American Review*. Copyright © 1994 by John Luther Adams.

Jennifer Brice. "Lullaby for Lloyd" appeared first in a slightly different version in *Permafrost*, Spring 1992. Copyright © 1995 by Jennifer Brice.

Hugh Brody. "Family Trees" is from *Means of Escape* (Douglas & McIntyre, Canada, 1991). Copyright © 1991 by Hugh Brody.

Jerah Chadwick. "Drifters" was published for the first time in *Ergo*, the 1993 Seattle Bumbershoot Anthology. Copyright © 1993 by Jerah Chadwick.

Nora Marks Dauenhauer. "Memorial Day in Kiev" and "My Aunt Jennie's Bed" are published here for the first time. Copyright © 1995 by Nora Marks Dauenhauer.

Lauren Carroll Davis. "Singing the Fins" is published here for the first time. Copyright © 1995 by Lauren Carroll Davis.

Martha Demientieff. "Mental Health Meeting" is published here for the first time. Copyright © 1995 by Martha Demientieff.

Jim Dodge. "Aweigh" appeared first as a privately circulated broadside and is published here for the first time. Copyright © 1989 by Jim Dodge.

Ken Dola. "Dressing Out and Barking Knuckles" and "Between the Steens, the Trout Creeks, the Rising of the Sun" are published here for the first time. Copyright © 1995 by Ken Dola.

Stephanie Mills. "Making Amends to the Myriad Creatures" was first published in a longer version by the E. F. Schumacher Society in 1991. Copyright © 1991 by E. F. Schumacher Society (Box 76A RD3, Great Barrington, MA 01230) and Stephanie Mills.

Melinda Mueller. "Endurance" and "The Later Biography of Raoul Wallenberg" are published here for the first time. Copyright © 1995 by Melinda Mueller.

Gary Paul Nabhan. A longer version of "Hummingbirds and Human Aggression: A View from the High Tanks" first appeared in the *Georgia Review*, Summer 1992. Copyright © 1992 by Gary Paul Nabhan.

James M. Nageak. "Ayagumagalha, the Wanderer," a story told by Justus Usisana Mekiana and translated by James Nageak, is published here for the first time. Copyright © 1995 by James Nageak.

Richard K. Nelson. "Bringing in the Storm" is an excerpt from *The Island Within*, North Point Press, 1989. Copyright © 1989 by Richard K. Nelson.

Sheila Nickerson. "The Dolly Varden Char: Its Name, Its Dance, Its Prize" was first published in *Northern Review*, Winter 1993. Copyright © 1993 by Sheila Nickerson.

Chet Raymo. "A Measure of Restraint" is from *The Virgin and the Mousetrap*. Used by permission of Viking Penguin, a division of Penguin Books USA, Inc. Copyright © 1991 by Chet Raymo.

Pattiann Rogers. "The Family Is All There Is" is from *Splitting and Binding*, Wesleyan University Press, 1989. Reprinted by permission of the University Press of New England. Copyright © 1989 by Pattiann Rogers. "Emissaries" was first published in the *Georgia Review*, 1993. Copyright © 1993 by Pattiann Rogers.

William Pitt Root. "Song of Returnings" was published in *Striking the Dark Air for Music*, Atheneum, 1973. Copyright © 1973 by William Pitt Root.

Nanao Sakaki. "Let's Eat Stars" is published here for the first time. Copyright © 1995 by Nanao Sakaki.

Paul Shepard. "Three Green Thoughts" is excerpted from a longer essay, "Five Green Thoughts," which first appeared in *Massachusetts Review*, Summer 1980. Copyright © 1980 by Paul Shepard.

Gary Snyder. "Raven's Beak River: At the End" was first published in *Sulfur*, 1988. Copyright © 1992 by Gary Snyder.

William Stafford. "Roll Call" first appeared in *My Name Is William Tell*, Confluence Press, 1993. Copyright © 1993 by William Stafford. "In the All-Verbs Navaho World" was first published in *Holding onto the Grass*, Honeybrook Press, 1992. Copyright © 1992 by William Stafford.

Terry Tempest Williams. "Buried Poems" first appeared in *Coyote's Canyon*, Gibbs Smith, 1989. Copyright © 1989 by Terry Tempest Williams.

THIS BOOK commemorates ten years of a program that has linked together a few hundred people interested in wrestling with important human questions. In the face of those questions, bonds of respect and friendship have been created. Without those bonds, the Sitka Symposium on Human Values and the Written Word would not have sustained itself for a decade, and this book would not have come into being. It is dedicated, therefore, with gratitude to all who have nurtured the Symposium over the years—faculty and participants who have attended, and fellow planners who have devoted the time and energy to make it work.

Among the many people who have had a part, particular thanks must be extended to some key individuals. First to Don Muller, Cheryl Morse, and Marylin Newman, fellow founders who shared the vision of the program, collaborated to bring it into being, and created and served on the board of directors. To Evelyn Bonner, Linda Halfon, Tina Johnson, John Straley, and Steve Will—the Island Institute board that supported the idea of an anthology—my thanks. And to Dick Nelson and Lauren Davis for years of past service on the board and for advice on the book.

Gratitude also goes to the Alaska State Council on the Arts and the Alaska Humanities Forum for ongoing financial support, and to BP Exploration and the Lannan Foundation for support in particular years. Sheldon Jackson College has donated staff time and facilities throughout the history of the program. And Old Harbor Books, the birthplace of the Symposium, has provided service extraordinaire year after year.

Since the inception of the Symposium, Gary Holthaus has been one of its most enthusiastic spokesmen, offering suggestions and encouragement that strengthened the program as it evolved. When the notion of this anthology surfaced, he helped nudge it from idea into reality. Other invaluable support and advice came from Barry Lopez, who shares the vision behind the work of The Island Institute. Bill Kittredge and Ted Chamberlin offered counsel as the book took shape. Scott Walker and the staff at Graywolf Press understood why the collection should be published. Shawn Newell and Bob Mayberry helped with proofreading and editing. Thanks, thanks to all. And to Dorik Mechau, something far greater than gratitude for standing by—through all the work and doubts and questions—steady as a rock, believing.

Contents

Foreword

. . . We didn't know who we were; we didn't know our
identity. We had become like a shell; our values
were empty. When you don't know your identity,
where do you begin?

—Rachel Craig, Inupiaq Elder,
Kotzebue, Alaska

WHERE THE ELDERS began, in Kotzebue, years ago, was with stories,
the stories of the elders who still knew the old ways. After gathering the
elders to talk with them, holding long meetings during the day and
dancing late into the night, the contemporary Inupiat, according to
Rachel, recovered almost all the oral tradition. It has been recorded on
tape and published in books and transformed into classroom material.
What came from the stories, Rachel says, was "a sense of connectedness
with previous generations, and something to pass on." The importance
of the past and the sense of a future that needed to know the elders'
stories gave the Inupiat "a feeling we were doing good work because we
were doing it for others, for someone in future generations." Many of
those stories were about the Inupiaq understanding of the land, and the
relationship of the people to it; they told of how they lived on the land,
and what it meant to be so closely connected to it. The sense of time,
both past and future, and the sense of place, live in the stories of all our
cultures. We tell them so we will come to know ourselves and our place
in the world, to find that connectedness that Rachel tells us the Northwest Arctic Inupiat found.

Something of the urgency that drove the Inupiat has also driven a
handful of Alaskans in Sitka to bring together the best storytellers from

several cultures. Where, when the dominant culture has "become like a shell" and our "values are empty," do we begin? One place to begin is with the stories of our elders. Every summer for ten years the best writers and thinkers from the United States and Canada have met in Sitka to engage in intense conversation with approximately fifty-five other participants to explore "human values and the written word." Everyone is expected to take part in the conversation. The number of participants is deliberately limited so that everyone has access to faculty, and so that the discussion is intimate, and no one need ever feel left out. I have been fortunate to sit in on many sessions of the Symposium, and every time have felt the way that younger Inupiat must feel: reconnected to myself and to my place, and with my head abuzz with new ideas to consider for years to come. Robert Hass writes, "This is that ideal thing: home-grown, community-based, sustained for a decade now by mostly voluntary and always inspired work, national in reputation, global in its concerns."

Originally they called it the "Sitka Summer Writers Symposium," and writers came not only from Alaska but from New York, Florida, California, Montana, and a host of other states. Though aimed at writers, this symposium is unique in that the focus is not on writing workshops and tips on publication, but on thought: the best thinking that participants and faculty can bring to bear upon current issues. At each Symposium the faculty has been asked to address a particular theme. It is possible for fledgling writers to get their material read and criticized, and to talk to established writers about publishing, yes; but the real purpose has consistently been to think hard about contemporary concerns and to share that thinking with the group. In the course of each Symposium every faculty member does a reading, makes a presentation, attends all the sessions, and talks with other participants. Barry Lopez, who has been twice a faculty member, indicates the kind of mutual respect that characterizes the Symposium. "The organizers had been careful to assemble a faculty that would help catalyze an enriching experience for everyone by breaking down the strict boundary between 'faculty' and 'student.'"

The themes have been grounded primarily in place and in stories. The power of that approach is lauded by one participant who wrote, "My time at the Symposium changed me in profound ways. . . . In the company of gentle friends, my writing, and theirs, helped me respond to the questions of where I was and who I'd become. . . . I was involved in Symposium topics that focused on a sense of place and a sense of purpose. For me, the timing couldn't have been more perfect." Chet Raymo, a faculty member, said simply, "The Symposium was a transforming experience . . . those seven days will leave their mark on my work," and poet William Pitt Root called his time at the Symposium "a pivotal moment" in his writing career. "Although aspects of wilderness have always been a part of my poetry . . . my experience at the Sitka Symposium still stands out . . . a chance to see other ways of carrying the message on."

Though many of the writers are concerned about the environment, and have written extensively about the world of nature, environmental concerns have not been the real heart of this unique experiment. The idea of place is important, that's true, but the idea of stories has been primary. Coming to understand how story works, and the nature and importance of narrative, even to a culture like ours that may seem to have left its oral tradition behind, has been perhaps the most important thread that has run through each session. The Symposia have attracted some of America's outstanding spokespeople, but they often seem to echo Martha Demientieff, a faculty member from Holy Cross, a village on the Yukon River:

> We're looking for something
> Crying, we search
> Seagull cries with us
> Wheeling, crying, looking,
> Where will we find our language?

Now the folks at The Island Institute who sponsor this event every year call it "The Sitka Symposium on Human Values and the Written Word." They are ready to broaden their audience to include a larger public. This book is but one step toward letting many more people into their thinking and inviting us to join in their dialogue. The essays, poems, and comments in this collection bring together the work of both faculty and students. You will find the quality of both high indeed, and may discover, as did Lopez, that the distinction between faculty and other participants has blurred. Reading these works and thinking hard about the world we live in, we are all invited, in the words of Martha Demientieff's poem, to

> . . . sit near each other and
> Remember, remember
> How to live in an altered world
> Bearing the pain over and over.

Gary H. Holthaus
Center of the American West
University of Colorado
Boulder, Colorado

Introduction

SINCE 1984, people have been gathering in Sitka, Alaska, for a week each June to talk. The gathering place has been a hexagonal room with two windowed walls and a stone fireplace, a room just large enough for fifty or sixty people to spread themselves comfortably around the perimeter and still be close enough to become familiar with each other's faces and voices. The parameters of the conversation have been set out by questions posed by a handful of Sitkans who make up The Island Institute, people eager to encourage thoughtful consideration about things that matter in the human experience. The questions have revolved around complex dilemmas on political, ethical, social, and environmental fronts, dilemmas faced by individuals, families, communities, and the larger society. Underlying these deliberate questions have been broader, yet more specific ones: what is my role, my responsibility, my work in relation to these issues?

The more definitive shape of the conversation has been determined largely by the individuals who have come. A group of recognized thinkers and writers—five to seven each year—has led the discussions. Poets and astronomers, anthropologists and novelists, natural historians, philosophers, linguists, and folklorists, they have been people whose work has reflected on the questions at hand. Their perspectives are rooted in Western traditions and native American traditions, in the written word and the spoken. Their ideas have juxtaposed aspects of the human experience that are seldom considered in relationship—the poetic imagination and the reasoned argument, perhaps, or the public shape of our private lives. The conversations have been developed further by the thoughts of those who have come as participants, people from varied walks of life who are concerned with the questions. College students and people with advanced degrees; twenty-year-olds and seventy-year-olds; scientists and artists; social workers and lawyers; land-use planners and ministers; aspiring poets and published novelists. They have gathered from around Alaska and from the far reaches of the rest of the country, and brought to the discussion their own knowledge—of family life, subsistence practices, urban living, environmental issues, spiritual questions, and academic pursuit. They have offered their experience of human curiosity, grief, exhilaration, frailty, cynicism, hope, and resilience.

The conversations of those weeks have also been tacitly shaped by what lies beyond that hexagonal room. The name Sitka is derived from Tlingit Indian words that describe a place on the outer or seaward edge of the island. It is a place distinguished as much by its geology, flora, and fauna as its human history. In a moment of distraction, one's eye goes out the window of that room to follow the dark shape of raven disappearing into the darker stand of trees. Between discussions one wanders down to the gravelly boundary where the North Pacific Ocean meets the fractured landmass that is Baranof Island, rising at acute angles to three or four or five thousand feet, crowding the town onto a narrow bench of horizontal land at the water's edge. One walks between hemlock, cedar, spruce over water-logged ground, spongy with mosses, green upon green upon green as only a rain forest can be. Or in a lucky moment, one waits for the humpback whale to rise again, to burst through the ring of bubbling water that has captured its prey. And the rain drips while mists hover in the trees. Or the sun glints off Sitka Sound, making things too bright to see. Coming back to the room, one re-enters it with a different eye, an altered sense of being—a kind of change that, however imperceptible, can only be brought about by the larger world beyond the human.

The reason for such a convergence of minds in such a place? The Sitka Symposium on Human Values and the Written Word. Known in its early years as the Sitka Summer Writers Symposium, the annual gathering initially established itself as something other than a writers' conference. Its founders wanted to consider the act and practice of writing in context, in relationship to other things they cared deeply about, for if the endeavor of writing is to have any lasting value, it must be connected to the realities and possibilities of our lives. For the tone of the meeting, they took their cues from the very word *symposium: a convivial meeting for drinking, conversation, and intellectual entertainment.* Conviviality and conversation have abounded. The intellectual entertainment has been a certain held attention, an engagement of spirits and minds. The shared cup has been filled with coffee more than wine. The sustenance has been the common partaking of ideas that have challenged assumptions, affirmed hopes, and reshaped lives.

Simple mathematics make it clear that the Sitka Symposium has not reached a large audience. Many a conference might, in a single session, enroll the total number of people who have come to Sitka over ten years. Those small numbers have been deliberate. They attest to a character that has made it possible for participants to return home, as poet William Stafford has said, "changed but safe, quiet, grateful." The reverberations of people's experiences in Sitka go out into the world in ways that might never be accountable. Still, the substance of the work that has taken place each June deserves to be shared more widely. The repeated responses—regard, inspiration, excitement—from people as varied as those who have taken part are indicative of a public appetite for reflective discussion of important questions.

Hence this anthology, a collection of writing by both faculty and participants who have attended during the Symposium's first decade. While no printed page will ever substitute for the tenor of those conversations or the ambience in that room, the ideas are in the words. If the Symposium's consideration of writing has any purpose, it is in passing on ideas, for the written word, whatever its shortcomings, can be a lasting testament to the best work of the human mind. The selections included here are not transcripts. Nor were they necessarily written in Sitka. They are linked together not simply by the *event* of the Symposium, but by the *ideas* that allow the Symposium to reverberate beyond the bounds of its annual six days. And though the selections represent only some of the many voices that have filled that room, they reflect underlying concepts that have run through the history of the program.

The location of this gathering—the mountain and ocean country of the Tongass Rain Forest—has proved to be key. Whatever the human question at hand, the place itself has forced a concession to more fundamental relationships: those we have to the rest of the natural world. This acknowledgment has been a cornerstone of the Symposium. It has not meant that the conference has always had an "environmental" focus, but that other pressing human issues have been considered against the backdrop of our essential connection to the natural systems that sustain us. In that light, we have looked at the underpinnings of cultural world views to see how they define our sense of obligation to our own communities and other natural communities. We have reflected on the human propensity to interpret the world in scientific, spiritual, and imaginative ways. We have examined the translation of personal beliefs and perceptions into public action and expression. We have contemplated the nature of the covenants we are party to when we subscribe to a particular set of values, when we call a place home or a cultural tradition our own.

The irrepressible human impulse for narration has provided the means to make sense of many of these questions through stories, another cornerstone of the Sitka program. The narrative form is as old as our species. We use it both consciously and unconsciously day to day. We rely on some stories the way we rely on nature. They have explained the world to us. Centuries old, they have shaped the psyche of cultures and civilizations. In the Western tradition, the written story has long been dominant, easing the need to listen carefully and remember. Among Alaska Native cultures, the key stories are just now being transcribed and translated into written form. With this recording comes a certain advantage of historic preservation, but a simultaneous loss of a tradition integral to the cultural contexts that sustained families and communities for hundreds of years before Western contact. Still, the narrative form renews itself. It instructs us, entertains us, and heals us. Through it, we can imagine and hope.

Our reflections on a story also allow us to examine our convictions. Its metaphors help us clarify the difference between truth and illusion. They encourage us to think about how we come by our beliefs and how we live by them. They show us possibilities for redefinition, for reassessing the fixed point of view that keeps fresh perspective at bay. They help us tolerate the necessary tension between freedom and restraint. We turn to story again and again to say what it is we believe, to shape and reshape our lives, to help us live more honestly, thoughtfully, carefully. Implicitly, Socrates has been another cornerstone of the Symposium: "The unexamined life is not worth living." In a twentieth-century context—in Alaska—that assertion has demanded an examination far broader than might have been conducted in ancient Athens. Tlingit, Athabaskan, Yup'ik, Inupiaq, Aleut, Haida, Tsimshian points of view, each with its own integrity, each reflecting on the other and on modern versions of Western tradition. For all, the essential questions remain. What is wisdom? What is justice? How do we know them in our hearts?

This collection opens with Mary Kancewick's thoughtful consideration of the possibilities inherent in the fertile ground where cultures meet, possibilities available to us if we take time to watch and listen, if we forgo presumption and practice tolerance. She gives us room to stand and consider what follows: a poem conveying a memory of those here before, a Yup'ik Eskimo story. Barry Lopez's "Landscape and Narrative" broadens our stance. He characterizes inner and outer landscapes that are brought together by narrative: "The purpose of storytelling is to achieve harmony between the two landscapes, to use all the elements of story—syntax, mood, figures of speech—in a harmonious way to reproduce the harmony of the land in the individual's interior." He gives us ground to take in the Chickadee Woman, a giant steelhead on the end of our line, the Dena'ina Indian "Ridge Where We Cry." The poetic reflections that follow lead us to Terry Tempest Williams' archaeologist, who uses poems to draw a community into its distant past.

Hugh Brody's story "Family Trees" takes his narrator into a not-so-distant darker history that has stained the human conscience. Gary Nabhan's essay puzzles over the nature of human aggression, and Chet Raymo turns to science to caution us about ourselves, recognizing "an integrity and balance within nature that demands of the earth's dominant species a judicious self-restraint." When we tip the balance, we are left to take up the challenge offered by David Grimes and Wes Jackson to become native, to devote ourselves again to the places where we live.

Such a charge is paramount, but not simple. It is complicated by other ties and other loyalties—those to work and family. William Kittredge's story "Do You Hear Your Mother Talking?" gives us a narrator who finds refuge in work and love, refuge from the unstable grounding of his childhood. Ken Dola barks his knuckles on the job while he watches the life go out of trees. In John Keeble's story, a family's house holds the pain of the loss of a daughter "and every bit of decomposable, flimsy, true substance of life." Melinda Mueller balances this life with a longing for another time and place, and Jennifer Brice's narrator struggles to find compassion for an adopted family member. Still, Ayagumagalha, the Inupiaq wanderer, takes care of his people, and Seth Kantner comes to share a community's stories. We stand by each other. We keep watch with poet Jane Leer.

Richard Nelson begins the last section of the book by throwing us into the embrace of a storm, an embrace that we too seldom indulge. He reminds us of a kind of attention John Haines and Pattiann Rogers argue is critical—an attention that allows us to understand so we can make amends; an attention like Paul Shepard's that is grounded in history but stays fresh; an attention that lets us hear the resonance of a place and gives us the courage to lift our own voices and sing with Lauren Davis the "wandering melodies [that] come . . . out of the air, the light, the colors of the rocks."

Therein lies our hope. In thinking about prophecy, Lewis Hyde closes this collection by reflecting on Thoreau and remembering his words: "It is not indifferent to us which way we walk. There is a right way . . . " If we can embrace that certain attention, if we can stand by each other and the places where we live, if our words can convey clearly what we believe and our minds stay open to possibility, we can help ourselves "sort the true from the false and begin to move," as Hyde suggests. "The prophetic voice seeks to have us see that the golden age is not in the past or the future. It is here," he tells us. "The heroic age will not be with us unless we will be its heroes."

What does it take to be a hero or heroine at the end of the twentieth century? Hyde does not suggest that it requires the extraordinary, but rather that we acknowledge, with the prophet, those things that are true in all time. Stories and metaphors reveal those truths to us. Our acknowledgment of them allows us to shape our lives around them. It is not, indeed, a matter of indifference which way we walk or what we say or how we behave. Our lives are determined by the causes and consequences of choice. To the degree those choices are our own, we can make them carefully. We can examine and consider, talk and listen, seek other opinions and perspectives, venture out and return again to what we know is home ground. It is these parameters that have defined the Sitka Symposium on Human Values and the Written Word. These are the things that carry it forward and out into the world through the lives of individual people—those whose words are collected here, those others whose voices reverberate in that room, those who will come in the future.

Carolyn Servid
The Island Institute
Sitka
June 1993

I

Connections: The Stories

The stories people tell have a way of taking care of them. . . .
Sometimes a person needs a story more than food to stay
alive. That is why we put these stories in each other's
memory. This is how people care for themselves.

—Barry Lopez, *Crow and Weasel*

HOWEVER it is that the human mind perceives the world, one of the most important devices it uses is metaphor. Often thought of strictly as a poetic or rhetorical embellishment, metaphor is much more fundamental to our everyday thoughts and actions. At its root are notions of relationship and connection: the ways in which things resemble each other. Our understanding of the world is based in an essential way on such relationships and connections.

Stories—in both narrative and poetic form—are the larger metaphors we use to make sense of our lives and our world. When we tell each other of our experiences, when we craft a tale that keeps an audience spellbound, we are describing our connections—to each other and to the places where we live. When we revisit classic works of literature, we recognize elements of ourselves and truths of the human condition. When we listen to the stories of another people, another culture, we look for relationships between their perceptions and our own. When we describe the patterns and movements of the larger natural world, we are coming to understand a narrative that both parallels and contains our own.

Of Two Minds

MARY KANCEWICK

I come to this writing by way of a maceration—and by way of a moment.

The maceration came first, the soaking, the softening. The Latin root, *macerare,* means "to steep." As I write this I watch a trapper choose a stiff piece of old moosehide to soak for a spring night in the eddy of the river flowing past his cabin. Later, with a sharp knife, he will cut the softened skin into babiche, wind babiche around birch, to re-lash a sled. The dogs that pull the sled over snow range around him now in the tall grass and bluebells—a blooming sprouted from soil macerated by the snow's recent melting. The word carries a sense of intent—an immersion for the purpose of absorption, a suspension towards transformation, towards transcendence. The crossed and layered thongs of babiche dry strong, are beautiful, are ready for new motion. The bluebells will be followed by wild roses.

My maceration, that in which this writing has its origins, is the soaking, the softening, of a European-American psyche, one stiffened into a shape of Western Civilization, in the eddy of Alaska Native village life.

Maxim has it that East is East and West is West and never the two shall meet—but of course they do, and at that meeting things happen.

Western political consciousness originated in early Hebrew thought, with laws set forth by Moses and Samuel, presented as covenants engraved on stone tablets. The inscribed musings of Greek philosophers, Plato and Aristotle the most famous among them, followed, and then the Roman Code, under the influences of Roman statesmen such as Cicero. The Middle Ages of Western Europe brought with them the thought-shaping writings of St. Thomas Aquinas, Dante, and others. The Protestant revolution contributed the visions of Luther and Calvin. The eighteenth century, known as the Age of Enlightenment, was enlightened by the rationalizations and models developed by Locke, Hume, Rousseau, Smith, Burke, Fichte, Bentham. Western political thought came to be identified with the idea of *constitutional* government, government based upon formalized principles agreed to by individuals who have come together to be governed. Thomas Jefferson in the *Declaration of Independence*, and Alexander Hamilton and James Madison and the other framers of the United States Constitution applied this Western conviction to the creation of a union of the thirteen colonies.

The thinking of the East has been shaped by Hindu political theory, by Confucian doctrine, the philosophies of Taoism and Buddhism. It embraces also the less-known ways of the indigenous peoples of North and South America, of Greenland, of Australia and New Zealand, of Africa. The East is understood by the West to approach politics and government from the touchstone of tradition, and to emphasize an organic social authority, one rooted in land-based history, one growing and developing from environment and circumstance rather than invented and agreed upon by independent, thinking individuals.

East has met West wherever Western powers have colonized their lands: India, North and South America, Greenland, Australia, New Zealand, Africa. It has been in the interest of Western colonizers, by their own values, to reject the potential validity or even existence of political thought and organization among indigenous peoples of lands colonized in the name of Western powers. As a result many such systems have been forcedly destroyed, and others reshaped Western-style.

East meets West today in Alaska, where the various indigenous peoples, the Inuit and Yup'ik Eskimos, the Aleuts, the Athabaskan tribes, and the Tlingit, Haida, and Tsimshian Indians, are currently struggling to accommodate themselves to the government of the United States. The Native peoples of Alaska are struggling to strike a balance with the new system, and in the process are becoming more conscious of the value of their indigenous ways, more articulate about them, and more determined to preserve those traditional ways that may yet serve them in the future they seek for themselves. In this process we of Western traditions have an opportunity to consider the impact of our ways and the future we seek for ourselves.

✳

Southwest Alaska. Land of the Yup'ik. A six-passenger bush plane flies me low over snow-covered muskeg, during the few hours of midday sun. I land in New Stuyahok just as the low-slanting light fades. Three-hundred-some Yup'ik people live in this village on the banks of the Nushagak River. In summer they live by fishing, in winter by hunting the caribou.

After being shown my place for the night, I am invited to join the women of a Yup'ik family for an evening steam. I slide in darkness over thick ice to the designated steam house, towel tucked under a parka-puffed arm. The steam of my breath wets my ruff; the cold turns it to hoar. My white halo reflects light from the moon onto a face that rivals its pale. The faces I pass in the night are warm-colored under their hoods.

In the tiny entryway of the family steam house, by the dim light of a single lantern, I shed my clothes. I leave them, rolled into a ball, on the plank bench. I slide on wet wood into steam, stopped and steadied on both sides by strong arms swiftly extended. The arm of the left tugs and guides me to an open spot to squat. The stove throbs red, the sole glimmer in the steamy dark. Someone tosses water onto the glow; the splash explodes into crackle and hiss. Sweat beads on my skin, running down me, braiding like rivers down my face, my chest, my shins. I taste salt on my lips. Someone passes a basin, a cloth, a dipper, a bucket of water. I wash, plopping the cloth, smoothing over limbs, wringing, dipping again, my soft sounds joining those of the others.

We hear the swish and creak of a sled passing outside, the panting of the dogs that draw it, the clink of the clasps that fasten their harnesses and lines. Someone names the driver, the lead dog, the number in the team. We hear children's voices drop into the night like ice shattering onto the road from house eaves. Someone names each child. After a time, the woman nearest me begins to hum. The sound vibrates in my chest, as it must in that of each of the others.

Our bones tremble together on the same notes. We become, all of us, parts of a single instrument, objects of the same strum.

*

Southeastern Alaska's coast and islands. Land of the Tlingit, the Haida, and the Tsimshian. I arrive in the springtime. My lungs fill with the smell of yellow cedar as women strip bark for baskets; as a master carver chisels a trunk into a totem. My tongue tastes the ocean salt in fresh-dried seaweed, the bitter bite of just-gathered herring roe.

I meet Tlingit elder Austin Hammond at a regional Native gathering in Juneau. He comes from Klukwan, a village in the Chilkat River region. We talk then, sharing frybread, but it is in Anchorage the next fall, when at a public hearing we meet again, that his message strikes me with meaning.

The hearing concerns Native subsistence, a way of life shaped by the harvest of resources from the land. The Tlingit elder travels to the meeting to present his people's deed, as recorded on a ceremonial blanket of his Sockeye Salmon Clan. The blanket has been passed from generation to generation in an unbroken line, the history of the land and its people woven into mountain goat wool, from a time before the Puritans' first Thanksgiving. His granddaughter holds the blanket for him, translating his Tlingit words. Her grandfather tells how the Tlingit land was formed, how Raven made the waters, how the trees and plants came to be, how the people realized their kinship with the sockeye salmon, how the rules governing the use of land and waters came of the need to protect that kinship. Her grandfather shows how the Tlingit people and their land and its resources continued as one for thousands of years, continues to this day. Her grandfather says, "You say this is your land. Where are your stories?"

*

Interior Alaska. Athabaskan land. I travel by riverboat down the Yukon, to Tanana, a mixed village of some five hundred Native and non-Native people.

It is July. Sweat makes my clothes stick. Mosquitos hover in persistent clouds over every bit of exposed skin.

An hour after landing I kneel in dirt and sun with a middle-aged woman, Koyukon Athabaskan, before nets stretched over grass. I watch her fingers mend, reconstructing by knotting in new string. I imitate. The two of us talk. She tells me she is a grandmother. I tell her I remember watching my grandmother mend lace curtains stretched over square wooden frames. I watch the Athabaskan woman cut even lengths of line with a small knife. She is a fisherwoman. She is the tribal chief of the village. She is the city manager. But what Eileen Kozevnikof tells me is that there is a child who calls her grandma. We kneel side by side, accepting the melding smells of each other's sweat, the smells of the potions we use to ward off the swarms of mosquitos. My fingers and hers move on the net in different rhythms, but she is pleased with the tight knots I make, the way I space, the care I take. She says, "We do this every spring."

I understand her to mean her life is this sort of pattern of connections, of knots and spaces; a pattern fashioned by reaping, rending, and reparation. I think that mine is too, that it has a different mesh, is designed to catch a different fish.

✳

Aleut country stretches across the Alaska Peninsula, along the Aleutian chain, and onto Kodiak Island. I land in Larsen Bay, on the northwest side of the island, in a penetrating November rain. I watch it fall on fields of yellowing wild celery, on the trees sheltering and screening the small homes. I am grateful to enter the house of a new friend, an Aleut woman of an age near my own. I sleep a dreamful sleep on her fold-out couch, under a dead parakeet in a hanging cage.

My friend has some number of grandmothers who married among the Norwegian men who years ago fished from the island. My friend has blue eyes, fair skin, blond hair. She grew up in the house she shares with me, a house with a view of the fish cannery, then operating. The two of us drink coffee, munch pilot bread, discuss opera. We also discuss her graduate work in public policy at the University of Texas in Austin, her marriage to a non-Native man, her divorce, her job as village tribal operations officer, and her plans to raise her two children in the village. "I've spent a lot of time outside," Sheila Aga Theriault tells me. "I've taken the time to understand you people. But your people don't try to understand my people, to understand me." She tells me that her parakeet enjoyed opera as much as she; that it escaped its cage the morning before, flew directly to a pot of boiling water on the stove, and landed in it feet first. She tells how she scooped it out, alive, but with legs cooked crisp. She smoothed salve on the crust and laid the bird on the floor of its cage, hoping it might somehow survive. It didn't.

Months later my Aleut friend sends me a letter. She writes that, due to local politics, she has lost her job as tribal operations officer, that there is no other work for her in the village, that she is going back to Texas. Her words sound fluttery, and I see that the water is hot all around her. I know my friend has stronger wings, a stronger heart, and a clearer mind than her pet parakeet. I also know this is not true for every young Native testing new waters. I feel the lightness of her letter in my hand, the sheets lying across my palm like feathers, like spread wings. I think how liberty is in essence the assurance that a chosen way of life may be perpetuated.

*

Northwest Alaska. Land of the Inupiat. In Shishmaref, a village on the wind- and wave-swept coasts of the Bering Strait, I meet young Inupiaq Albert Ningeulook. We walk a long way together, through the first snow of the season, a fine snow, sifting through the air like meal. It is late September. We walk through town, a place of mostly wooden structures built in clusters, past the old village site where the people dig for artifacts to sell to outside buyers for cash, to the beach. Mostly he listens while I talk. I confide in him all my doubts about the rightness of a non-Native person like myself traveling, working, living in the villages; my fears of rejection, my loneliness, my indirection. As I speak, my companion picks tiny spiralled shells from the cold sand and places them in my hands. He places them open side up, so my eyes fall into the space curving from their always delicate lips. Sand drops from the fine faint embossings of their surfaces to catch in the warp of my wool mittens. He says to me, "You are happy. You just don't know it."

Before I leave the village, he presents me with a red mug of thick glass onto which he's scratched my name, and "Shishmaref." I think, yes, to be empty and to be open is to be full of possibility, and yes, this is what it is to be happy.

In the course of visiting with Alaska Natives, I began to understand in a different way, with a different mind, concepts I had learned in a Western context, concepts such as those "self-evident truths" set forth in our *Declaration of Independence* from Britain—concepts of individual rights and property, of life, liberty, and happiness; and the truths hidden in history, which affect an understanding of constitution, consent, representation, and equality under the law.

In Kotzebue, at a hearing in a high-school gym, Inupiaq poet Robert Mulluk expressed a thought with relevance as much for those of us of Western traditions as for the Native people he addressed:

> This is what we have to do; we have got to look beyond the horizon because, when you look into the horizon, then you think that is the end—but it is not. You walk to the horizon, and again there is another horizon. You can go all the way around the world in this manner. If we can look at it in that aspect, we will be better off. Otherwise, we will get too caught up in one simple thing, or one matter, or one problem. We have got to look at it from all angles.

As he spoke, children on fat-tired bicycles pedalled on the thick ice of Kotzebue Sound, their elbows extended with effort, wheels sliding circles around the grandmothers sitting at holes chopped in the ice to jig for tomcod. The ice extends to the horizon visible from shore, but the seal hunters know that some miles out there is open water. Alaska itself marks a horizon where East and West meet. We need to see what lies beyond this horizon, towards an extension of both our perspectives. We are dependent upon each other in the creation of conditions that will insure a future. Might it not be that Eastern and Western peoples manifest complementary hemispheres of a most wonderfully fashioned intelligence, and that to realize the potential of the whole we must connect our codes, our various ways of cunning and courage; that in this way we dramatically expand what is possible and begin to realize what is meant?

One winter I lived across a slough from Athabaskan elder Howard Luke. He built his home on an island in the Tanana River and for a time I cross-country skied past his place almost every afternoon, setting my skis in the snow-machine trails that trace the river's meanderings. I would stop, always, at the stick that marked the place where he ice-fished, and nod a greeting in the direction of his cabin. It seemed the right thing to do; I don't know if he ever saw me, ever knew.

Howard Luke spends his days at the University of Alaska in Fairbanks, counselling and working with Native young people from throughout the state. This is what he says he tells them, when they ask him the way to approach the future:

> A lot of them are asking me, they say, what shall I do, Howard? Shall I go through college or study the culture? To one of them I said, well, what your dad told you? "Well," she told me, "he said, he told me, well, you're eighteen years old now, you take up anything you want." And that's not the right thing to say. So she asked me, and I told her. I said, if I were you, I would take up college and get through, get through the thing, and gradually, like I'm talking to you, pick up your culture. . . . Just like, see, I make a bunch of stuff and I just show them how it's done, and how they drive moose, and what you do if your gun gets jammed . . . and your luck . . . so they know.

At a hearing in Fairbanks, members of the Alaska Métis Association (an association of Indians of mixed Native and non-Native blood), undertook to remind listeners that the United States Constitution is itself an example of the creative potential of connection between cultures. The extraordinarily innovative and successful political experiment of the United States of America drew a good deal of its inspiration from the arrangements of the Iroquois Federation functioning then along the continent's northeastern coast.

I spent a day researching this claim in a university library. It did not surprise me to find that Felix S. Cohen, author of the seminal treatise in the field of Federal Indian law (*Handbook of Federal Indian Law*, 1942, 1982) supports this interpretation. Cohen wrote in 1952, in an article in the prestigious journal *The American Scholar*, that American historians "have seen America only as an imitation of Europe," and that this is a mistake. He asserts that "the real epic of America is the yet unfinished story of the [native] Americanization of the white man." He attests that "politically there was nothing in the Empire and kingdoms of Europe in the fifteenth and sixteenth centuries to parallel the democratic constitution of the Iroquois Confederacy, with its provisions for initiative, referendum and recall," and that it was American Indian political practice that inspired John Locke and Thomas More, as well as Montesquieu, Voltaire, Rousseau, "and their various contemporaries."

The historians who have studied the tribes and the period agree that the five (later six) federally governed Iroquois Indian nations practiced the concepts of natural rights and popular participation, political ideas that European philosophers had until then only theorized. The Iroquois Federation based its constitution, "The Great Law of Peace," on "self-evident truths" about government of the people, for the people, and by the people, which were quite foreign to the old monarchies of Europe, such principles as leadership serving the people and the people's right to impeach; checks and balances in government (no action could be taken without the approval of all five represented nations); the separation of the duties of civil chiefs and religious leaders; and such basic rights as those to political and religious freedom of expression, against the unauthorized entry of homes, to political participation by women, and to a relatively equitable distribution of wealth.

Sociopolitical scientist Bruce E. Johansen has done the most recent research concerning the suggestion of Native influence on the framers of the U.S. Constitution. He wrote, in a 1979 work *(The Forgotten Founders: American Indians in the Sociopolitical Thought of Franklin and Jefferson),* that "the Iroquois and other Indian nations fired the imaginations of the revolution's architects," and especially influenced the thinking of

Jefferson and Franklin, who saw in the near Indian communities "what colonists wanted for themselves: societies free of class stratification and oppression." Many of Franklin's writings, Johansen indicates, show that "as he became more deeply involved with the Iroquois and other Indian peoples, he picked up ideas from them concerning not only federalism, but concepts of natural rights, the nature of society and man's place in it, the role of property in society, and other intellectual constructs." He quotes Franklin to have observed that "happiness is more generally and equally diffused among savages than in our civilized societies," and finds that "Jefferson thought enough of [such] happiness to make its pursuit a natural right, along with life and liberty. In so doing, he dropped 'property,' the third member of the natural rights trilogy."

The Alaska Métis Association's reminder of the United States debt of political ideas was stated in a spirit of admiration for the resulting application of principles. The criticism intended was that of lack of respect, the too-quick forgetfulness of the Native contribution. I heard the same sentiment, expressed with the same sorrow, by an old Gwich'in Athabaskan woman holding my hand and shaking her head. We sat together in her tiny cabin on the thin mattress of her bed. Her village, Venetie, in her language, "the banks," rests on a real curve of the Chandalar River, not far from the imagined line of geography, the Arctic Circle. Myra Roberts' grandson, a fisherman, trapper, and sometimes fire-fighter, translated her words for me:

> When Columbus sailed across the ocean, the first person that ever stand there was a Native person to meet him, gather him round with a feast, with a good pipe to smoke—a good pipe.

A good pipe. How could we have forgotten?

Criticism may be what fills the grail of all quests. In an analysis of Mexican society and United States–Mexican relations, Mexican poet and essayist Octavio Paz explains that "criticism is the imagination's apprenticeship in its second turn, the imagination cured of fantasies and determined to face the world's realities. Criticism tells us that we should learn to dissolve the idols, should learn to dissolve them within our own selves. We must learn to be like the air, a liberated dream." Criticism, and especially self-criticism, is a sign of a creative connecting. It is a coming up against an "other" that forces the "one" to reassess, reevaluate.

I've described something of the maceration that has readied me for a new shape. I promised a moment as well.

The Latin root of moment, *momentum*, means movement. The English word is used to mean very brief, very important, the increasing force of something. My moment contained all of these.

The moment crucial to this writing occurred a few days after my moving to an isolated cabin on the Tozitna River. On the momentous day, I stepped north along the riverbank, enjoying the suck of spring muck on my boots. I paused at No-Name Slough, stepping carefully there because tall grass under the water makes depth deceptive. On the far side of the slough I paused again on a banked iceberg, to watch the newly released water rush by. I stood on the iceberg as if it were a great summit I had scaled, and some time flowed by with the water before I thought to move on. Halfway through a step intended to put me on a trail through the willows, it happened: The stand of brush before me shook with a roaring so definite and deep it echoed in the facing bluffs. I turned and ran.

At fifty yards, no panting nearing behind me, no crashing but my own through the bush, I stopped behind a hefty low-branching spruce and looked back, ready to climb. I saw a glossy brown hump of a back move with slow deliberation through the thinning willows towards the water's edge. My heart beat with the same heavy floating. It wasn't coming after me; didn't even know of my existence, maybe. I quick-stepped on, my breathing still rough, the flush of my skin dropping slowly to the tips of the fingers still pressed hard to my palms, to the toes curling with unaccustomed urgency over the stones and roots of my path. At a hundred yards I turned again, I saw two curves of self-absorbed fur. A sow and a cub? Although one mound of glistening brown was smaller than the other, both shapes were big, very big. Beginning to believe in their unawareness or disinterest in me, I continued to watch, mindful that if they chose they could move very quickly. One raised its head. It was a moose. Two moose.

I was stunned by the misperception caused by reliance on preconception—which serves so often as a life preserver in a flood of emotional reaction. If I had not turned around, I would have sworn I had encountered a bear. If I had turned around only once to look, I would have sworn I had seen that bear. I would have dramatically wiped my brow. It would have made a story. If I had turned twice, yet not lingered those few minutes more, I would have sworn I'd almost met not only one bear, but two, and would have told my story over and over, I'm sure. I knew that moose growl much as bears do, had encountered moose before at that slough, but my mind was set to perceive threat as: bear.

My maceration in the flow of village life prepared me to testify: my moment at No-Name Slough made clear to me why I needed to do so. I've tagged my mental machinations with Latin-rooted terms to niggle you, without undo melodrama, as to our cultural links to the fallen Empire of Rome. Consider this thought of Felix Cohen:

> When the Roman legions conquered Greece, Roman historians wrote with as little imagination as did the European historians who have written of the white man's conquest of America. What the Roman historians did not see was that captive Greece would take captive conquering Rome and that Greek science, Greek philosophy and a Greek book, known as *Septuagint*, translated into the Latin tongue, would guide the civilized world and bring the tramp of pilgrim feet to Rome a thousand years after the last Roman regiment was destroyed.

At a hearing in Fairbanks an Athabaskan in his late twenties—with a neat moustache and wearing a jaunty cap; whose father figured prominently in the land claims movement; who himself runs an agricultural self-help program for Athabaskan communities—stepped with some defensiveness to the microphone. Alfred Ketzler, Jr., said, "In the bathroom here in this hotel, there's a slogan on the wall of the toilet. It says Indians are the proven fact that the niggers screwed the buffalo." And he said, "Out of forty kids that went to [my high] school there's only twenty-two of them left. Eighteen of them are dead."

We must listen to the words of Native peoples speaking from deep inside themselves. We must allow their words to echo from the bluffs in us. We must consider. Let the fuss subside, and consider:

> We had laws long before your nation was organized and came into being. In fact, we already enjoyed life, liberty, the pursuit of happiness and equal protection of laws and due process of law. Our tribal laws already insured these rights and these are laws that are violated, that are desecrated, and that are dishonored. There are a lot of Natives walking around in Alaska that are walking around with injured souls. I, for one, am one. . . . I have a deep injury that I walk around with, without honor, it seems.
> —Franklin Williamson, Kake

> Native people are different. . . . People that are non-Native don't quite understand our way of thinking and somehow, if we could close the gaps so they can better understand us, we better understand them, I think many good things can happen.
> —Eleanor McMullen, Port Graham

> If we can accept them, why can't they accept us, who we are, and then we can work more harmoniously together instead of devising laws how to govern each other? . . . We would like to have more control of our own lifestyles. . . . If we can accept theirs, they should be able to accept ours. . . . The Native people came a long ways to learn the non-Native ways, lifestyles, and we're finding out their lifestyle is what we already had, but for some reason they still don't recognize that.
> —Gene Strong, Skagway

We have believed our way to be best, believed assimilation with us to be in everyone's best interest, believed it to be a privilege, believed, seemingly incurably, that in the end all ways of life should be this one best way, necessarily and absolutely. But it might be that there is no "one" without an "other," that the nature of being, and of all continuing, is as heterogeneous as it is changing.

As a result of maceration, a thing, a being, opens up, fills itself with all the suppleness, the promise of a new growing. The babiche that was moosehide, that now lashes a sled, can in a later emergency be chewed by a man or dog for food. The bluebells will be followed by wild roses, and they by marsh grass of parnassus. Each will have its moment.

Berry Pickers' Shadows

Jane Leer

Something happens when the smell of crushed
cranberry leaves and mosses rises up
around your knees, when the stoop of your back
freezes and the bent elbow straightens, then returns
to the bucket, when the corners of your eyes
watch for the bear's black shadow—
the sense of women here before,
the same stoop and bend, the same basket
bucket plopped berry-full between hunkered
thighs, the same full sour scent of a decomposing
blanket of earth beneath your feet, and the shadows
you sense are not bear, but the ground's
memory of those gathering before.

Man Who Left

ELSIE MATHER

BEFORE MY VIEW was blocked by newly built structures, I could always look out the kitchen window to look at a church steeple not far from our house. It is white with perhaps eight sides that taper to make a point at the top. The simple shape is not particularly striking or beautiful, but over the years my appreciation of it has deepened because I seemed to have absorbed something new each time I looked at it.

It forever changes in color from pure white to shades of gray or blue depending on the sky changes. Some days the sides that are visible to me are each a different shade of whatever color is dominant. At other times the steeple blends into the sky as though it doesn't exist. Yet other times it contrasts sharply against the sky as though it commands your attention.

Recently I have been working on a traditional Yup'ik story that was heard by a Yup'ik elder when he was a young man. He died several years ago when he was nearing eighty. I first heard this story on tape about eight years ago and have since listened to it many times. And like my experience with the church steeple I have, over the years, absorbed different aspects of it, understanding a bit here and there. Sometimes the story is sharp and clear. At other times it is remote, its message almost completely meaningless.

I have come to liken it to a symbol. Perhaps that is the way to best look at it. There is no one set of words that could adequately describe what the story is about. Those of us who have a penchant for analysis could take some lessons from the old storytellers who simply tell these stories without explaining what they are about or what lessons we are to learn from them. They intuitively know that, in the end, analysis and explanation can limit the listener's ability to make meaning in their own terms.

Also in our quest for novelty and new information we tend to ignore the value of repetition. We forget that understanding and knowing occur over one's lifetime. Older Yup'ik people remind us to listen even when we have heard something over and over again. They tell us that as we go on with our life we will some day come to an understanding of something we have listened to. Some of us never do understand, but just having heard the words or the phrases can give us a sense of participation in our respective cultures.

Stories connect us to our place, our past, and to each other, and they can continue to speak to us about our human condition. They enrich our lives and give us new questions about life.

The following story was told by Phillip Charlie of Tuntutuliak around 1980 to Dorothy Cyril Dahl, who was in that village taping stories to be aired by the Bethel KYUK radio station. Mr. Charlie was about seventy years old at the time.

I would like to thank Phyllis Morrow, Professor of Anthropology at the University of Alaska, Fairbanks, for her help in the translation. I also thank Mrs. Diane Carpenter, of the Pacifica Institute in Bethel, Alaska, for reading the manuscript and for her kind suggestions.

In transcription of the narratives we try to represent on paper the oral performance by the use of line breaks and spacing. These breaks roughly correspond to pauses, intonation contours, grammatical groups, and shifts in "story scenes." For further information on this, see Woodbury in J. Sherzer and A. C. Woodbury, eds., *Native American Discourse: Poetics and Rhetoric* (Cambridge: Cambridge University Press, 1987).

For the benefit of those unfamiliar with Yup'ik culture, brief comments might be helpful about some recurring themes and motifs that are generally a part of stories that are considered to have occurred in the ancient past. During that remote time, people and animals could speak with each other. Humans who could transform into an animal or animals took their hood off from the chin to show their human face. The marmot in this story "gave herself" to the man and in the end the allusion is that she, along with her child, went back to her own home as a marmot. In this and another story Mr. Charlie tells, the feeling is that to be transformed into an animal or an object such as a rock is to become free of human problems and suffering.

A theme that occurs in this story and others is that of supernatural participation in the drama of revenge and punishment. The aid of a supernatural power is generally evoked through song, or through a combination of singing and dancing. In this story a great wrong was done to the wife and child by the husband who abandons them and takes another wife. This deed is considered so atrocious that mere human revenge pales compared to what is meted out to the man by a supernatural entity. In this case an earthquake came about when the woman evoked the powers through her dancing and singing. She sings the song five times. The numbers four and five are significant numbers in some Yup'ik rituals.

MAN WHO LEFT
told by Phillip Charlie

Now then,
there was a man
who lived by a river.

He didn't know anyone else.
He never saw another person.
There was no one else to be seen.
He just lived there alone in his house.
He lived there very peacefully.

———

It is said that
there were cliffs across the river from his place.
Kaimat they were called.

They are dry cliffs where loose dirt continually shifts downward.
I don't know what they call that dry tundra ground in English.
That *kaimaq*. [singular form of *kaimat*]
They use it in flower pots as dirt for the plants.

It was that kind of ground.
They were rocky cliffs.

And that was where that man lived
with nothing to worry about whatsoever.

———————

And so he lived.

But sometimes
he would think about things,
"Aling . . ." [expression of frustration, wonder]
When he traveled on the ocean,
when he went down there,
he would sometimes think,
"Aling, why is it that I have never
seen anyone else?
I never see another human being like myself."

———————

In the evenings,
after hunting on the sea,
he would go back to his house along the river.
And on his way he would sometimes see those little
        animals called marmots
on the cliffs along the river.

(I don't know what they are called in English.)

———————

And so it was.

———————

And so one evening
he was down on the ocean.
It was in the falltime
when nights were starting to be very dark.
It was pitch black that night.
It gets that way when there is no moon.

———————

He had been paddling out in the ocean
and was on his way home.
(Perhaps he was old enough to have gray hairs
     on his temples
for he would not have stayed young forever.)

So when he reached the mouth of his river
he saw that the tide was coming in.
His house wasn't far from the mouth of that river.

So, since it was very calm out
he sat still in his kayak
and let the tide carry him up the river
moving now and then to keep his kayak turned forward.

———————

He was close to those cliffs,
those rocky cliffs
across the river,
where there were sandbars
along the shore.

———————

It was very very dark out
back then when there were no flashlights around.
You could not see anything.

———————

And then,
in a little while,
while he was traveling,

hm!
a ray of light
hit the tote hold of his kayak!
And the light was coming from the riverbank.

Then,
that light came closer

as if it were approaching him.
And when it was on him
he thrust his paddle into the sand below
to hold himself in place
and turned his head
and saw
a doorway above him on the riverbank!
A doorway!

That man,
that *nukalpiaq* [adult male; accomplished male hunter],
had traveled back and forth along there
aaaall that time and had never seen what he was seeing now.
Yet there was that doorway
with a grass mat hanging from the top
and the pattern of the woven grass
stood out sharply against the light.

———————

And he thought,
"Now then,
what could this be!?"

———————

Then the man
got up on the beach,
pulled up his kayak,
and secured it.

He walked up further
and found a path
of steps leading up
and followed them.
When he got to the entryway
he went in.
He went in and there inside was a woman,
a young woman.

She was wearing a parka
of marmot fur.

And near her
was a beautiful new parka
also made of marmot fur.

———————

And as he entered
the woman said to him,
"Waqaa! [expression of greeting with the underlying question
        as to the purpose of the visitor]
How did you get here?"

The man said
that he came
as soon as he saw
her place,
that he had never seen it before.

And the woman said,
"Aling, aaaall this time
you lived up there
upriver
and I here.
Aling,
I would walk around here
and then you would just pass by
without stopping."

"Well,
this is the first time I've noticed your place."

———————

So then
since he didn't feel hesitant

he said to her,
"Well then,
come with me
and we'll be husband and wife."

And the woman answered,
"Yes, I will.
I'll go with you."

So she rolled up her parka and her sleeping mat
and they went down to the river.

And then they went upriver.

———————

And so now that woman, whoever she was,
became his wife.

Now he had someone to talk to.

———————

And so things went well with the two of them.

———————

Well,
time came for them to have a child
and they had
a boy.
It was a boy.

Oh! how his father loved that boy
after longing for someone all those years.

———

That was how it was.

———

And then,
since the child couldn't stay a baby forever
he naturally started growing.
And now he was starting to crawl.
His father would help him along
and he would crawl to him.

Later he
started to take steps
and would toddle over to his father.
That baby,
their child,
was now at that stage.

———

It was in the springtime
when their child
was that age,
that the man,
that father,
went out hunting
and was gone all day and all that night.
He didn't come home!

He disappeared!

And the two of them
just stayed there
in their house.

———————

The father never came home.

———————

Well then,
one day
in the early morning
when the sun was starting to rise
the woman and her child
were sitting outside of their house.

And suddenly,
while they were sitting there
they saw a little bird,
a robin.
Those birds
that sound so pleasant
when they are singing in the trees
are robins.
We hear them these days too.

———————

That little bird lighted beside them.
And after landing there
he opened up his hood from the chin.
And then they saw that
it was a young man!

A boy!
He was a young man!

And he said,
"Waqaa, waqaa,

I have been very concerned about you two.
And since you are still waiting for your husband to return
I came here to tell you
that there is no use in expecting him back.

_____

You see,
this spring
when summer was beginning
there came a hunter
to a village
over there.

And then
he took
the youngest of those sisters living there as his wife.

He *is* your husband."

_____

That little boy,
that child,
kept staring at the young man.

"Well,
since someone might notice I'm gone
I'll go back.
I just came to tell you.
If you should decide to do something about your situation,
look which way I go.
I will go only in a certain direction.
Watch me closely

and see where I go.
So in case you decide to go there
you will know the way.

Then he flew off.

———————

He flew on
and then
disappeared behind the hill
back there.

———————

And so they went back into their house
and ate.
Then
the mother said to her child,
"Now I see what your father did.
He went off somewhere
to live with other people.
I had thought he truly needed someone to live with,
and I felt sorry for him.
That is why I gave myself to him."

And
feeling sorry for the child
she started crying.

———————

Well then,
that woman started to sew a pair of skin boots,

waterproof skin boots.
She made two pairs of them.

She made two pair.

When she was done with them she oiled them.

Autumn time was not far off.

It was the time when
the ground was sometimes covered with frost.

———————

And then
when she finished the boots
they filled a grass bag
with food.

And she stuffed
her parka,
her beautiful parka,
into the bottom of a grass bag.
She also made something in which
to carry her baby on her back.

So they got ready in the morning
and left
following the direction the bird had taken.

———————

That night they camped out
and ate some of the food they brought.

And again the next day
they went on
and camped out again in the night.

And again they traveled the third day.

───────

And then
they reached the valley,
and when they were atop a mountain
they saw a marshy lowland below them,
and there was a river
and they could see the mouth of the river.

So they walked down
to the mouth of the river
where they could see signs that many people had been there.
There were old campfire sites with used roasting sticks.
People had been roasting something in the fire.

───────

And so they walked along the river going inland
following a bend in the river.
And at the third bend
they sighted a large village. They also saw a *qasgi* [men's
    firebath or community house].

And on the edge of the village
was a small house.
There was this small house
sitting by itself away from the others.

And so,
they went into that house.

When they were inside the porch
they saw a little old puppy.
A little puppy was tied up on one side in the porch.
And then
when that puppy saw them
it yapped,
"Waw-aw! Waw-aw! Wa-au-au-au, waw-aw!"

Then someone inside said,
"Grandchild, your little puppy out there . . .
go check on it.
The boys might be mistreating it again."

And right after someone inside said that,
a young girl with a dark face appeared from the entryway
        in the floor (in the porch).

And after gawking at them,
looking from one to the other,
she dashed inside.

And then
the grandmother in there asked her,
"Well,
what is it?"
And her grandchild replied,
"Look,
there is a woman out there
carrying a baby on her back,
who must have come to this village
from somewhere."

And the grandmother said,
"It's no surprise.
That man
would not have lived alone.
So now someone must be looking for him.
He came from somewhere, where he had a family.
Tell them to come in."

Then that little girl shot up again from the
        entryway in the porch,
"She wants you to come in."

―――――――

And so
they came in and stood across from the grandmother.
And since the little girl,
that poor little urchin,
had a place of her own there,
she fixed up a mattress for them
there in her place across from the grandmother.
She acted as their hostess
and then they all ate.

―――――――

And then,
the woman ventured to ask them,
"Well then, have either of you heard anything? What is
        the news this past spring?"
And the old woman replied,
"You see, this spring,
when summer was near,
there came a hunter with a kayak.

And he took one of those sisters,
their youngest sister,
for a wife."

————————

And so then
the woman explained all to the grandmother
and said that
she herself had felt sorry for him
back where they lived.
She knew that he was looking for a companion
and she took him as her husband
thinking that he really needed someone,
and then he just disappeared.
"He left us just like that," she said.
"And so,
we are here now
because we were led to this place."

————————

And after a while
a young boy came in.
He came in
and it was that bird,
that bird that revealed itself as a boy,
the one that landed beside them.
The woman recognized him.
Here he was the little girl's older brother.

————————

And so
the woman and her child stayed there that day.

Then
the old woman said,
"Say,
there are dances held here in this village,
and there will be a dance this evening.
And whenever there are dances
that man and his wife sit in the back
and the wife always has her arms around him
during the dancing.
There will be dancing again tonight!"

"Ii-i [I see],
then, I'll go and see the dances."

So,
that woman,
that guest,
said to the young girl,
"Well now,
if there is dancing tonight
they are probably going to start soon
since it is starting to get dark,
since it is getting dark.
So go watch them.
When a certain number have had their turn,
after five dances,
come over.
I'll go too and dance over there
where they are dancing."

"Ii-i" [Yes].

And so
that young girl went out of the house.

———————

And was gone for a long time.

———————

After a while she came in
and said that
the villagers had done their fifth dance.

So the woman got ready.
She had secluded herself in the corner earlier
        and had washed her hair.
And although she had no soap
her hair was clean and neat, lying flat against her head.
She had washed her hair,
getting ready for the dance.

She put on her fine parka
of marmot fur,
and since she wasn't wearing a dancing headdress
she put one on
and went over (to the dance).

———————

And so,
she went into the porch.
Back then when they had oil lamps
there were two lamps lit in the porch.
Inside,
the people were drumming and dancing.

———————

And then there was silence.

———————

It was very very dark outside.

———————

Then one of the men inside said,
"Is that all? That must be the last of the dancers.
There's such a long break!"

And so it happened
that as the people of the *qasgi* waited
there appeared through the entryway in the floor
a head,
facing away from them, facing the outer porch.

How black the hair was!

———————

Then she pulled herself up
wearing a marmot parka,
a beautiful parka of marmot fur.

She got up and walked toward the front of the *qasgi*
and the people all stared at her,
never having seen the likes of her before.

———————

Wearing a dancing headdress
she was facing towards the front—away from them.

When she turned around, aaah, there
in the back was her husband,
with his wife's arms around him.

————————

And when her husband saw her
he went down on his back
and wedged himself underneath that bench,
the sleeping bench in the back.
He wedged in under there.

————————

So then,
one of the old men said,
"Well, go on
and sing for her,
so she will dance."

Turning herself to face them,
that woman,
that stranger, said,
"No,
I myself will sing.
I will do the singing myself.
You will not sing for me.
Just accompany me with your drums."

"Mm-mmh,
we'll do that for you then."

————————

How fascinating she was in her marmot parka!

"I will not sing the song correctly,
but if I sing it a certain way
it will be understood."

––––––––––

And so that young woman,
with her husband back there,
raised her arms,

Song: "That mountain up there,
that mountain up there.
Sayanganii-ii.
May a piece of rock from there roll toward me.
Its blue-gray rocks.
Its blue-gray rocks."

The people on top of the *qasgi*
looking in through the smokehole
cried, "Oh! Why is it turning dark above the water?"

And again she sang,
"That mountain up there,
that mountain up there.
Sayanganii-ii.
May a piece of rock from there
roll towards me.
Its blue-gray rocks.
Its blue-gray rocks."

One of the people looking in said,
"Oh!

It is starting to thunder.
The sky is turning black! It is getting dark!"

———————

And the woman raised her arms again,
"That mountain up there,
that mountain up there.
May a piece of rock from there
roll towards me.
Its blue-gray rocks.
Its blue-gray rocks."

Again the people up there said,
"Oh!
It's hailing out here!
And there are pieces of something hard coming down.
They seem to be tiny pieces of rock!"

And then one of the old men—an old man—
told the woman,
that stranger,
to stop her dancing,
that she had danced enough.

And the young woman replied,
"Ahh,
I'm having such a good time,
for I really wanted to dance."

———————

"That mountain up there
(She is singing for the fourth time),

that mountain up there.
May a piece of its rock
roll towards me.
Its blue-gray rocks.
Its blue-gray rocks."

"Ouch! Ouch!
Look, it's raining rocks now!"
someone looking in up there said.
"Let that stranger," said one of the old men,
"stop dancing. That is enough."
"Aa-h, yes,
I'll stop after one more time." And now,
she is singing for the fifth time.

This time
she thrust her arms up high,
"That mountain up there,
that mountain up there.
May a piece of its rock
roll towards me.
Its blue-gray rocks.
Its blue-gray rocks."

"Q'ruuk!" [sound of a loud crash]

And she threw herself into the entryway!

———————

After a bit
she came into the old woman's house, where the young boy
        had been sent earlier.
"Whew!

I didn't think I could do what I did.
I'm glad
that I accomplished
what I set out to do."

From somewhere came a rumbling sound
and sounds of something crashing.

And so,
after all the rumbling and crashing stopped
the woman said to the young boy,
"Why don't you go check on that village;
go see what happened."

The boy went over to where the *qasgi* had been
but it wasn't there.
There were no houses.
And as for the place where the *qasgi* had been,
the ground there was all inside out.
It was all torn up!

When it was daylight the next morning
they saw that the whole village area beyond them
was aaaall broken up.
And then,
that young woman said [to the old woman and the two children],
"Well, my dear ones,

you will live here always.
Nothing will happen to you.

As for us two, we'll go back."

_____

And so they returned
to their little place.
They went to their house first.
They went there first
and stayed there
for a number of years.
And perhaps they stayed there all winter.
They stayed there in that place.

And when they had used up everything,
everything they needed,
the woman said to her child,
"Now,
we'll go downriver to my own place,
my own house."

And so this time
they went down there
to her real house.

That woman took her child down there with her.

_____

And so it was
that man

who lived by himself
and who was longing to have a companion
was the one that marmot felt sorry for.
And thinking that
she would truly be his support
she had taken him as her husband.

But he, being willful,
met his destruction
when the ground swallowed up the village.
He was destroyed along with the others.

And so,
the woman lived on,
her pathway in life straightened out.
All the painful things in life were destroyed.
All pain was healed.
And may all the causes of sadness be over for her now.

That is all.
That is the end.

Drifters

Jerah Chadwick

Among her people she tells me
since ancient times, hunters
on spring ice, shifting
leads, one false step, almost
inaudible fracturing, then
the gurgling drum of cracks and scramble
for solidity. *We knew them*

by their animal eyes
and appetites, those who survived
by chipping ice and chewing clothes' leather
even after weeks of drifting

You could not get near
and if you trapped and dragged them home
you'd have to tie them
to the roof posts
They would wail and waste away

We learned to leave cooked food
and clothes outside the village
to avert our eyes
and show no fear, coaxing
each one to speech and recognition

Now, bed, booze, powder
pills, blackouts
of broken faith with the body
"Look the lamps are lit,
come warm yourself," we call them also

Those Who Have Been Taken Over by the Sea

Landscape and Narrative

BARRY LOPEZ

ONE SUMMER evening in a remote village in the Brooks Range of Alaska, I sat among a group of men listening to hunting stories about the trapping and pursuit of animals. I was particularly interested in several incidents involving wolverine, in part because a friend of mine was studying wolverine in Canada, among the Cree, but, too, because I find this animal such an intense creature. To hear about its life is to learn more about fierceness.

Wolverines are not intentionally secretive, hiding their lives from view, but they are seldom observed. The range of their known behavior is less than that of, say, bears or wolves. Still, that evening no gratuitous details were set out. This was somewhat odd, for wolverine easily excite the imagination; they can loom suddenly in the landscape with authority, with an aura larger than their compact physical dimensions, drawing one's immediate and complete attention. Wolverine also have a deserved reputation for resoluteness in the worst winters, for ferocious strength. But neither did these attributes induce the men to embellish.

I listened carefully to these stories, taking pleasure in the sharply observed detail surrounding the dramatic thread of events. The story I remember most vividly was about a man hunting a wolverine from a snow machine in the spring. He followed the animal's tracks for several miles over rolling tundra in a certain valley. Soon he caught sight ahead of a dark spot on the crest of a hill—the wolverine pausing to look back. The hunter was catching up, but each time he came over a rise the wolverine was looking back from the next rise, just out of range. The hunter topped one more rise and met the wolverine bounding toward him. Before he could pull his rifle from its scabbard the wolverine flew across the engine cowl and the windshield, hitting him square in the chest. The hunter scrambled his arms wildly, trying to get the wolverine out of his lap, and fell over as he did so. The wolverine jumped clear as the snow machine rolled over, and fixed the man with a stare. He had not bitten, not even scratched the man. Then the wolverine walked away. The man thought of reaching for the gun, but no, he did not.

The other stories were like this, not so much making a point as evoking something about contact with wild animals that would never be completely understood.

When the stories were over, four or five of us walked out of the home of our host. The surrounding land, in the persistent light of a far northern summer, was still visible for miles—the striated, pitched massifs of the Brooks Range; the shy, willow-lined banks of the John River flowing south from Anaktuvuk Pass; and the flat tundra plain, opening with great affirmation to the north. The landscape seemed alive because of the stories. It was precisely these ocherous tones, this kind of willow, exactly this austerity that had informed the wolverine narratives. I felt exhilaration, and a deeper confirmation of the stories. The mundane tasks that awaited me I anticipated now with pleasure. The stories had renewed in me a sense of the purpose of my life.

This feeling, an inexplicable renewal of enthusiasm after storytelling, is familiar to many people. It does not seem to matter greatly what the subject is, as long as the context is intimate and the story is told for its own sake, not forced to serve merely as the vehicle for an idea. The tone of the story need not be solemn. The darker aspects of life need not be ignored. But I think intimacy is indispensable—a feeling that derives from the listener's trust and a storyteller's certain knowledge of his subject and regard for his audience. This intimacy deepens if the storyteller tempers his authority with humility, or when terms of idiomatic expression, or at least the physical setting for the story, are shared.

I think of two landscapes—one outside the self, the other within. The external landscape is the one we see—not only the line and color of the land and its shading at different times of the day, but also its plants and animals in season, its weather, its geology, the record of its climate and evolution. If you walk up, say, a dry arroyo in the Sonoran Desert you will feel a mounding and rolling of sand and silt beneath your foot that is distinctive. You will anticipate the crumbling of the sedimentary earth in the arroyo bank as your hand reaches out, and in that tangible evidence you will sense a history of water in the region. Perhaps a black-throated sparrow lands in a palo verde bush—the resiliency of the twig under the bird, that precise shade of yellowish green against the milk-blue sky, the fluttering whir of the arriving sparrow, are what I mean by "the land-scape." Draw on the smell of creosote bush, or clack stones together in the dry air. Feel how light is the desiccated dropping of the kangaroo rat. Study an animal track obscured by the wind. These are all elements of the land, and what makes the landscape comprehensible are the rela-tionships between them. One learns a landscape finally not by knowing the name or identity of everything in it, but by perceiving the relation-ships in it—like that between the sparrow and the twig. The difference between the relationships and the elements is the same as that between written history and a catalog of events.

The second landscape I think of is an interior one, a kind of projection within a person of a part of the exterior landscape. Relationships in the exterior landscape include those that are named and discernible, such as the nitrogen cycle, or a vertical sequence of Ordovician limestone, and others that are uncodified or ineffable, such as winter light falling on a particular kind of granite, or the effect of humidity on the frequency of a blackpoll warbler's burst of song. That these relationships have purpose and order, however inscrutable they may seem to us, is a tenet of evolu-tion. Similarly, the speculations, intuitions, and formal ideas we refer to as "mind" are a set of relationships in the interior landscape with pur-pose and order; some of these are obvious, many impenetrably subtle. The shape and character of these relationships in a person's thinking, I believe, are deeply influenced by where on this earth one goes, what one touches, the patterns one observes in nature—the intricate history of one's life in the land, even a life in the city, where wind, the chirp of birds, the line of a falling leaf, are known. These thoughts are arranged, further, according to the thread of one's moral, intellectual, and spiritual development. The interior landscape responds to the character and subtlety of an exterior landscape; the shape of the individual mind is affected by land as it is by genes.

In stories like those I heard at Anaktuvuk Pass about wolverine, the relationship between separate elements in the land is set forth clearly. It is put in a simple framework of sequential incidents and apposite detail. If the exterior landscape is limned well, the listener often feels that he has heard something pleasing and authentic—trustworthy. We derive this sense of confidence I think not so much from verifiable truth as from an understanding that lying has played no role in the narrative. The storyteller is obligated to engage the reader with a precise vocabulary, to set forth a coherent and dramatic rendering of incidents—and to be ingenuous.

When one hears a story one takes pleasure in it for different reasons—for the euphony of its phrases, an aspect of the plot, or because one identifies with one of the characters. With certain stories certain individuals may experience a deeper, more profound sense of well-being. This latter phenomenon, in my understanding, rests at the heart of storytelling as an elevated experience among aboriginal peoples. It results from bringing two landscapes together. The exterior landscape is organized according to principles or laws or tendencies beyond human control. It is understood to contain an integrity that is beyond human analysis and unimpeachable. Insofar as the storyteller depicts various subtle and obvious relationships in the exterior landscape accurately in his story, and insofar as he orders them along traditional lines of meaning to create the narrative, the narrative will "ring true." The listener who "takes the story to heart" will feel a pervasive sense of congruence within himself and also with the world.

Among the Navajo and, as far as I know, many other native peoples, the land is thought to exhibit a sacred order. That order is the basis of ritual. The rituals themselves reveal the power in that order. Art, architecture, vocabulary, and costume, as well as ritual, are derived from the perceived natural order of the universe—from observations and meditations on the exterior landscape. An indigenous philosophy—metaphysics, ethics, epistemology, aesthetics, and logic—may also be derived from a people's continuous attentiveness to both the obvious (scientific) and ineffable (artistic) orders of the local landscape. Each individual, further, undertakes to order his interior landscape according to the exterior landscape. To succeed in this means to achieve a balanced state of mental health.

I think of the Navajo for specific reason. Among the various sung ceremonies of this people—Enemyway, Coyoteway, Red Antway, Uglyway—is one called Beautyway. In the Navajo view, the elements of one's interior life—one's psychological makeup and moral bearing—are subject to a persistent principle of disarray. Beautyway is, in part, a spiritual invocation of the order of the exterior universe, that irreducible, holy complexity that manifests itself as all things changing through time (a Navajo definition of beauty, hózhóó). The purpose of this invocation is to re-create in the individual who is the subject of the Beautyway ceremony that same order, to make the individual again a reflection of the myriad enduring relationships of the landscape.

I believe story functions in a similar way. A story draws on relationships in the exterior landscape and projects them onto the interior landscape. The purpose of storytelling is to achieve harmony between the two landscapes, to use all the elements of story—syntax, mood, figures of speech—in a harmonious way to reproduce the harmony of the land in the individual's interior. Inherent in story is the power to reorder a state of psychological confusion through contact with the pervasive truth of those relationships we call "the land."

These thoughts, of course, are susceptible to interpretation. I am convinced, however, that these observations can be applied to the kind of prose we call nonfiction as well as to traditional narrative forms such as the novel and the short story, and to some poems. Distinctions between fiction and nonfiction are sometimes obscured by arguments over what constitutes "the truth." In the aboriginal literature I am familiar with, the first distinction made among narratives is to separate the authentic from the inauthentic. Myth, which we tend to regard as fictitious or "merely metaphorical," is as authentic, as real, as the story of the wolverine in a man's lap. (A distinction is made, of course, about the elevated nature of myth—and frequently the circumstances of myth-telling are more rigorously prescribed than those for the telling of legends or vernacular stories—but all of these narratives are rooted in the local landscape. To violate *that* connection is to call the narrative itself into question.)

The power of narrative to nurture and heal, to repair a spirit in disarray, rests on two things: the skillful invocation of unimpeachable sources and a listener's knowledge that no hypocrisy or subterfuge is involved. This last simple fact is to me one of the most imposing aspects of the Holocene history of man.

We are more accustomed now to thinking of "the truth" as something that can be explicitly stated, rather than as something that can be evoked in a metaphorical way outside science and Occidental culture. Neither can truth be reduced to aphorism or formulas. It is something alive and unpronounceable. Story creates an atmosphere in which it becomes discernible as a pattern. For a storyteller to insist on relationships that do not exist is to lie. Lying is the opposite of story. (I do not mean to confuse ignorance with deception, or to imply that a storyteller can perceive all that is inherent in the land. Every storyteller falls short of a perfect limning of the landscape—perception and language both fail. But to make up something that is not there, something that can never be corroborated in the land, to knowingly set forth a false relationship, is to be lying, no longer telling a story.)

Because of the intricate, complex nature of the land, it is not always possible for a storyteller to grasp what is contained in a story. The intent of the storyteller, then, must be to evoke, honestly, some single aspect of all that the land contains. The storyteller knows that because different individuals grasp the story at different levels, the focus of his regard for truth must be at the primary one—with who was there, what happened, when, where, and why things occurred. The story will then possess similar truth at other levels—the integrity inherent at the primary level of meaning will be conveyed everywhere else. As long as the storyteller carefully describes the order before him, and uses his storytelling skill to heighten and emphasize certain relationships, it is even possible for the story to be more successful than the storyteller himself is able to imagine.

I would like to make a final point about the wolverine stories I heard at Anaktuvuk Pass. I wrote down the details afterward, concentrating especially on aspects of the biology and ecology of the animals. I sent the information on to my friend living with the Cree. When, many months later, I saw him, I asked whether the Cree had enjoyed these insights of the Nunamiut into the nature of the wolverine. What had they said?

"You know," he told me, "how they are. They said, 'That could happen.'"

In these uncomplicated words the Cree declared their own knowledge of the wolverine. They acknowledged that although they themselves had never seen the things the Nunamiut spoke of, they accepted them as accurate observations, because they did not consider story a context for misrepresentation. They also preserved their own dignity by not overstating their confidence in the Nunamiut, a distant and unknown people.

Whenever I think of this courtesy on the part of the Cree I think of the dignity that is ours when we cease to demand the truth and realize that the best we can have of those substantial truths that guide our lives is metaphorical—a story. And the most of it we are likely to discern comes only when we accord one another the respect the Cree showed the Nunamiut. Beyond this—that the interior landscape is a metaphorical representation of the exterior landscape, that the truth reveals itself most fully not in dogma but in the paradox, irony, and contradictions that distinguish compelling narratives—beyond this there are only failures of imagination: reductionism in science; fundamentalism in religion; fascism in politics.

Our national literatures should be important to us insofar as they sustain us with illumination and heal us. They can always do that so long as they are written with respect for both the source and the reader, and with an understanding of why the human heart and the land have been brought together so regularly in human history.

The Chickadee Woman

ELIZA JONES

THIS WAS ONE of the stories told in the Upper dialect of the Koyukon-Athabaskan language by the late Jenny Pitka of Stevens Village. The stories were tape-recorded by her niece Sally Hudson of Fairbanks. Sally gave me the tape to transcribe and translate so that the stories can be preserved and enjoyed by others. *Chickadee Woman* is one of the many stories that were traditionally told by Athabaskan people. Here I am presenting the English translation of the story that I had transcribed. The vocabulary and structure reflect Koyukon language use.

There is some confusion in this story about whether or not the woman left behind was a chickadee or bank-swallow woman. Jenny Pitka called her a bank-swallow woman at the beginning of the story, but referred to her later on, and more often, as a chickadee. So I chose to call her chickadee woman.

The story of women, young or old, left by their tribe to die, but who manage to survive by their wits and the aid of some higher power, is told by different Athabaskan groups. The late Madeline Solomon of Koyukuk told a similar story about an orphan girl who was abandoned to die during a starvation. She not only survived but saved her people with all the rabbits she snared and saved after they left her. The story was one of three stories that Madeline Solomon told that were published in a booklet called *K'adonts'idnee* by Alaska Native Language Center, University of Alaska-Fairbanks.

Some background information may be necessary for the reader to understand the story. In the past, chiefs or well-to-do men often had two or three wives, as long as they could take care of them. The women were often each other's sisters or cousins. This was an accepted practice and most of the time the women got along together. The first wife was considered the primary wife and had the highest status, and she was the boss of the other wives. In the traditional seasonal rounds, the families left their permanent winter settlements and moved around in search of game, usually caribou. It was important for the families to hunt caribou for the meat, but more importantly for the fur and sinews to make clothing. They usually left sometime in January or early February and moved around until sometime in April when the snow started thawing and it got too difficult to travel. The women worked hard making warm clothing for their families before they left. Fur-lined mittens and boots were a must, especially for the children. The men made or repaired sleds and snowshoes for the trip. They took along a *neebaale*—caribou skin teepee—to live in while traveling. Only the babies and toddlers too small to walk rode in the sleds. The children all had snowshoes to walk in. They traveled as far as they could go in one day and made camp. It was the women who usually set up camp, shoveling out a place for the teepee. They put it up and put spruce boughs down for the flooring. They also cut wood and then cooked. The men usually hunted for rabbits and spruce grouse while the women and children set up camp. Sometimes they stayed in one camp up to a week. When they did, the women set snares for rabbits and ptarmigan. They also made and set a fishtrap for black fish in a lake nearby. The fish was good eating and good food for the dogs if they had any. The men went out hunting caribou every day with bows and arrows, of course. Traveling like this was very enjoyable as long as the weather wasn't too cold.

THE CHICKADEE WOMAN
I dedicate this story to Jenny Pitka and her family.

In the time very long ago
there lived a Hawk Owl man and his wife, who was also a Hawk
     Owl.
A Chickadee family lived there.

It was fall.

They lived there until midwinter when the days started to get longer.

Then it was time once again for the whole family to move out and
    travel in search of caribou and other game.

To get meat for the family, but more important, to get fur and sinew
    to make clothing for the family.

When they hunted that way they would camp here and there while
    the men hunted in the area for caribou.

The Hawk Owl man married a pretty Chickadee woman to be his
    second wife before they left.

This made the Hawk Owl woman very mad and jealous.

Both the Hawk Owl and Chickadee family went on this trip.

They traveled all day and made a camp.

The big ordinary-looking Hawk Owl wife went out in the dark and
    searched in the sled of the pretty young Chickadee woman.

There she found some food, including some kinnikinnik berries stored
    in fish oil.

She ate some of the berries.

She came back in the house.

There was some fish oil on her hand when she came in.

She rubbed the oil around the mouth of the Chickadee woman while
    she slept.

When they woke in the morning the woman had oil around her
    mouth.

"Look at that. Looks like she stole some food from the sled," the
    Hawk Owl woman said of the Chickadee woman.

The Hawk Owl man was mad but he didn't say anything.

This went on all winter while they traveled.

Every night she'd sneak out and eat the Chickadee woman's food.

The Hawk Owl woman wanted her husband to think that the
    Chickadee woman was eating up the food supply.

This pretty young woman didn't try to defend herself when this
    happened.

Finally one day . . .

    [Intake of breath]

Once again Hawk Owl woman searched in the Chickadee woman's
    sled.

She rubbed oil around the Chickadee woman's mouth again.

"Look at her, she been stealing the food supply. Look at the oil
    around her mouth," she told her husband.

The man looked at the Chickadee woman.

She looked like she just ate.

There was fresh oil around her mouth.

"No, I didn't steal anything," she said, but no one believed her.

"No, I didn't do what she said I did. She just made it up," but to
    no avail.

They left her behind when they left that camp.

There was an old lady with them.

She was a Chickadee woman like herself but old.

That woman left a pot of hot coals for her.

When she saw that they were putting the fire out by throwing snow
    onto the fire she took some of the hot coals and hid it for her.

She knew that the young woman that they were going to leave behind
    didn't have anything.

She walked up to her and hugged her before she left and whispered,

"Take those hot coals and build yourself a fire after we leave.

Try to build yourself a fire on the river bank," she told her.

She also left a wooden drill and a tool made of caribou foot bone, and
    a sewing awl with her.

What could the Chickadee woman do after they left her?

She just stayed there.

After every one left,

leaving her behind,

she struggled to build a fire.

She managed to start the fire using dry spruce twigs.

Then she started scavenging, in the area where the people lived, for
  anything they might have left behind.
In the places where the unskilled woman lived she found lots of
  sinew.
In some places she found a whole strand that they left behind.
In the area where a skilled seamstress sat and sewed she found only
  minute amounts, or end pieces, of sinew.
She plied, plied, and plied those.
She plied them and made snares . . .
She was able to make a whole snare from the sinew left behind by the
  careless seamstress.
She only got enough to make a partial snare from each of the places
  where the skillful seamstress lived.
Then it is said that she went out to set some snares for rabbits.
She had nothing to eat. Nothing.
The only thing she had was some oil in a little skin pouch given to
  her by her grandmother.
It was the kind they used to rub on their faces.
She tasted a little bit and moistened her lip with it when she got real
  hungry.
Her grandmother must've had a feeling that her granddaughter was
  going to make it.
She went to check her snare and to her surprise and relief she caught a
  rabbit.
She skinned it and picked and saved all the sinew from that rabbit
  before cooking it.
She made more snares with those.
She also pulled all the sinew from the feet before she cut them off.
She continued to live at that place.

She traveled long distance from her camp though in search of more
  rabbits.
Once in a while she built a fire for herself and spent a night where
  there were lots of rabbits.

Soon she had <u>enough rabbit fur to make a woven or knitted rabbit-</u>
    skin blanket.
Even though a knitted blanket takes a lot of skins she knitted one.
She knitted it and stretched it.
She stretched it by spreading it out on a level place and securing the
    edges with pegs.
She left it that way for some time.
It became a good blanket.
It is said that she wrapped herself in that.
Yes, she spent the winter living in a house she built.

In the spring she moved out to the river.
She was all alone.
It was warm now but because she didn't have anything else to wear
    she was still wearing her knitted rabbit-skin parka and rabbit-skin
    pants.
She lived by her poor self when . . . *[Intake of breath]* . . .
there she was after the ice went out, when she heard people for the
    first time since being left.
She heard young men coming down the river.
She heard them singing.
"What can I say to them? What can I tell them to make them
    land?" she thought.
She was sitting on the bank.
She was looking for them.
There were two young men paddling down in canoes on the other
    side of the river.
When they were within hearing range she hollered, "My buttocks
    gets too hot."[1]
That was all she hollered.
It is said that they landed there.

1. She said that both to catch their attention and because she's still wearing her winter fur clothing. She didn't have any summer clothing to change into.

Then she told them her story:
She was left to freeze but that her grandmother left her some things
    to help her survive.
"I really need help, that is why I asked you to land," she told
    them.
So where was the Chief? Where was he?
"Here! Take my blanket."
One of the young men gave her his leather blanket.
The other young man did the same.
Using that she made herself a dress and a pair of pants.
They went up into the mountain, taking her with them.
They lived up in the mountains.
Both men were married to her.

They made a good living for her, with plenty of food and all the
    materials she needed to make things.
They were living where there were lots of caribou.
They hunted and brought home all kinds of little things to her.
She accumulated lots of goods.
She had porcupine quills and everything she needed to sew with.
With all those she started sewing.

The men she married told her that the women in their family made
    fine needles from the bones of marten penises.
They are tough and pliable.
They sewed very fine stitches with those kind of needles.
They made some.
They gave them to their wife.

Then she started sewing.
She really sewed a lot.
She tanned hides.
She tanned caribou hides.

For the big old Hawk Owl woman who caused her so much grief, she
    laid the hides on the rocks and poured some fine gravel on them
    and rubbed them into the hide while they were still raw.
Then she dried them.

Late in the summer she also made some dried meat to give her when
    they went back to the village.
Her husbands had told her that they would eventually return to the
    village.
She covered the meat with fine gravel and dried it.
It is said that she stored those away from the rest of the meat.
For her grandmother who saved her life, she made a parka of summer
    caribou hides trimmed with quills.
Summer caribou hides are prized for parkas.
She also made her a pair of pants.
She made a whole set of clothing for her grandmother.

Oh dear! It is said that that fall they left to go to back to her village.
They arrived at the village.
The people were so happy to have visitors.
They took turns visiting them and shaking their hands in the house
    that they stopped at.
Even way back then it was customary for people to shake hands.

Soon her grandmother came to see her.
She sat down facing her granddaughter to visit with her.
She took a bag out from back against the wall for her grandmother.
She dressed her grandmother in the clothes she had made.
That was for saving her life.
She came back out all dressed up.
She also saved all of her grandmother's favorite food for her.
She gave her the food including dried meat and dried fat.

Then the big old woman who lied about her, saying she stole food,
    saw the old woman in her new clothes.

She rushed over to visit the woman who came.

She gave her a lumpy caribou parka and she also gave her some dried
    meat.

She sat down and tried to eat the dried meat.

Each time she bit into the meat she bit down on gravel.

She couldn't eat it, it was covered with gravel.

It is said that she said, "What is wrong with this? Did someone
    dry this especially for me?"

That was the meat the Chickadee woman dried for her.

That is as far as I know the story.

The Dolly Varden Char:
Its Name, Its Dance, Its Prize

SHEILA NICKERSON

It is said we are named
for a dress print, a flower-sprinkled
dimity worn by a coquette in Dickens.
But fiction and clothes came later.
We danced at the first ball of the river,
winning the prize for beauty:
the right to swim from lake to sea.
Every stripe, spot, and pattern was there,
in colors not found above, and we won.
Ever since, the other side of water
has been attempting imitations. See
how their fashions change, their flowers fade.
Even their novelists fall short.

Aweigh

JIM DODGE

VICKY AND I were steelhead fishing on a secret riffle of a nameless Pacific
Northwest river, perhaps the best ironhead water between the Russian
and Bella Coola, to which you may receive directions for a thousand dollars' cash. It was late afternoon, the sky the color of wet ashes, the river
high but beginning to clear. I was drifting a roe-glo through the upper
stretch of the run when I felt a slight pause in the *tick-tick-tickity* rhythm
of the pencil-lead sinker bouncing along the stony bottom. I set the
hook. The rod tip bowed and began to pulse, the heavy, solid throb running through my shoulders.

"Fish on!" I hollered to Vicky forty yards downstream.

She turned and looked at me, yelling back, "Really?"

For some reason, this is the usual response of my fishing companions,
leading me to believe they regard me as either an astonishingly inept
fisherman or a reckless liar.

"Really!" I assured her at the top of my lungs, lifting my doubled rod
as proof before turning my attention to the battle.

Actually, it wasn't much of a battle. The fish was sulking in the strong
mid-channel current. I tightened the star drag slightly and applied some
pressure. The fish turned lethargically and headed downstream. I lightly
thumbed the spool; at the added pressure, the fish swung toward shore
down by Vicky, who had just reeled in and started walking my way, no
doubt to offer encouragement, consultation, and general assistance.

As my line sliced toward her, she stopped and peered into the water,
then shook her head. "Hey," she called, "you've got a big ol' sore-tail salmon."

"No," I begged her.

She pointed empathically a few feet offshore. "I can *see* it thrashing. Big, beat-up sore-tail."

I took the Lord's name in serious vain—no wonder the fish wasn't fighting—then tightened the drag to reel the fish in for quick release. The fish offered little resistance until it was about twenty feet away, then made a sullen move toward swifter water. When I clamped down, it swung back, passing in front of me. Sure enough, it was a spent salmon, its rotting fins worn to nubs, the battered body mottled with patches of dull white fungus.

But something wasn't right. The sore-tail was languidly corkscrewing along the bottom, a movement that didn't match the steady quiver I felt through the rod. Then I saw why: The sore-tail, in some blind expression of its spawn-till-you-die imperative, was engaged in a last gasp courtship of the fish actually connected to my line, a steelhead longer than a yardstick and as deep as a Dutch oven.

Hearing Vicky move up behind me, I whispered, "That sore-tail you saw isn't the fish I have on. It's trailing my fish, which is one humongous *hog* of a steelie, putting on some spawning moves."

"Sure it is," Vicky said.

I worked the steelhead a few feet closer, telling Vicky without turning my head, "Step up easy and see for yourself."

Vicky stepped up easy, very easy, but not easy enough.

The riffle was about fifty yards wide. With the power of a nitro-fueled dragster, the steelie crossed it in one second flat, leaving me blinded by the mist sprayed from the spool mingled with smoke from the drag. Struck dumber than usual, I simply stood there as the whopper steelie made a sharp right at the opposite shore and streaked downstream. I watched the line melting from the spool. I felt like my nervous system was being stripped from my body through the solar plexus, a rush beyond sensation toward something as clean and empty as my spool was about to be if I didn't stop the fish. But I didn't want to stop the fish. I didn't want the feeling to end.

The spool was almost down to the backing when the steelie abruptly swung back into the heavy current and dove to the bottom, slowly lashing its head.

I wanted to tell Vicky to go home and pack some grub because I was going to be there all night, but when I finally got my slack jaw working I discovered I couldn't utter the few words I could remember.

Train wreck in the cerebrum. Synaptic bridges collapsed.

I concentrated on the basic sounds, managing something close to "Biffeegaaaah."

Vicky cocked her head. "You what?"

"Big," I gasped. "Godzilla."

At the moment, though, it felt more like I was hooked to Godzilla's heart, thirty pounds of pure throbbing force, the rainbowed rod pulsing steadily as the fish hung in the current, gathering power for another slashing run.

Then the hook pulled out.

I felt like a lover had just hung up the phone after telling me, "I'm sorry, but it's over."

Like I do when the Dream Joker whispers, "You won ten million in tonight's lottery" and I wake up broke as usual.

Unplugged a heartbeat short of Divinity, a nanosecond shy of Solid Full Circuit. Lost. Looted and left behind. Mentally exhausted, emotionally gutted, spiritually bereft.

Vicky helped me back to the car.

But as I fell asleep that night, I remembered the wild power of the steelhead's cross-river run, remembered it from my bones out, in nerve-meat and blood, that rush of glory as I emptied into the connection, joined for a moment, each other's ghost, then blown away like mist on the wind; and my gratitude for that moment's nexus overwhelmed the despair of its loss—as if one can truly possess or lose anything, or the connection ever break.

In fishing, as the moment of experience enters the future as memory, it's prey to seizures of enlargement and general embellishing. I feel sure, however, that that steelhead weighed close to twenty-eight pounds. It's possible—and, given a few more years of voluptuous recollection, almost certain—that the fish would have tipped the Toledoes at over thirty, making it easily conceivable that I'd hooked what would have been a new state-record steelie. But even taking the distortions of time and memory into account, ruthlessly pruning any possibility of exaggeration, carefully considering the Parallax Effect, the Water Magnification Variable, the Wishful Thinking Influence, and the El Feces del Toro Predilection, I would lay *even* money in the real world that that steelhead weighed at least twenty-six pounds, and would gladly wager a new car of your choice against a soggy cornflake that it was twenty-four minimum.

In that spirit, I trust you will understand that I offer a blessing when I wish for our coming years that a big one always gets away.

In the Country Above

NANCY LORD

A DENA'INA INDIAN story tells of a man who fell in love with a woman he found in the woods chewing spruce gum. He took her home and they lived together, but she ate only brush and sometimes she disappeared and came home soaking wet. One time he followed her and found her swimming with beavers. She was a beaver-woman. She took him into her beaver house, taught him to swim and to eat tender branches. When fall came she told him he could go, but he didn't want to. She changed him into a beaver and they lived at the lake all the time after that. Now and then they changed into people, but mostly they were perfectly happy to remain beavers.

I don't know if this story is meant to be instructive or cautionary, or simply an entertainment, but I think about it as I walk to the lake above the cabin where we spend summers. Here, some distance down the outflow creek from the lake, beaver have built two new ponds that have flooded the trail and opened the forest.

I stand below the first dam and touch a piece of it, a butt end of alder, faceted with the cuts of chisel-wide teeth. I wonder: how is it possible that mud and *sticks*, none of them larger around than my wrist, can be holding back that eye-level expanse of flat, sun-glistened water? As I watch, fish surface with a sound like soap bubbles bursting, leave tiny ringed ripples. They're no more than fingerlength, rainbows that might have washed over the older dam at the end of the lake. Across the pond, a bush shakes; a bird I can't see is working through it, picking buds. Bird song is everywhere—the wistful, burry tones of the thrush, the trilling of warblers. Water trickles through the dam. A breeze rustles past, turning

69

alder leaves to show their paler sides. With a crack of wings, two ducks take off from the far end of the pond; pintails, they whistle across a cloudless sky.

Only two years ago this was a shady forest of dark, moss-hung spruce and twisted birch, head-high thickets of devil's club, mossy humps of the mouldering logs. Passing through on the trail we could just hear the gurgle of creek, buried somewhere within. But the beavers have altered the landscape. There are more in this country now than we've ever seen, and they've moved outward from the lake, felling enormous trees, engineering waterways. Each spring, we see ousted young ones down on the inlet, paddling through saltwater in search of new territories.

I look across the pond to a sunny slope of meadow, a purple patch I know to be new violets. After a winter of heavy snows and periodic volcanic dustings, spring has come to this part of Alaska, finally taking the past patches of gray snow from the woods. Late May, and the ferns are just unfurling, the devil's club leafing on its cudgel end. It's possible now as it never is later in the year to move through the country, to see its beginnings, its contours, and its history.

Ken calls from up ahead. Always the pragmatist, he's checking out the blueberry bushes, examining buds, predicting a good harvest. He wants to know if I remember when our first pie was, last year. It was when we were still fishing hard, still in July. I remember because I hadn't wanted to take the time to pick berries, but later I was glad we had.

I continue along the trail, thinking again of the Dena'ina. They hunted beaver, roasted their tails on sticks, used their fur for hats and sleeping robes. They lived with beaver, shared the country with them, respected them. The story suggests the Dena'ina believed a beaver's life was as legitimate as any other. It was not a ridiculous idea, in their world, to imagine a human choosing a beaver's life.

But the Dena'ina who used to be here are gone. After European, Russian, and American contact, their descendants lived in villages along the coast, where they adopted the Russian Orthodox religion and lived by fishing and working in canneries. A village site just a few miles from here wasn't abandoned until the late 1920s, when its remaining inhabitants moved north to join another village and send their children to school. Other Dena'ina, today, have disappeared into the prevailing culture.

Uphill through a tunnel of alder, we straddle the center of the muddy path, the tracks of a moose. We whoop at the top, giving notice to any bear on the other side. There it is, through the birch leaves: the lake.

We call it "the lake" or "the lake above our camp." On maps, among thousands more Alaskan lakes, it hasn't any name. Locally, we've heard two names: Horseshoe Lake, after its shape, and Hayden Lake, after our neighbor, who lives a couple of miles distant and who, when we asked him the lake's name, gave it his own.

I'm very fond of our neighbor and, after fifty summers here, he's earned his connections to this country. Still, naming pieces of the landscape after ourselves, after *people,* doesn't seem right. We leave enough mark on the country as it is.

The Dena'ina didn't name places after people. Neither did individuals, as far back in history as anyone knows, ever coin new names; the names were already there, reaching back through generations of oral tradition. When Dena'ina place names were collected from those who still speak the language, remarkable consistency was found among the speakers. Names were reported with care and with obvious affection for associations with them. A hill is known as Where an Animal Is Crouching because, from a certain vantage, it looks like a large animal preparing to spring. A hunting area is called Where Horns Are Gathered. A river is called Where Someone Put a Man's Head Under Water, commemorating a time, a story, when two men fought over a fish.

A mountain ridge we can see from our camp is known as Ridge Where We Cry. Shem Pete, one of the oldest living Dena'inas, reported in 1982, "They would sit down there. Everything is in view. They can see their whole country. Everything is just right under them. They think about their brothers and their fathers and mothers. They remember that, and they just sit down there and cry. That's the place we cry all the time, 'cause everything just show up plain."

The Dena'ina knew some of their lakes as Lake of Creek that Flows Swiftly, Grass Is There Lake, Overturned Trees Lake, Water Lily Lake, Lake in Which There Are Beaver Lodges. The lake above our camp would have had a name. We can only imagine what it might have been.

We cross the lake by creaking rowboat, escaping mosquitoes—the first of the season, the oversized, sluggish ones that wintered inside niches of tree bark. Ken rows; I sit in the stern, stare into the black water, the sun hot on my head. *Plok.* I turn to see widening rings near the shore.

I look back at the dead, broken tree that always looks to me, especially in evening light, like an antlered moose. In that low spot past it, twice, I've seen moose sunk to their knees, browsing. A week before, a bear was grubbing through the same area. Ken saw it here; I saw it later, looking over the bluff at our camp, a large blond bear with a dark stripe down its back.

There's beaver sign everywhere. Fresh, yellow cuttings. Flattened trails emerging from the brush, ending in water. The first house is partway down the lake, sprouting green alders from its roof. We creak past. I watch for a reddish beaver we've often seen here—the same one, or different ones from year to year, I don't know—but none appears. Another fish jumps. This is a good fishing spot; the rainbows like to shelter amid the underwater branches.

Ken stops rowing, fills a plastic bag with lake water, drinks from the corner of it as it spurts from pin holes in its side. I say what I say every time we come to the lake: "This is my favorite place in the world."

The lake narrows, turns. Lily pads cross the narrows. Dead, gray, weathered-to-a-shine tree trunks stand in water at the edges, a sign that the lake has risen over the years. Around the curve, down the lake's other leg, we would come to the outlet, the beaver dam, the best of the blueberry bushes. We spot a single loon on that side; it dives and comes up again. Another beaver house rises like a haystack against a stretch of grass-covered flat. The mountains lie that way, the high passes the Dena'ina crossed to first come to this country, sometime between three hundred and a thousand years ago. Today, the mountains are lost in billowy clouds.

We land the boat on a point.

We hike away from the lake, into sun-dappled forest. We kick up clouds of ash, circle hollows of devil's club, climb over downed trees. Salmonberry are already in bloom, pink petals wide and silk-smooth. Here and there, last summer's highbush cranberries are still hanging on, reduced to wrinkled red shells. The Dena'ina used all of these plants. They ate the berries, but they also boiled the highbush cranberry bark as a cure for upset stomachs and colds. They ate the shoots, flowers, and berries of the salmonberry and made a tea from its leaves. This time of year, they ate the leaf clusters of the devil's club; they spit chewed stalk onto wounds as a painkiller, wrapped fractures in bark, and harvested the root to treat toothache.

The pit, when we come to it, is obvious. It's deep, a depression in the ground, perhaps four feet lower than the forest floor. It's not the depth that's so remarkable, but the exact rectangular shape, the outline of two rooms. One is perhaps fifteen by twenty feet, the other a third that size. Rimmed with ridges of earth, they're joined with a break in the wall between them. Another break opens the large room to the outside.

I've been here once before, but I'm still taken by surprise, still overcome by something I can't easily explain. I want to hold my breath, stop time, go back. People lived here. The country remembers. The land holds this memory in ridges of earth, in deep holes, in the cry of a jay and the smell of softened spruce pitch. The people of this country lived here. I don't want to move. I only want to be frozen in their presence, the marks they made, the lines they drew.

It was a long time ago, and it wasn't. It was before Captain Cook sailed by in 1778, before epidemics of smallpox, measles, whooping cough, flu, and tuberculosis wiped out entire villages. It was not so long ago that the land's forgotten. A wall. A doorway. How many feet walked through? How many stories were told?

A spruce tree—one of the largest in the area—grows from one corner of the main room; another, somewhat smaller, stands in the pit itself. Either must be at least a couple of hundred years old.

We call them house pits. They're common in this part of Alaska, wherever the hunting was good and there was water to drink and a reasonable winter climate. They're what's left of the traditional Dena'ina houses—barabaras, as they were called by the Russians. Winter homes. I try to picture this one as it had been—dug into the ground but then framed with short walls of posts and logs, surrounded with sod, a roof of overlapping sheets of birchbark or perhaps caribou hides, back when this was caribou instead of moose country. I try to see the barabara in snow, smoke curling from the hole in the roof, snowshoe trails beaten around it. A cache built off the ground, on peeled poles, filled with bales of dried salmon. The smell of boiling meat. Sounds of people talking, babies. Winter was a time of rest. January is known, in Dena'ina, as The Month We Sing.

Right now, King Salmon Month, the barabara would be silent, empty, the country's new grass closing in around it. The people would be on the beach below, camped in less substantial houses, feasting on fresh salmon, splitting and hanging salmon to dry in the smoke of an alder fire, beginning again the cycle of preservation that would see them through another winter.

Summers on the beach, we catch salmon to sell to Japan. We eat a few, hang some in our smokehouse. In The Month Leaves Turn Yellow, we leave the beach, not to this country above, but to a country away, a house in a city.

Archaeologists have excavated a very few house pits, but they never found much in the way of artifacts of historical record. "Excessively tidy," one archaeologist said of the Dena'ina. Unlike the Eskimo, who inhabited much of the same area at an earlier period and who left a wealth of stone, bone, and clay artifacts behind, the Dena'ina had a wood-based culture. They did without stone lamps, burning instead the tails of candlefish, an oily fish. Their containers were made from spruce root, birch bark, hollowed out logs. They walked about on wooden snowshoes, hunted beaver with clubs, furnished their homes with grass mats. They burned their dead. If I were to dig into this pit, I would most likely find only fire-cracked rocks from the hearth or from cooking—from being dropped, hot, into bark bowls filled with water.

We leave the pit, walk silently, farther into the woods. Everywhere, I think I see unnatural depressions, two walls forming a right angle; I know pits are here and I can't see them exactly, or what I see are only dead trees fallen and rotted, covered with moss. I know there must be more than one house to the village. We pick our way through brush, over more deadfall. We step to the rim of another pit: deeper than the first, smaller, two rectangular rooms of different sizes connected with a pass in the wall between, unmistakable.

The woods open to more sun, another lake without a mapped name, more beaver houses. An old cabin still stands on the hillside, just up from the shore. Half the roof has fallen in; across the other half lies a wooden sled, bleached white as bone. The front door opens inward to a mess of abandoned debris: torn fiberglass insulation, rotting clothes, an old boot, broken glass, rusted cans, a bare bed frame, swollen paperback books, an overturned washing machine. A television set, sitting upright on the floor, is entirely whole, in need only of a dusting.

I've been here before, though not for years. Moose antlers that were mounted over the door have fallen to the ground. Before, I pondered the meaning of a set of bird wings—white ptarmigan wings—nailed beside the door; all that remains now are the rusting nails with a bit of fiber caught beneath them. I look for a spruce root sewing basket I remember, its side rotted out where it lay against the floor, spilling buttons, but I can't find it.

Ken examines the woodpile, cords of rotten spruce. He finds the old well, bends aside an alder to free the hatch and look inside at the cribbing, the cool, clear water deep down.

All I know about the people who lived here I know from our neighbor, Hayden, who recalls delivering them once to the Anchorage airport, their cardboard suitcase tied together with the starter cord from an outboard. He remembers them, walking through the airport door, nervous and so out of place, "holding hands like two little kids."

Doris was Dena'ina, from the village to the north. Chet was white. Summers, they fished down on the beach. They were here in 1958; I know this because one of them pounded empty twenty-two shells into the end of a cabin log, spelling out their initials and that year. Hayden remembers when they bought their generator, television, washing machine. It was Doris's "Indian money," the one-time payment each member of her village received for oil exploration on their land. He also recalls that Chet got more and more "Indian" until he forgot how to write his name and could only sign papers with an X.

Out behind the cabin, under a big spruce, there's a dog's house of bent alders, branches, and grass. A rusted chain circles the tree, buried in the wood where the tree's grown around it, thick as scar tissue. Nailed to the tree, high, are two bear paws; most of the fur is gone now, exposing bone knuckles, and lichens have begun to cover the bone like new fur. I only know that the Dena'ina used dogs for hunting bear and that they tied bear paws around a dog's neck as part of its training.

Five years ago, the last time I was here, I pulled on the dog's chain. I was interested in how much new earth had built up around the tree. I pulled and dug and slowly tore the chain from the ground, and at the end I found, not only the end of the chain, but the dog's very skull.

The surface of the lake, down past the cabin, is creased. A small brown head: the apex of an expanding wake that flows behind, widening, widening and softening, merging at last into smooth water. I suspect there are more beaver here now than at any time since before the Dena'ina came through the mountains.

Ken and I sit on the slope above the lake and eat our lunch of brownies and apples. He's eager to leave; we have work on the beach, nets to finish hanging and a log to float on the high tide. He looks at his watch. It feels odd to both of us, to be where we can't see the ocean, to not have the tide as our timekeeper. I wish we didn't have to go. Who, today, dreams of living with beavers? For all the natural beauty here—the lake reflecting spruce and mountains, the bunchberry flowers growing beside me, the *sweet-sweet-sweet* of a sparrow—I feel the loss, the absence, the missing continuum.

Those of us who come here only as visitors will never know what it was to live here, to be a part of this place. If I ever learn why people attached ptarmigan wings beside a door, I will still never, really, understand the meaning of that act. We can never know the feeling of looking down from a known place and wanting to cry—not at how beautiful the wild country is, but for our brothers and fathers and mothers, our history and our place where "everything show up plain."

Ken and I love this place, but we are starting with it almost from scratch, and without knowing what it is to live in it entirely, eating its animals and plants, making our lives out of wood. It is all we can do to begin our own year-to-year traditions, our own stories. We name our places: The Lake Above Our Camp, Where the Striped Bear Was, The Beaver House Where There Are Trout, Where the Berries Are Biggest. Down on the beach, we bought a fishing site from our neighbor, Hayden; he called it Eagle Set, after a tree where eagles liked to perch; the tree fell down and disappeared and the eagles roosted elsewhere, and still we call that location Eagle Set. The stories we tell are of people at airports, old cabins, a chain and a skull, ptarmigan wings beside a door and then no ptarmigan wings—nothing left but a spot of fiber between a nail and a rotting log.

The beaver, still swimming, looks like he's doing it for fun. I can only imagine that he may be trying to tempt us to join him.

In the All-Verbs Navaho World

WILLIAM STAFFORD

"The Navaho world is made of verbs."

Left-alone grow-things wait, rustle-grass, click-
trunk, whisper-leaf. You go-people miss the hold-still
dawn, arch-over sky, the jump-everywhere glances.
This woman world, fall-into eyes, reaches out her
makes-tremble beauty, trolls with her body, her
move-everything walk. All-now, our breathe-always
life extends, extends. Change. Change your live-here,
tick-tock hours. Catch all the flit-flit birds,
eat the offer-food, ride over clop-clop land,
our great holds-us-up, wear-a-crown kingdom.

Raven's Beak River: At the End

GARY SNYDER

Doab of the Tatshenshini River and the Alsek Lake, a long spit of
gravel, one clear day after days on the river in the rain, the glowing
sandy slopes of Castilleia blooms & little fox tracks in the moose-print
swales,
& giant scoops of dirt took out by bears around the lupine
roots, at early light a rim of snowy mountains and the ice
fields slanting back for miles, I find my way

> To the boulders
>   on the gravel   in the flowers
> At the end of the glacier
>   two ravens
> Sitting on a boulder
>   carried by the glacier
> Left on the gravel
>   resting in the flowers
> At the end of the ice age
>   show me the way
> To a place to sit
>   in a hollow on a boulder
> Looking east, looking south
>   ear in the river
> Running just behind me
>   nose in the grasses
> Vetch roots scooped out

by the bears in the gravels
Looking up the ice slopes
  ice plains, rock-fall
Brush line, dirt sweeps
  on the ancient river
Blue queen   floating in
  ice lake, ice throne   end of a glacier
Looking north
  up the dancing river
Where it turns into a glacier
  under stairsteps of ice falls
Green streaks of alder
  climb the mountain knuckles

Interlaced with snowfields
  foamy water falling
Salmon weaving river
  bear flower   blue sky singer
As the raven leaves her boulder
  flying over flowers
Raven-sitting high spot
  ear in the river,   eyes on the snowpeaks,
Nose of the morning
  raindrops in the sunshine
Skin of sunlight
  skin of chilly gravel
Mind in the mountains, mind of tumbling water,
  mind running rivers,
Mind of sifting
  flowers in the gravels
At the end of the ice age
  we are the bears, are the ravens, are the salmon
In the gravel
  at the end of an ice age

Growing on the gravels
  at the end of a glacier
Flying off alone
  flying off alone
  flying off alone

Off alone

Buried Poems

Terry Tempest Williams

There is a man in Boulder, Utah, who buries poems in the desert. He is an archaeologist who knows through his profession that eventually his words will be excavated, that although they may not be understood now by his community, at a later date his poetry will be held as an artifact, mulled over by minds that will follow his.

This man is alone, walled in by the wilderness he loves and neighbors who don't understand him. They say he spends too much time with the dead, that his loyalties are to bones, that the land could be better used for the planting of corn than the digging of corpses. They say he talks too little and thinks too much for a town like Boulder.

He has lived among the locals for decades, but he is still an outsider. It is the Anasazi who keep him here. They are his neighbors, the ones who court his imagination. It is their echoes reverberating through the canyons that hold him.

He listens and he studies. He pores over the artifacts that come into the museum where he works. When no one is around, he pulls out his glasses, slips on his white cotton gloves, and carefully turns the objects over and over as though some wisdom might speak to him from a sandal or basket or cradle board.

Occasionally, a local or two drop in. He invites them outdoors and encourages them to sit between sage. He takes his hand and sweeps it across the valley and tells them this site was once occupied by over two hundred individuals, continuously from A.D. 1050 to 1200, that this is twice the population living in Boulder today. He tells them the Anasazi were born farmers and hunters and gatherers—planting beans, squash, and corn as they supplemented their diet with big game and rodents. He tries to convince them that the Anasazi, through their technology of manos, metates, pinched pots, and atlatls, were remarkable people well adapted to an inhospitable environment. And then he stops himself, realizing how carried away he has become. He lets the visitors wander among the ruins.

On another day, some neighbors ask, "Are you finding anything good out there?"

"It's all good," the archaeologist replies, "corn cobs, charcoal, and chipping debris. . . . "

The neighbors are unimpressed. He gives in.

"But one time, we were excavating in a particular site and uncovered three ollas—corrugated vessels used for carrying water. Next to these pots were two large balls of clay that had been kneaded. You could still see palm marks from the anonymous hands that had made them. Beneath the pots and clay balls was a burial, the delicate placement of female bones."

He pauses as he rubs his hand over the soil. "I honestly believe she was a potter. We have found no reference to anything like it in the literature. It is most unusual."

The locals look at him, puzzled, and shake their heads. It doesn't register. He sees it in their eyes. They ask him for evidence and he says they buried it for another generation to uncover. They look at the dry land and they look at him, and they walk away.

The man leaves the museum for the day, locks the door behind him, and retreats to his spot in the rocks. He pulls out his pencil and spiral notebook from a front pocket of his cowboy shirt and begins writing. Poems come to him like wild horses to water. He writes a few lines, tears the paper, and burns the edges with his lighter. He writes another verse, tears it from his notebook, antiques it with fire, and places it in a pile that he holds down with his boot. By the end of the afternoon, he has a dozen or more poems. On his way home, he buries them.

The man knows the ways of these people. They ranch and they farm. They know the contours of the land, and if a white triangle of paper is sprouting where corn should be, they'll pull it up. Or if the cows are out grazing and happen to kick a sheet of paper into the air, it'll get read by the wranglers. And when women are planting borders of zinnias around their homes and uncover a poem with their trowel, they'll call their neighbors just to pass the words along.

Which is exactly what happened. Within a matter of days, the whole town of Boulder was reading each other poetry.

Some think they are love poems written by an Indian. Others guess they are clues to a buried treasure left by John Wesley Powell or Father Escalante. And still others believe they are personal messages left especially for them by a deceased family member, which is how they became known as "the ghost poems."

The archaeologist listens. He walks about town with his hands in his pockets. People are talking across fences, over melon stands, and inside their automobiles. Some individuals are even offering to buy them from their friends. But the finders of the poems won't sell. The man who buries the poems quietly slips into the convenience store and buys another notebook and lighter and returns to his place in the rocks.

His poems become shorter, more cryptic, until, finally, they are a series of pictographs—the pictographs found in Calf Creek Canyon, Coyote Gulch, and Mimi's Grotto.

The town eventually seeks him out, asking if he knows what these picture poems might mean. He refers them to different canyons, invites them to his slide shows, and tells them stories about the Anasazi who once lived where they do now. He explains how these drawings on canyon walls are a reflection of Anasazi culture, of rituals, and all that mattered in their lives. Now, he tells them, we can only speculate. The townsfolk are listening. He sees it in their eyes.

A local hands him a poem and says, "Read this. My boy found it buried near the overhang behind our ranch."

The archaeologist reads the poem out loud.

SOUNDS

The ruin clings to the cliff
Under the arching sandstone.
It is quiet now.
No longer do you hear the laughter,
The everyday sounds:
Women making pottery—the slap, slap of clay,
People cooking,
Men returning from the hunt,
The builders,
Children playing,
The cries of sorrow when a loved one passes on.
They are gone now—
The Anasazi.
The survivors.
The adaptors.
The only sounds now
Are those of the wind
The raucous sound of the raven, and
The descending sound of the canyon wren.
The guardians.*

By now, the town of Boulder has hundreds of these poems in its possession. They hang in the schoolhouse, where the children are taking up
the mystery. The community still wonders who is responsible for these
writings, questioning just how long they will continue to be found. But
poems keep appearing in the strangest places: in milk cans, on tractor
seats, church pews, and irrigation ditches. And rumor has it, the canyons
are filled with them. It just may be that the man who buries poems in the
desert has turned the whole damned town into archaeologists. The next
thing we'll hear is that the locals want to preserve the wilderness for its
poetry.

*Poem by Larry Davis, an archaeologist in Boulder, Utah.

II

Measures of Restraint

A balance that does not tremble cannot weigh.
A man who does not tremble cannot live.

—Erwin Chargaff

HUMAN HISTORY is made up of the collective stories of individual lives. It is shaped by scientific and humanistic inquiry from traditions as varied as the Greek, the Chinese, the African, and the Eskimo. We live our lives not in isolation, but against this backdrop, in the context of the natural world of which we are an integral part. From the historical backdrop we can get a sense of how best to behave as a species. From the rest of the natural world we can come to understand our place in a larger scheme.

We live with a conscience—individual and collective. Local and family histories define it for us most immediately, distant people and events shape it more abstractly. Through the living of our lives, we are creating a body of knowledge that rests on both possibility and limitation. The vitality is in the tension between the two. We must dream, but our dreams must be bound by a vision that looks both forward and back. The best we must remember, the worst we must not forget.

Family Trees

HUGH BRODY

SHE ARRIVED with a great clamour of hugs and shouts that was followed by a peculiar quiet. She settled herself into the spare room—hardly more than a narrow bed and a dressing table with a jar of flowers. Aunt Sonia had come for her summer visit.

Each year she said to me: "You are my favourite relative."

So I sat for some part of every day of every August, on a Persian rug that served as a bedspread, in her tight little room with a view over an English suburb.

What did Aunt Sonia look like to us children? She seemed so large, so grand, so loud, so important. Her bedspread was so dense with intricate perfection. Her clothesbrush, set out beside a cigarette case on the dressing table, was silver-backed. I had a sense of immaculacy and riches. A wonderful superiority.

She gave informal lessons in who we all were. "I'm going to tell you about cousin Olga. An artist. The voice of an angel. She was the best—of Vienna, Berlin, Warsaw." Her authority was unquestionable.

Her voice had a complete intensity: the sounds concentrated and unfamiliar, the emphases extreme and unexpected. Fifteen years later I realized that she had a heavy central-European accent.

She said: "You must represent me, you understand? You must be my representative in this English-speaking world."

She urged me, without ever saying the words, never to forget that *real* civilization came from a world that had been effaced.

She said: "You must learn to see the invisible. You must search always for those who have been disappeared."

She insisted that English was not quite a language of real culture. "Certainly not since Shakespeare!" And I sometimes got the impression from her that Shakespeare read better in German translation. "But now," she said, "after all that has been said in German, with the war, we can no longer regard German as a decent language." Still, she told me there were words in German that could not be found elsewhere. These, she said, we must understand. So particular words—Schadenfreude, Weltanschauung, Gemütlichkeit—broke into her English like exotic birds. Magnificent, somehow ominous for their perfection, and—to me—incomprehensible.

She said: "You must speak to me in French. To overcome the disability of Englishness." I agreed: since she did the talking, I was not much tested. My French lessons began with little commands. "Ouvre la fenêtre." "Une cigarette, s'il te plaît." These sounds seemed to be full of beauty and truth (I knew what they meant!), and added to my childish belief that one's own language, the original language, holds very little of that which *must* be understood.

The historical silences of our home were broken each summer by little more than the use of a rather fractious German. I remember that everyone cursed the cat with the particularly inappropriate "Jesus-Maria!" Adults spoke German when they thought it best the children not understand. They may have exchanged in this secret code a multitude of thoughts and anecdotes about that other, ornate home deep behind their eyes. But I doubt it. I suspect that they used German to mention chocolates that were rationed or things that propriety, not suffering, deemed better concealed.

These summers of childhood faded behind webs of growing up, and with the inevitable moves out of small rooms and away from strange, warm sounds or the cursing of the cat. In a way, in the way that is the nature of growing older, I forgot who Aunt Sonia was.

Then, many years later, after decades of forgetful travel, I returned to London. Now, with children of my own, I wondered what had become of Aunt Sonia. Suddenly I wanted to reach across all the times and distances between me and my antecedents. As if, in knowing more of the origins, the present would make better sense. As if, by visiting her again, in whatever room, I could set my own children—or the child in myself—on firm ground.

I wrote her a note, and suggested we meet. She replied with an invitation to tea. She gave me directions: turn left outside the underground station at a northwest corner of the District Line, left again, and look for the house with five rose bushes and an iron gate.

As a child I had imagined her home in London to be as splendid, as ornate and unquestionable, as she herself. But behind the gate and the rose bushes was a drab, suburban maisonette.

She welcomed me at the door and led me to a tiny kitchen where she pressed me to eat central-European delicacies. She talked about plays she had seen on television and articles in newspapers. She spoke with all the passion, with all the accents, of the European émigré. And I listened for echoes.

How natural it seemed to sit there. The comfort of family ties without their customary reproaches. I visited often.

I discovered that she was very small, very compact. Her clothes were always neat, enclosing her firmly. Her hair was gray and set in a wave. She wore a patch of powdery pink on each cheek, and thin lines of lipstick. I realized that she was an energetic, impatient woman. And bossy, too. Not someone for whom a mellow nostalgia or pained dredging through the past was anything like a habit. Far from it: she buried events under the energies of today. I asked her questions about her life, but she refused to return to the Europe of her childhood. She said: "I was twenty-five when I left Vienna, a few weeks after the German Anschluss." And she told me: "I would never again set foot in those parts of the world!"

She talked about characters in her life, but apart from their history. She avoided any real journey into prewar days. Nonetheless, I began to feel I could look through her eyes at footprints leading to and from the history that, in some measure, was also my own. And one day I asked her if she kept any old pictures of herself when young, the house they had lived in, Vienna before the war. She pulled a box from the back of a cupboard: a collection of photographs—a tattered archaeology of her life and culture.

All of the pictures in the collection predated the war, and none of their subjects had ever cared to visit England. They included oval portraits and groups by the sea. Self-conscious but often full of laughter: bright and various forms of another era's here and now.

Among the photographs I found in Aunt Sonia's archaeological box was a tiny portrait of my great-grandmother. I asked if I could keep it. "Of course," said Aunt Sonia. "Take any of them." But I took just the one and put it in my wallet. I never knew my great-grandmother. My desire to have her photograph may have come from a need to carry the image that reached furthest back in family time.

The picture's quality is surprisingly good: a large, pale woman squints out of a backdrop of studio clouds. At first glance her expression appears severe; a closer look shows a wry smile, an inner comment, perhaps, on the whole business of posing. The way in which she holds her head, long necklaces, the weight of a dark, plush coat—the impression is of confidence, solidity. The picture was taken in the early 1930s.

Last year, talking to Aunt Sonia on the telephone, I asked what happened to her grandmother, my great-grandmother. The solid woman of the photograph.

"She perished," said my aunt.

"Where? How?"

"She was killed by the Russians."

"By the Russians? When?"

"At the beginning of the war."

"In 1940? Were the Russians killing Jews in Poland? Wasn't it the Germans, the occupation in the east? Wouldn't it have been '41 or '42? Anyway, what *happened?*"

"She perished."

The next time I visited her, I asked Aunt Sonia to help me draw up a family tree. Herself at the centre. The others perched in branches above and around. The leaves of the tree fluttered in Austria, Poland, the Ukraine, and then across the world. An autumnal scattering. Ernestina, Theodora, Gershon. And here, the children, Maria, Leon, Chaim, Marie-Elizabeth. A diaspora of names, arranged in clusters. Gregor, Jacob, Miriam. And on the other side, Jakub, Szmul, Hillel. Now who was on my uncle's side, yes, Irena, Ludwik, Evgenie, Oskar, Mordechai. And their uncles and aunts, over here: Adam, Louisa, Joseph. The grandparents were Isaiah and Christina.

As she filled in the slots, Aunt Sonia muttered questions to herself. "Who *were* the Einbach children? The Zelkowicz parents? The Liebman grandparents?" At one point she said, as if reciting a line she had read in the Talmud, "The soul of the world is locked up in names."

I thought: I am asking Aunt Sonia to make a journey, albeit cryptic, to a history that seems not to be on her mind. And yet—how naive it would be to expect otherwise!—the names came pouring out. And with the names a ghastly conjugation. Bronislava, she perished. Ludwik's brother, he perished. The sisters, they perished. She perished, he perished, they perished. I put a thin red line through the victims.

All family trees are a journey to the graveyard. Other families' naming would have been worse: many of my relatives escaped: leaves did fall in England, Canada, Australia, and Israel. No, the weight of Aunt Sonia's story lay in the word "perished." These were not men and women and children who *died*. They did not end their lives in a particular year, or at a particular place, or as a result of particular diseases. No long illness, no sudden heart attack, no tragic accident. Nothing comic. No one run over by a tram. Not even a mysterious suicide. Nothing that let death affirm life. They "perished."

I looked at the names we had written. I pressed Aunt Sonia for details, asking her to recall what she knew of circumstances that might differentiate each one of our family within the amassed slaughter. She looked up from the white sheets of paper I had spread on her kitchen table and asked, "Can anyone bring a loved one to mind with only a memory of the eyes?"

"Isn't that one of the reasons for making a family tree," I said.

She replied: "Without a name I can't bring anyone to mind."

"And here are the names; you remember so many," I told her.

"I can bring them back to life," she said. "I can bring back their lives. But that's all. As for the deaths . . ."

She paused, then said: "I haven't heard, I never heard." She paused again. "I can't remember. Why don't you ask Cousin Elsa? She would know."

I wanted to know.

But for Aunt Sonia, I decided, the details of this family tree, the actual history, from the beginning of a name to its end, would be too terrible to endure. The bits and pieces of the tree that she marked out for me were a form of quick memory, a flicking on and off of lights. As a whole, the making of our family tree was a reference—detailed and personal— but only a reference to an episode. A madness. From which Aunt Sonia had, more or less, removed herself.

I did ask Cousin Elsa for details. Older than Aunt Sonia, and someone who fled east behind the retreating Russian lines, she knew far more. She recollected circumstances. Her child died of starvation in Lvov, 1940. Her husband died in Dachau in October 1943. Her brothers-in-law were shipped to Auschwitz in '44. Her favourite brother, a member of the Polish underground, was tortured to death. Also '44. Weeping, she said: "I should have died too." I stopped asking.

I had learned enough. I could tell my children, should they ever need to know, how their family came to England. More or less what hap-pened to their grandparents, great uncles and aunts. I could tell them about Aunt Sonia. I could tell myself. It had been enough, almost, to spend time with Aunt Sonia, to listen to her, as I had those summers long ago, and to have seen her box of photographs.

I began wondering, what is the difference between knowing and not knowing the facts? Aunt Sonia knew that people were killed by the hun-dreds and hundreds of thousands. Among them individuals she loved; family members, who in part gave her her life, perished. So of course she knew. Yet I found myself thinking that she kept the knowledge general-ized in order not to wish, day after day, like Cousin Elsa, that she too had died.

The night after my conversation with cousin Elsa I had a dream about Aunt Sonia. She had grown very tall and elegant, her hair was long and fair. She was walking down some unfamiliar boulevard, carrying a para-sol. She stopped and turned to look at me. She said: "There must be some belief, some hope." I felt a sudden shame, as if the beam of her eye carried guilt deep into me. She seemed to wait for an answer, but none came. So she said: "One seeks to be more than a crippled survivor." Still I made no answer. She said: "The grief will be yours." The words seemed to wake me, already true in part.

The following weekend I went to see Aunt Sonia. I tried to be normal, attempted to gossip. But she was distracted. I asked her what was on her mind.

"I've been thinking about what happened. About the turning point," she said.

I felt uneasy, a moment of distant dread. As if she had anticipated questions I had decided never to ask.

"I left Vienna," she said. "I went to Paris. I believed that France was safe. I thought the Nazis would never take France."

She paused.

"I wasn't the only one. We heard that many German generals believed that the French army was too strong for their blitzkrieg. I shared the opinions of the German generals! But they were executed." Her voice became very quiet, she seemed so small in her neat cardigan and permed hair. "I had to run again. That was the turning point."

"In what way?"

"In what way! Europe had ended! Berlin, Vienna, Paris—all in the hands of the insane barbarians. All culture was finished."

"So you came to England." I had heard this part of the story many times before.

"I came to London, to wait. To see what was going to happen. To choose a place to go. Palestine? Australia? I wasn't sure. But definitely not here!"

She laughed and shrugged. Then she talked for a long time, in a quiet voice, without sadness or anger. Bit by bit she had settled in England in a rather English way. She felt safe. Protected. And in a Birmingham factory, where she was sent to work on a shoe-making machine, she met a shortsighted, unglamorous, movingly decent Englishman. They became lovers. He moved in with her. The wider protection of the nation had its echo in a narrow domestic safety.

When Aunt Sonia told me about the Birmingham man, it was to explain why she did not leave Europe. She laughed about the unlikely passion they felt for each other. She said, "I think he appreciated a bit of noise." Before the war ended—though at a time when its outcome was no longer in doubt—he left her. And married a neighbour. "Not young, not beautiful. But more suitable," she said. "Really I didn't mind." Then she started to spend time with our family—with its brand-new generation. The summer visiting had begun.

A few weeks after Aunt Sonia had told me about her journeys in the early years of the war, she talked about the immediate aftermath of the war. The period during which she learned who had survived. She suddenly said: "The names I knew were Heydrich and Eichmann and Himmler."

I said: "I suppose you mean you can't know the names of the men who really committed the murders."

She did not answer.

I sat there, at her kitchen table, imagining the names of the young men who flicked a whip, fired a revolver, tied a noose around a neck, managed the daily gassings. Grief was clutching at my stomach. I had nothing to say. But she broke the silence: "No names. No details. Specialists track some of them down. I am not a specialist."

The next day she sent me a postcard. On it was written a cryptic little message: "Heydrich, Eichmann, Himmler. Another family tree. The family of murder."

I imagined her as she wrote that, thinking: Our family tree is over here, with those that perished marked through with a thin red line. Their family tree is over there, with those who were said ultimately to be responsible for the murders marked in bold. No details surround the names of the dead; no details of the actual murderers either. Both family trees wrapped, smothered, in silence.

I thought: I must accept the silence. I feared the grief. But I wrote Aunt Sonia a reply to her card. I said: "Everywhere the small facts remain deeply hidden. There is an inevitability about the ignorance: in the midst of genocide, individual death is hard to isolate. What can we know of my great-grandmother's murder other than as one of a batch?" I did not tell her that I had begun to imagine, over and over, the moment when she was the one who climbed on the bodies in a pit, the moment when she became the next one to be shot. Images built from her photograph, and from an archive of old pictures. No colour. Nothing vivid. I began to know how difficult it was to get beyond her having simply perished. Aunt Sonia had turned the tables on me: I kept thinking we had talked about the family tree enough.

Aunt Sonia, however, surprised me.

I visited her a week or so after receiving her postcard and sending her my letter. She said she wanted to talk about why we had written to one another. I said: "Isn't there a problem of circumstances? I mean, if a member of a family is assaulted or killed, other members—the survivors—memorialize the wound and grief by knowing as much as can be known. The name of a rapist or a murderer, the details of a punishment." She listened with unusual attention, murmuring once: "They are buried under heaps of bodies."

I went on. "The trouble is, we are cut off from both the crime and the criminal. Between those that 'perished' and the gross figures of Heydrich, Eichmann, Himmler, there is little more than a sense of some foul gang. They had power, then were defeated. Of course we know that members of the gang survived and scattered about the world, ageing in hiding. Odd ones are winkled out and dragged into the light. Then we are given the personal stories we need. But these stories do not establish for sure that this or that one killed in such and such a manner on an actual day some particular relative. These stories at the trials, or even those in the detailed work that comes from searching archives, offer nothing that can be marked beside the red lines on the family tree."

I looked at her, thinking I wanted to stop these thoughts. I said: "Is that what you meant by your postcard? On our tree the labels without settings, and on the other side the selected names in bold."

I had finished, or, more likely, had puzzled myself to a long pause. She said: "I don't think so. No. I don't think that is so."

I said: "So what do you mean? Or is it all too horrible to talk of any more?"

She looked at me and smiled. "I don't know. Now I am tired."

The attempt at the family tree, the repetitions of the word "perish," the thoughts and conversations between us that followed, some coincidence of things, the moment in our modern histories, whatever there was, for both of us, in the air—for some such set of reasons Aunt Sonia began to do research.

At first it was a bit of a book here, a bit of a book there. Quite soon she was a devoted—dare I say "fanatical"?—extramural graduate student of the Holocaust.

The first phone call came on a Sunday evening. I remember I was in the middle of getting the children to bed. I had begun telling the latest story about giants and mountains. I picked up the phone, eager only to get off it again. When I heard Aunt Sonia's voice I suppose I resigned myself to the weekend news update. But she had a different kind of news on her mind. Her voice was slow, without its usual quickfire qualities, without its energetic confidence. She sounded measured, didactic:

"I've been reading. Listen. In Hungary they didn't begin the killing until 1944. Did you know that?"

"No."

"Not until the war was as good as over. But that's not the point. The point is, the Hungarian police did it. I mean, two thousand local police pushed them all into the trains." Still her voice paced out each fact, step by step. "They counted them, seventy-five to a car, and drove them in with whips. Seventy-five to a car. Old people were dying right there at the station. The police forced them in. It took sixty-five days to send four hundred thousand to be gassed. The murderers. The police were murderers."

She said more. She restated this discovery, measured it out in different ways as if to be sure, as if to be able to present this history with neither doubt nor embellishment. In each part, from each angle, she always ended with the police. *They* surprised her.

The next call came a couple of days later. At Tuesday lunch time. Not a moment she would usually phone me. Again the slow voice. I thought: Is she a little drunk? My attempt, no doubt, at a first line of defence.

"I've read something else. There were over fifty thousand concentration camp and slave labour guards at their posts at the end of the war. Fifty thousand! Who were they all?"

Then on Wednesday night:

"Romania was one of the worst. I've discovered that Himmler complained that the Romanians were being too efficient. Twice. Two different complaints. The German camps couldn't cope with the number of people they were sending to be slaves or killed. That was in 1941, and I think in '42."

Friday:

"Heydrich had a plan. All worked out. And he thought people all over Europe would help him. And lists. In January 1942—just before he was blown up—he showed all his lists. He even had marked out three hundred thousand in England. These were the people he expected to be exterminated here."

I said that I was not surprised that there were plans and lists. The Germans are famous for efficiency. This exasperated her.

"No, no. That's not it. They didn't just have plans. They had an expectation. They were sure that they would be helped. That there would be *co-operation*."

The phone kept ringing. Over the coming weeks Aunt Sonia passed on the facts she could not bear to keep to herself. The details she could not live with. The discoveries that ate at the foundation of her hopes. I heard about the Ukraine, Poland, France, Greece, Czechoslovakia, Holland, Norway. . . . I became used to her new, strange way of talking to me. I was drawn into the rhythm of her calculations.

The research, like the voice, was relentless—and had its pattern: Aunt Sonia was mapping out the spread of that other family tree. She was marking innumerable, innumerable dots, and then joining them together. From trunk to branch to twigs to leaves. From Lithuanian guards to German gas-chamber manufacturers, to businessmen with slave labourers on their production lines, to mechanics who fixed death truck exhausts, to Latvians who assisted the murder squads, to Poles who extracted teeth from corpses, to railway workers, to researchers into the useful poisons.

Aunt Sonia, marking and joining these dotlike facts, was drawing a baobab of immense proportions. Limbs of this huge tree reached the width and breadth of the Europe the Germans managed to dominate. Branches spread through civil service offices, police stations, nationalist political organizations, churches. Its leaves fluttered down in quiet back-yards, seemingly harmless living rooms, and on homes in every town and village of the war zones and occupied lands.

The last of the history phone calls was the most troubled and the long-est. Her voice had now lost its measured tones. She spoke much faster, yet without restatements, no emphatic or balancing repetition. At the beginning of this call she tried to tell me something about Italy and Bulgaria—the countries to which, apparently, the arms of the monstrous tree did not quite reach. A reprieve. I clutched at the reprieve. Encour-aged it. I said: "Ordinary people were on every side. For and against. The Resistance. Socialists as well as prison guards. Attempts on Hitler's life. Men and women in every country who risked everything to save Jews."

But she changed tack altogether and said, "I don't suppose you know about Evian."

"Evian?"

"The conference. They talked about refugees."

"Who talked about them?"

"Everyone. England. America. Australia. Mexico. And others."

She told me that this was the beginning of restrictions. At the very moment of despairing need, they restricted immigration.

"They shut them in," she said. "They turned groups back at the Swiss border. Do you know why? Can you imagine such a thing? Because the Swiss government, in its wisdom, ruled that racial discrimination was not a good enough reason to be a refugee. Not a good enough reason!"

She hesitated. Then shouted down the phone at me: "Are you still there?"

"Yes."

"I thought you'd gone. I'll tell you. Even Finland, even the one coun-try whose rulers defied the extermination plans, even the country where they said 'kill us first if you plan to kill our people.' Even from Finland fifty Austrian refugees were sent back to Austria, back to the Germans. Why? Because their visas were not 'in order,' because they came from the Austrians and not from the Finns."

"I didn't know."

"Of course you didn't. So I'm telling you. You have to know. And something else. Do you know something else?" She didn't wait for my answer. "I've discovered about the Americans. Thousands of Jews could have escaped, would have been allowed out, if there had been boats to carry them. The Americans said they could not provide boats. No ships available." Her voice was getting louder: "They said there weren't any boats—and at the same time they were shipping tens of thousands of German prisoners of war! And not just the Americans. The British too. They refused to let children escape. And something else. There were deals with the Nazis that would have saved thousands more. Yes." She shouted. "Eichmann offered lives for gold! But the deals fell through: the British and Americans created currency and shipping difficulties. Always difficulties. Delays. No deals were possible. A million could have been saved." She shrieked at me, in a sort of climax for her facts: "They were condemned to death, by our allies. And do you know? They wouldn't bomb the railway lines to Auschwitz. They said there were technical reasons. They let the trains keep running!" And after this scream, she said quietly, "That was the four hundred thousand Hungarians. The ones the police had loaded." Then her voice faltered. I realized that she was at a loss. And, lost, she asked about the children.

Aunt Sonia never mentioned her research again. But she did not return to any ordinary way of talking. In fact, she could no longer stop herself from talking. She had always been a chatterbox. But now, in her endless stream of words, now she was compulsive, frantic. Words like small bricks with which she built a high, thick wall. It was infuriating. Then alarming. She alienated everyone. She appeared to be self-obsessed, drowning in her own trivia. So noisy. And so inconsequential.

Then, suddenly, "elle se tut." I borrow the use of the expression from a French short story I once read. And I think her end is best expressed in

French. "Elle se tut." She shut up. I was told by her doctor—an old family friend—that it could have been an overdose. Perhaps, just possibly, an accident. Who knows?

Her silence, at first, was the silence of the world. All around and within me. I went to her house. I stood in the kitchen, in order to remember her. Her absence, like all the absences of the dead to whom we stand adjacent, if only for moments, was like a blanket over the soul, a brief suffocation. In grief we close our eyes, we gasp, we gulp for air. We try and muster the facts.

I stood in her kitchen; and when I breathed again and opened my eyes, I asked myself: Why did she choose silence? Something to do, I was sure, with the roots of the spreading tree. Where did these roots find their sustenance? What social compost, what system of society made this tree take its shape and then grow with such relentlessness? Until its deformity became the norm, its leaves the colour of every time of year.

I thought: Here is the unbearable discovery. For she had to continue, had no choice but to continue, to live on the earth where this tree had its roots. No possible land existed without the hummocks and furrows of its system. The soil of its nurture—the earth of Europe—has not been, can not be, remade or replaced. Its leaves lie skeletal everywhere. Cut off stumps and old branches are the framework of our way of life. Both trees—our family of labels and the latticework of murderers—occupy a one and only terrain. There could be no more innocence. With her new facts, Aunt Sonia could no longer have hope.

She left me a letter. I don't think of it as a suicide note. We had often written to each other. But this was strange, a surprise. It was like a work of scholarship. Quotes were linked by questions. The quotes came from letters I had written to her. The questions were hers. This strange document reached me after "elle se tut," after the silence. As I read the quotes and questions I felt that, even after all these years, I was still the little boy sitting on the Persian rug in the spare bedroom of our family home, being told that I must continue to be her representative. It was the last of our conversations.

In quoting Aunt Sonia's final letter, I realize I am quoting quotes and paraphrases of myself. A curious turning inward of the circle. A resolve, on Aunt Sonia's part, to carry the issue forward—if only into another generation. She may have been offering me the escape that had, after more than half a century of trying, failed her. In this letter she said:

> . . . You wrote to me on May 8th, 1972. You told me about your first trip to the Arctic. You said: "I looked down from the windows of a Twin Otter aeroplane. We were circling the settlement, beginning to land. We had flown for nearly two hours. Over nothing but nothing. Tundra and then the ice of Hudson Bay. No fields. No walls. No *property*. And the ice, both of the lakes and the sea, is every shade of blue and green. This supposed emptiness is full of unbelievable beauty."

She followed this with the question: Is emptiness what you needed? And went on: I don't think so.

> You wrote in July: "The tundra is marked by such subtleties. Of plants that thread themselves into the permafrost and tuck themselves into the shelter of rocks and tussocks, and whose flowers are small and delicate and vivid with a miniature brilliance. And the subtlety of the tracks of animals—lemming trails worn into the earth, weasel and fox prints across a snowbank. And above all, or subtlest of all in the human scheme of things, signs of people. Graves and cairns and tent rings and the remains of an old turf and bone house. These are everywhere yet make no difference to the surface of this world. Layer upon layer of men and women whose remains are solid, made of stone and bone and shaped wood, and at the same time ghostly, delicate, integral to the landscape."

She wrote after this: Were ghosts what you needed?

> I think not. I remember you told me that the people of the north have avoided—what did you call it?—the neolithic catastrophe. You meant, I think, that when there was no agriculture, when human beings were hunters, they had a way of life in which men and women acknowledged their dependence on one another and therefore were equal. That there was no ownership of the things people needed in order to live. No private lands. No private fishing. That they did not tyrannize children. Nor tyrannize themselves with worries about their children. You wrote in a letter, in January 1980:

"This is a world without fields. I look across from where I live, and see land. Resources, not development. I travel with hunters. They are individualists, but there is no competition. They harvest, but with no sense that their taking will leave less for others—or that their failure could come from others' success."

And Aunt Sonia asked: Is there, after all, a system beyond mass murder? Have you travelled to where there is, or was, or can be envisaged, a redemption? You said only a year ago, in a springtime letter: "The men and women of this camp sit and wait. They appear to sift the world around them without anxiety, as if thinking were no more anxious, no more hesitant, than drinking tea. They are waiting for the wind to change direction, the animals to move farther to the north, the children to feel well, for things to be *right*. They are calculating without the paraphernalia of outward rationality; they are intuiting without self-conscious insistence on intuition. In a fully human way, they think. So with calm, they wait."

The final line of this letter was her question: "What did you think they were waiting for?"

The Later Biography of
Raoul Wallenberg

MELINDA MUELLER

1.

Loss
is always particular,
never general.

Though thousands are dead
in an earthquake or
the trenches,
there is no dispensation.

For each
will have to be suffered
a separate
unmitigated grief.

So, in our last
glimpse of him, he
believed.

2.

There have been late,
chill rains making a mâché
of petals under the apples' dark-
stained trunks.

There have been lilacs foaming
against clouds,
curds of violet and gray set
above the leaves'
round hearts.

And on well-fed afternoons
crows leave aside their signature
guttural cries
and clatter their beaks like castanets,
with one liquid note
at the finish.

There has been one thing, and another,
and another. This love
of the physical world never
goes unpunished.

3.

Incidental details attend
any life.

For what we don't know, then,
write something else in its place:
the one chair kept vacant
by the table,
out of respect.

For a life, this:
In the night sky, the planets
are those lights that
do not flinch.

Hummingbirds
and Human Aggression:
A View from the High Tanks

GARY PAUL NABHAN

I

THIS IS NOT exactly what I'd call a resort, nor have I come here for
sport. Instead, I've pulled into a pit stop on the devil's highway, in February 1991, for a reckoning of sorts. I've come to see if anything grows
in the tank tracks scarring the desert floor, to watch creatures battling for
riches in patches along dry washes, and to reflect upon human aggression.

My camp in Arizona's Stinking Hot Desert is more than twenty-five
miles away from the nearest permanent human habitation, but less than
four from a stretch of international border. That stretch, among the hot-
test on earth, has pulled me into its camps six winters over the last sixteen. This year differs in a subtle manner; I feel a tension carried in the
atmosphere that I have failed to observe before. I sense this weight in the
air is somehow balanced by the war in Kuwait. I am not sure, however,
whether I am the one bringing this tension along, or whether it is en-
demic to this land of little rain but remained hidden from me in the past.

The origins of this tension have become my consuming passion. Like
a lab scientist peering through a microscope to identify some debilitating
disease, I've fixed on a global issue through concentrating my attention
on this desert microcosm. I hope to discover a morality that is not an ab-

straction, one that emerges out of the local ecology, and that I can adhere to in this place. This morality must address a fundamental issue: "Are human societies fatally stuck in a genetic script of aggression against one another, whether or not such behavior is now adaptive?"

With every step I take around camp, I seek clues. I find myself kicking up bones, grave markers, ammunition shells, historic warheads, and missile debris. At night, I glimpse vapor trails of various nomadic tribes coming in for a little water; the cliffs echo with the calls of owls, these hooting souls reminding me of their presence.

Maybe I can echo-locate myself for you. I'm below an ancient watering spot along the Camino del Diablo, where over four hundred deaths have been recorded during the last century and a half. Some of these wayfarers died of thirst, some from broken dreams, some from ambush. Here, it is not hard to imagine hunters in pursuit, and the hunted in hiding or in flight. Over millennia, various tribes have converged here as their migration routes intersected. They bartered, haggled, or battled over scarce resources, and they shifted the boundary lines of their territories. My camp below High Tanks is loaded with the dispirited bodies of these past encounters, for the historic cemetery and much of the prehistoric archaeology once evident here have been bulldozed and tank-trampled by more recent military maneuvers.

I should explain, by the way, that I speak of two sorts of tanks. The latter are those of the U.S. Marines, armed and armored all-terrain vehicles. The former, the High Tanks, are usually called *Tinajas Altas,* as they were named in Spanish prior to the battle of the Alamo, when they were still part of Mexico. The High Tanks form a series of nine plunge pools, waterholes no bigger than bathtubs, naturally carved into the bedrock of a shady drainage that cascades five hundred feet down an abrupt granitic ridge.

Such cascades are seldom covered by waterfalls here in southwestern Arizona, where precipitation is so variable from year to year that all averages and ranges have lost their currency. Rain may fail twenty-six months at a time, but bombs fall out of the sky quite frequently, because the tanks lie in a bombing range jointly administered by the Marine

Corps Air Station in Yuma and a Bureau of Land Management office in more distant Phoenix. The area is often closed to "public access" during periods of bombing exercises, tank maneuvers, and mock battles. Here, in the late 1970s, the U.S. military reputedly prepared for the ill-fated helicopter raid into Iran's arid turf to free American hostages, and more recently it prepped for Operation Desert Storm.

I ponder that operation and my own genetic history as an Arab-American. A week before missiles were exchanged across the Saudi Arabia–Kuwait border, a Middle Eastern geographer sent me a few pages from Sir Arnold Wilson's 1928 history, *The Persian Gulf.* I was simultaneously intrigued and appalled to read how, eleven centuries ago, a state of anarchy prevailed from Oman to Basra. Taking advantage of the general chaos, Muhammad bin Nur wrested control of the region: "He cut off the hands and ears, and scooped out the eyes of the nobles, inflicted unheard-of outrages upon the inhabitants, destroyed the water-courses, burnt the books, and utterly destroyed the country." Nur's tyranny was met with "the vengeance of an infuriated people," who disposed of his deputies but then went through seven Imams of their own in less than thirty years. The area continued to be fraught with "intestine quarrels," Wilson tells us; then, "about the middle of the twelfth century, the Nabhan tribe acquired the ascendancy and ruled over the greater part of the interior of the country until the reestablishment of the Imamate in A.D. 1429; this tribe, however, continued to exercise considerable influence for quite two centuries longer . . . until . . . finally suppressed."[1]

Stunned, I learned how my own Nabhan kinsmen fought off Persian invaders, skirmished with a petty sheik from Hormuz, and then dealt with the dread Mongols who, at one time, held nearly all of Asia Minor. During this epoch, a few lasting monuments were introduced: underground *qanat* waterwork technologies, stone dams, arid-adapted crops, and Persian-influenced temples. To be sure, the long chronicle of bloodletting, upheaval, and desert destruction dwarfs these material accom-

1. London: George Allen and Unwin, pp. 82–83.

plishments. My paternal ancestors had no doubt been as absorbed in the warring, the warding of territory, and the hoarding of resources as any of them. Do genes for pugnaciousness lie latent within me? How much of the same bellicosity can be found in the history of Everyman?

I ask these questions to the desert, not rhetorically but literally: to the desert that is an open book waiting to be read, the desert that so casually pulls up its shirt, like Lyndon Johnson, to show us its scars. And I ask these questions to the Sonoran Desert in particular—but because the Sonoran is hitched to every other desert in some essential way, the answer I hear has bearing on the Persian Gulf.

II

The sound of divebombing jars me from my slumber. Some hummingbirds call this place home, others migrate through it, but they all fight tenaciously for its resources. I hear metallic shrieks and *zings*—the latter not unlike the sound of glancing bullets—as they dive or chase one another. I try to roll over and cover my ears, but the high-pitched chittering has penetrated the tent walls. I must get up, go out, and face the music.

The morning sun has not yet come over the Cabeza Prieta range across the valley from us, but the fighting began well before daylight. I am camped in a wash that is a haven for hummingbirds, but to arrive here they crossed a veritable hell, virtually devoid of the nectar and insect foods that their hyperactive metabolisms require. For miles in any direction, the surrounding desert flats and rocky slopes have little to offer the migrants of late winter. However, along a couple hundred yards of superficially dry watercourse leading down from the tinajas into the desert valley, the shrubbery is unusually dense. The native bushes form nearly impenetrable hedges of foliage along the banks of the wash, and some of these verdant walls look, at first glance, to be splattered with blood. But the color in fact is supplied by thousands of crimson, floral tubes of *chuparosa* for which the shining warriors battle.

Chuparosa simply means "rose-sucker" or "hummingbird" in Spanish. I am speaking of flowers so custom-fit for pollination by hummingbirds that they bear the bird's name wherever they grow. The chuparosa flower is elongate for hummingbird bills and tongues, a chalice filled to the brim with nectar each dawn. The bushes bloom through late winter in frost-free zones, tiding the birds over until the coming of spring stimulates other plants to blossom. Their bright color can attract hummingbirds from some distance away. In turn, the winged creatures transport the "sperm of floral sex" from one bush to the next, ensuring cross-pollination. The birds' iridescent heads become discolored by the thousands of pollen grains plastered onto them as they probe the flowers, hovering at their entranceways.

As I marvel over the perfect fit between hummer and blossom, another hummer comes along—and a high-speed chase begins. The Rufous Hummingbird and Costa's Hummingbird dogfight over the flower that is seemingly suited to fit both their needs, while I wonder how their belligerence is viewed by the Bambi Bunch, those who see all animals as cute, cuddly, or constantly in balance and at peace. In the blazing sun of a Tinajas Altas morning, I take a hard look at the desert, its creatures and flowers, trying to keep my own rose-colored glasses from tainting the picture, from stereotyping as nature films and glossy magazine features so often do. I concede that Nature behaves unlike model members of either the Tooth-and-Claw Hunting Club or the Benevolent Sorority of Nurturing Networkers. Nature, to my knowledge, has not recognized that adherence to any anthropomorphic construct is a requisite for existence. I try to put such filters aside, wanting to read the desert's own patterning without superimposing others upon it.

Rufous Hummingbirds do not nest here; they migrate up through California when the ocotillo blooming begins, and some continue as far as Alaska. The wandlike ocotillos are spread widely over the rocky ridges and flats of the Sonoran and Mojave deserts. Their populations burst from bud sequentially—south to north—providing migrants with a bridge extending northward. Sometimes, when cold winter weather has postponed ocotillo flowering several weeks, the hummers try to migrate anyway—in advance of peak flowering. Ocotillo fruit in these years are left with low reproductive success when their pollinators miss their date.

The ocotillo-flowering fest is an event that will begin here in another week or so. In most years, I recall, migrants such as Rufous arrive in late February just prior to the opening. They pack into the chuparosa patches already occupied by Costa's and Anna's, adding to the territorial tension. Physiologist William Calder, who discovered a remarkable life-long fidelity of hummingbirds to their nesting sites, has also observed Rufous individuals allegiant to particular stops along their normal migration route. Even though Rufous do not nest at Tinajas Altas as do Costa's and Anna's, their stake in this place is more than a one-shot deal. Unlike certain birds that become territorial only around courtship, breeding, and nesting, Rufous Hummingbirds even lay claim to sets of resources en route to their breeding ground. Accordingly, they fight tenaciously to keep other hummers out in the cold.[2]

This fact stuck me as curious, for I had supposed that birds become territorial only when needing to exclude other males of their own species from access to potential mates, or to guard enough food to raise a brood. Melees between migrants didn't make sense at first. I wove my way down the wash, wondering about this seeming incongruity. I then recalled that a mentor of mine, avian biologist David Lyon—who had introduced me to the subversive science of ecology two decades before—probed this very problem three hundred miles to the east of Tinajas Altas, in the Chiricahuas.[3]

When I contacted Lyon later on, he responded to my questions on hummingbird behavior with the fine particularism that characterizes the best of ecologists: "Where *were* you?" he asked. "There are great differences in territoriality in the winter depending upon the area. But all of these little rascals are opportunistic and will set up territories any time of the year if rewards are sufficient."

If rewards are sufficient. Lyon views the driving force of hummingbird

2. William A. Calder, III, et al., "Site-fidelity, longevity, and population dynamics of Broad-Tailed Hummingbirds: a ten year study," *Oecologia* 56 (1983), 359.
3. David L. Lyon, James Crandall, and Mark McCone, "A test of the adaptiveness of interspecific territoriality in the Blue-Throated Hummingbird," *The Auk* (July 1977), 448–49.

territoriality as the defense of dense caches of food during times of the year when there are few alternative energy resources. Because hummers must consume close to half their weight in sugar each day to maintain normal activities, finding a concentrated source of food for their fifty to sixty meals per day is a palpable problem. Territories at the Tinajas, then, should be most pronounced when chuparosa nectar production is sufficiently high to make the exclusion of other birds worth the price of the energy expended in defense. Imagine a chuparosa patch as an oil field thick with wells, in a country with few other energy resources developed. That's where the troops will hover.

Lyon has verified that territoriality among different species of hummers is truly adaptive, and not simply a misdirected means of venting innate aggression on other species that a male has mistakenly identified as competing for his potential partners. For his test, Lyon enticed a Blue-throated Hummingbird to establish a territory in an area circumscribed by ten sugar-filled feeders, two placed in the center of the area and eight in a circle on the periphery. Over the following period, he held constant the amount of sucrose available to the bird, but once a day he moved the eight on the periphery farther out from the midpoint, enlarging the area over which the sugar sources were distributed.

Lyon was not surprised when the Blue-throated male took to chasing other hummers out of the artificial territory, regardless of the area it covered. In fact, this male at first spent twice as much time in dogfights around the hummingbird feeders as males typically spend defending natural patches of flowers. The trouble came as the feeders were spread over a larger area. The Blue-throated initially attempted to defend the expanded arena, but the number of competitors entering it increased to two-and-a-half times what they were in the original small territory. In the smaller arena, the territorial male chased after the majority of all hummers trespassing into his turf, irrespective of their species identity. When the sugar was set out over the largest area, he was forced to become more selective in his combat; he needed more time to pursue competitors across the longer distances between feeders, and more time flying to reach the various feeders to refuel himself.

The Blue-throated male shifted his strategy. Rather than wearing himself out with incessant jousting, he opted for adaptability. He had tolerated the presence of females of his kind all along, but now he also permitted Black-chinneds to forage on the periphery. Although they outnumbered the other hummers at this time, Black-chinneds were small and therefore the easiest competitor to expel when resources became scarce. Magnificent Hummingbirds, another species slightly larger than Blue-throateds, posed more of threat. And yet, by afternoon, most of the Magnificents in the oversized territory were tolerated as well.

At last, defense against all comers became tenuous. A few competing Blue-throated males were allowed to feed without being ejected. Still, whenever other Blue-throated males were chased, they were pursued a greater distance than that flown to repel other species. If another bird was seen as a competitor for *both* food and sex, the aggressive tendency of territorial males toward him remained in place.

Place per se is not what the birds are defending. They are after a finite amount of nectar, pollen, and bugs required to stay alive and to pass on their genes. If they can glean those foods without much territorial pyrotechnics, they will do so, whether from a small area or a large one.

Their lives cost something, as do ours. On a late winter day, an Anna's Hummingbird must spend one minute out of every nine feeding in order to fuel its metabolism. Its hovering and flying demand ten times the calories per ounce of flesh that people need when running at full clip. If you give a hummer a feeder full of "junk food," it will reduce its foraging effort to a tenth of what it would be otherwise. Nonetheless, a male does not fill up all this newly found "leisure time" with warfare. Even when you give him a territory literally dripping with sticky-sweet sucrose water, his foraging efficiency increases tenfold while his time pestering intruders only doubles.

Put in terms of an ecological maxim, a male hummer will defend a patch of riches only to the extent that it is truly "adaptive" to do so. When battling becomes too costly relative to the food security it brings, he will relax what many observers have assumed to be unrelenting, genetically determined hostility. Here is where the genetic determinists (and fatalists) have led us astray: they claim it is our "animal nature" to be aggressive, yet even animals stereotyped as interminably warlike can suspend their territorial behavior. They opt for peace whenever their essential needs are met, or when the cost of territorial behavior becomes too high. And as ornithologist Amadeo Rea has pointed out to me, "Hummingbird fighting, warfare, etc., are not really homologous to human activities of the same name. How many dead hummers do you find in the chuparosa patch? How many bloodied, maimed victims? Their fighting . . . is probably only to exclude, not destroy, a rival male."[4]

The Aztecs called the hummingbird *huitzitzil,* "shining one with (a weapon like) a cactus spine." Yet for all its feistiness, the hummingbird does not embody the incessant irascibility attributed to it by certain historic and modern observers. Do such ascriptions actually tell us more about the Aztecs—or the sociobiologists—than they do about the bird itself? If human warfare is not homologous to that found in other animal species, what is its derivation? I track back into another desert to answer these questions, a colorblind botanist seeking clues that those with normal vision may not be able to detect. And I turn my vision from the hummingbirds—most of which have taken flight by this time—to the human being, whose tracks are still evident all around.

III

For weeks, the tension had mounted. Young, hormone-charged men stood on the south side of a line, like so many hummingbirds waiting for the ice to break up north, for the season to burst with activity. First Lieutenant John Deedrick likened the mood on the front lines to the waiting in a blind while hunting deer: "Just like being in a tree stand. You're cold and miserable and you just have to wait."

Then, the Desert Storm let loose like an ejaculatory release from an eighteen-year-old: after an all-out war of some one hundred hours, the boys were done. The troops were coming home, having freed the oil

---

4. Rea, a retired curator of birds and mammals at the San Diego Museum of Natural History, made this remark to me during a telephone conversation in May 1991.

fields of Kuwait from a despot's control. American soldiers were regaining the solid manly image that had been deflated during the sixties. "By God," George Bush exclaimed, "we've kicked the Vietnam syndrome once and for all!"

Lingerie sales in America reached a new all-time high, as women swooned for the victors. The boys were a bit embarrassed: "I think it's kinda shallow that a girl might want to make it with me just because I was over there. . . . Fun, but shallow."[5]

As anthropologists Fontana and Kroeber see it, ever since farming overtook hunting as society's primary means of support, young men have been trying to figure out what they can excel at that women cannot. The hunter's prowess, tenacity, and dignity, which once won him access to the most attractive and fecund mates, evaporated when both men and women began to share in the chores of agrarian society. Women had already been tending plants for centuries, domesticating them and possibly bringing in far more calories than male "breadwinners." As landscapes became tamed and men spent less time on the mythic wild proving grounds, they abdicated a primordial connection that had given them their meaning. What many people came to feel, Kroeber and Fontana have recently said aloud: "Women could do all the work necessary for society's physical survival. Males were potentially persons of great leisure. Or . . . ," as they rather bluntly state, "males were potentially all but useless."

Men swerved off course, from the sacramental and nutritionally justified bloodletting of hunting to that of warfare, even when the gains did not justify the risks. Another hunger grew in men's loins that made them want to taste blood, to be on top. And this hunger, seldom satisfied, sticks with many men today. Never in history have men been so useless; a woman can now go to a sperm bank and be fertilized without ever having to touch her child's biological father. No wonder Robert Bly's "Gathering of Men" has captured center stage in a formerly floundering

5. Unidentified serviceman, speaking in the spring of 1991 on a radio call-in program, "The Jones and Boze Show," broadcast over station KXCI in Scottsdale, Arizona.

men's movement. It sees the male loss of meaning beginning with the Agricultural Revolution, which took men out of contact with the wild, disbanding the fraternity of the Big Woods.

No boot camp or campus fraternity hazing has ever made up for that lack. Far from the mythic rite of passage that it once was for males in many societies, military service too has become an objectified routine of monitoring computer printouts and calculating missile trajectories from remote locations. The bombing of targets has become so depersonalized by the jargon that one might as well be playing Pac-Man. The young technicians simply "took out targets" and euphemistically referred to any human presence in those debilitated places as "collateral damage."

American audiences responded to the Gulf War with much the same fervor they usually reserve for the made-for-TV Super Bowl. Arab-bashing has become a new spectator sport: "Operation Desert Storm" cards come with bubble gum in packages remarkably similar to those in which our boys find the faces of Larry Bird, Bo Jackson, and Michael Jordan.

Even if the government's pathological lies about the war disturbed some Americans, it was fortunate for Bush that Saddam Hussein still seemed downright evil, while we only seemed sick. Of course, that perception was largely influenced by the White House media machine. Who else could be better cast in the role of the innately aggressive hummer than Saddam Hussein himself? Rather than emptying out the flowers of all their nectar, he shrewdly set fire to the scarcest resource underpinning our global economy: fossil fuel. While more than five hundred wells burned like battle torches day after day, enough oil was going up in smoke to meet a tenth of the world's daily consumption.

"If Hell had a National Park, this would be it," mourned the Environmental Protection Agency's director, William Reilly, on the "Today" show just after his return from Kuwait on 7 May 1991, hardly two months after the Gulf War "cease fire." The fires, of course, had not ceased: it would take months to extinguish all of them, and as each month passed with the blazes unabated, they added to the atmosphere as much as a million tons of sulfur dioxide, a hundred thousand tons of nitrogen oxides, and 2.5 million tons of oil soot—the latter amount being more than four times the monthly emissions from the entire United States. All told, the war contributed 4 percent of the world's total carbon release by the end of 1991, thereby accelerating global warming over the long run.[6]

And yet, President Bush still claims that Desert Storm made the victory swift, and the long-term damages minimal. Unfortunately, his antiseptic war was never that at all; over a hundred thousand were dead within a month, with twice that many wounded, crippled, or contaminated with toxins. Many more people were deprived of potable water and food for months on end, and it is now estimated that only one-tenth of the deaths occurred during the "official" war. Environmental destruction proceeded on an unprecedented scale and left unsanitary remains that will persist indefinitely.

To console us, William Reilly announced in doublespeak (during that same "Today" interview) that "President Bush cares as much about the environment as he did about winning the war."

However, the current condition of the fragile desert left behind by a million troops does not give credence to this platitude. Scars left by helter-skelter driving of military vehicles will be seen in the vegetation and soils for anywhere from 100 to 1,000 years. In some places, observers found the desert biologically sterile following the war; elsewhere, remaining plants were covered with a crust of soot, oil, and wind-drifted sand. Massive defense berms interrupted watercourses, and countless bomb craters were not exclusively the result of Iraqi actions. Further, the U.S. Air Force admits that it left behind nearly nine thousand tons of undetectable explosive materials in desert areas. In terms of exploded refineries and burning lakes of oil, the culpability is blurred. "Who knows who set what off?" asked Tony Burgess during a telephone interview. Burgess is a desert ecologist who spent three weeks with Friends of the

6. Tony Burgess, "Trip report to Saudi Arabia and Kuwait, for Friends of the Earth," unpublished manuscript.

Earth in the Gulf assessing environmental damage: "The country was so trashed. It literally was a vision from Hell."[7]

We have only an inkling of how far that hellish apparition will spread, but Burgess has assured me that the oil fires are bound to have profound, pervasive global ramifications. Using the greasy soot particles resulting from the burning oil fields as but one example, Burgess told me that "effects from the Kuwaiti smoke plume have already been picked up in Australia and Hawaii," more than eight thousand miles away from their source. From the snows of the Himalayas to the headwaters of the Blue Nile, acid rain and carbon soot have been accumulating at unprecedented levels.

Petroleum engineer John Cox regards the magnitude of carbon soot from Kuwait, Iraq, and Saudi Arabia to be more concentrated and therefore more devastating than what would be expected were a nuclear winter to occur. He explains why the Kuwaiti smoke plume has already been so widely dispersed: "If you are in a rainy area, a very high proportion of the smoke is going to be washed out. If, however, you are in an area that is already dry—and the microclimate around Kuwait is very dry—and you have an intense temperature, then the chances are that the smoke cloud will go to a much greater height than the nuclear war simulations suggest. . . . [There will be] a major effect upon the growth of vegetation and crops."[8]

This is not the maverick opinion of one self-styled expert, but that of the Greenpeace organization as well, which claims that the Gulf War already ranks as one of the most ecologically destructive conflicts ever. According to André Carothers, Kuwaiti officials have begun to concede that the environmental damages of the war have been more crippling than any material losses incurred during the hundred days of armed conflict.[9] And that, to my mind, is the fatal deviation, the divergence of our path from that of our sometimes pugnacious biological ancestors and

7. Information and statistics in this paragraph were gathered during a telephone conversation with Tony Burgess in June 1991.
8. "Waging War against the Earth," *Environmental Action* (March/April 1991), 22.
9. "After the Storm: The Deluge," *Greenpeace* (Oct./Nov./Dec. 1991), 17.

neighbors on this planet. Although sociobiological scholars may still smugly argue that "we are far from being the most violent animal," the damage our kind has done is suffusive enough to be all-encompassing.

Hummingbirds skirmishing over chuparosa, or Kuwaitis and Iraqis battling over an oil field may appear to be parallel parables of territorial disputes over scarce resources in the desert. But the latter battle has the capacity to damage a broad range of resources required for life now and in the future—indeed, to damage irreparably the capacity for life support within our planet's atmosphere. Gone are the days when ritualized warfare affected control over only one waterhole, one food-gathering ground, one territory.

The verbal antagonism between Saddam Hussein and George Bush on television was a pathetic throwback to esoteric jousting by medieval sportsmen, who lived in a time when the stakes were low and the damage local. We can no longer speak of competition for a single, concentrated resource; a life-support system dependent upon widely dispersed, vitally important resources is now under threat. Compared to other centuries, the number of wars within and between nations has increased during this century, despite pacifying efforts by the United Nations and other mediating bodies. If Bush or Hussein had the mentality of a hummingbird, it would be clear to them that the resources crucial to our survival are no longer economically or ecologically defensible through territorial behavior. These resources are too diffuse, too globally interdependent, to be worth the risks both leaders have placed before us. But what a hummingbird can surmise with its senses in a matter of hours or days, our species must muddle through, argue about, and even shed blood over for decades.

IV

I am back, in the dead of the summer, on a desert wash near the international border where hummingbird bushes like chuparosa exhibit a few last, ill-fated flowers withering in the heat. A fire has burnt a patch along the border today. Dusty whirlwinds are everywhere, turning and churning in the drought-stricken air. A hummingbird whirs by me. I turn to see if he is being chased, then back to see if he is in hot pursuit of another. He is not. We stop on opposite sides of the wash, which is wide enough to let us pause for a moment without feeling on top of one another.

As I pause, I think of the O'odham name for Tinajas Altas: *O'ovak,* "Arrowhead Sunk." The Sand People tell about two of their fellow O'odham who climbed to one of the ridges overlooking the steep-sided canyon where the precious pools of water are found today. One of these two warriors challenged the other to a contest: who could shoot an arrow all the way across the canyon to the far ridge?

As my O'odham friends tell it, the first man's arrow cleared the canyon, but the other's did not. Instead, it glanced against the bedrock in the drainage, skipped along, then sunk into the granite. Wherever it had struck the rock, however, a pool of water formed, and the O'odham and their neighbors have used these plunge pools ever since. Retelling this story, my friends express their gratitude for the unlikely appearance of water, wherever it emerges in the desert.

I turn to the hummingbird and think, "Who, then, won the contest? The warrior demonstrating the greatest facility with weaponry, or the one who helped make a lasting resource for all people?" Laughing at myself, at the long and winding trails my answers take, I leave the wash with one last gesture to the hummer. "You must be my teacher," I offer, palms open to his direction. "We're here together." I am beginning to learn what we share in common—this earth—and what differences in behavior I cannot bear to let come between us.

A Measure of Restraint

CHET RAYMO

ON SEPTEMBER 13, 1987, two unemployed young men in search of a fast buck entered a partly demolished radiation clinic in Goiânia, Brazil. They removed a derelict cancer-therapy machine containing a stainless steel cylinder, about the size of a gallon paint can, which they sold to a junk dealer for twenty-five dollars. Inside the cylinder was a cake of crumbly powder that emitted a mysterious blue light. The dealer took the seemingly magical material home and distributed it to his family and friends. His six-year-old niece rubbed the glowing dust on her body. One might imagine that she danced, eerily glowing in the sultry darkness of the tropic night like an enchanted elfin sprite. The dust was cesium-137, a highly radioactive substance. The lovely light was the result of the decay of the cesium atoms. Another product of the decay was a flux of invisible particles with the power to damage living cells. The girl is dead. Others died or became grievously sick. More than two hundred people were contaminated.

A beautiful, refulgent dust, stolen from an instrument of healing, had become the instrument of death. The junk dealer's niece was not the only child who rubbed the cesium on her body like carnival glitter, and the image of those luminous children will not go away. Their story is a moral fable for our times—a haunting story, touched with dreamlike beauty and ending in death. It evokes another story that took place almost a century ago, another story that illustrates the risks that are sometimes imposed by knowledge. It is a story of Marie and Pierre Curie, the discoverers of radium, as told by their daughter Eve.

The story begins at nine o'clock in the evening at the Curies' house in

Paris. Marie is sitting at the bedside of her four-year-old daughter, Irene. It is a nightly ritual; the child is uncomfortable without her mother's presence. Marie sits quietly near the girl until the restless young voice gives way to sleep. Then she goes downstairs to her husband, Pierre. Husband and wife have just completed an arduous four-year effort to isolate from tons of raw ore the tiny amount of the new element that will win them fame. The work is still on their minds: the laboratory, the workbenches, the flasks and vials. "Suppose we go down there for a moment," suggests Marie. They walk through the night to the laboratory and let themselves in. "Don't light the lamps," says Marie, in darkness. Before their recent success in isolating a significant amount of the new element, Pierre had expressed the wish that radium would have "a beautiful color." Now it is clear that the reality is better than the wish. Unlike any other element, radium is spontaneously luminous! On the shelves in the dark laboratory precious particles of radium in their tiny glass receivers glow with an eerie blue light. "Look! Look!" says Marie. She sits down in darkness, her face turned toward the glowing vials. *Radium. Their radium!* Pierre stands at her side. Her body leans forward, her eyes attentive; she adopts the posture that had been hers an hour earlier at the bedside of her child. Eve Curie called it "the evening of the glowworms."

Marie and Pierre Curie and their new element became famous. By the middle of the first decade of this century they had begun what can only be called a radium craze. A thousand and one uses were proposed for the material with the mysterious emanations. The curative powers of a radium solution—called "liquid sunshine"—were widely touted. It was soon discovered that radium killed bacteria, and suggested uses included mouthwashes and toothpastes. Health spas with traces of radium in the water became popular. Entertainers created "radium dances," in which props and costumes coated with fluorescent salts of radium glowed in the dark. It is said that in New York people played "radium roulette," with a glowing wheel and ball, and refreshed themselves with luminescent cocktails of radium-spiked liquid. The most important commercial application of radium was in the manufacture of self-luminous paint, widely used for the numerals of watches and clocks that could be read in the dark. Hundreds of women were employed applying the luminous compound to the dials. It was a common practice for them to sharpen the tips of their brushes with their lips. Many of these women were later affected by anemia and lesions of the jawbone and mouth; a number of them died.

By 1930 the physiological hazards of radioactivity were recognized by the medical profession and the reckless misuse of radium had mostly ceased. But the mysterious emanations—which properly used are an effective treatment for cancer—had taken their toll. Marie Curie discovered the secret of the stars; her tiny glass vials contained the distilled essence of the force that makes the universe glow with light. She died of radiation-induced leukemia, with cataracts on her eyes and her fingertips marked by sores that would not heal. Like many of the gifts of knowledge, radium had proved a mixed blessing. The poet Adrienne Rich has described Marie Curie's death this way:

> She died   a famous woman   denying
> her wounds
> denying
> her wounds   came   from the same source as her power

The evening of the glowworms! Eve Curie's evocative phase might also be used to describe the dance of the Brazilian children, their bodies luminous with cesium-137. In these two stories we are drawn at last and emphatically into the circle of the Janus-faced god. Death and beauty, wounds and power: The piercing horns of the dilemma of science, demanding from the seeker of truth a measure of restraint.

As I write these lines, I recall glowworm evenings I experienced as a child in Tennessee, running barefoot with my young companions through the lush green grass of the long sloping lawn, catching up fireflies in our hands. Stars in the silky night glimmered in concert with insect scintillations—tiny flashes of cold brilliance reflected in a canopy of over-arching pines, as in dark water. The insect lights seemed a miracle, a conjuration of elfin magic; a dozen fireflies in a bottle made a fairy light. Now, forty-five years later, I have before me as I write the image of another firefly light: a photograph of a tobacco plant made to glow with the phantasmic radiance of the firefly's luciferous gene. I have clipped the photograph from the pages of the journal *Science* and tacked it up on the wall above my desk. It expresses what is best and worst in our quest for knowledge.

To make the autoluminescent tobacco plant, genetic engineers first located the firefly gene—the DNA segment that gives rise to the enzyme that catalyzes the firefly's light-producing chemistry. The purloined gene was then introduced into the cells of tobacco plants, and the plants watered with a solution of the chemicals necessary for the luminescent reaction. The plants then emitted a faint but detectable light. The photograph was made by placing a genetically altered plant in contact with photographic film for twenty-four hours. The result is a scientific artifact that qualifies as a work of art.

One hardly knows how to react to experiments such as this. One admires the knowledge and skill that enabled the genetic researchers to achieve so remarkable a transmutation of living matter—a plant made luminous with an animal's gene. Certainly, one is moved to a deeper respect for the chemical machinery of life. Still, I turn to the photograph of the genetically altered plant with a sense of foreboding. The tobacco plant seems to rise out of the paper like a will-o'-the-wisp or friar's lantern, those flickering phosphorescent lights that are sometimes seen over marshes and swamps at night, that in folk legend beckon unwary followers into the mire.

The transgenic researchers do not consider their experiments frivolous or dangerous. They are confident that the firefly's etheric gene can be spliced with other genes as a valuable marker in genetic experiments. Researchers need to know quickly if and where transplanted genes have been activated. The firefly's light, issuing from the cells of another organism—human cancer-fighting cells, for example—can be an ideal signal. There is no doubt that the tobacco-cum-firefly experiments, and others like them, will lead to discoveries of potential benefit to society:

Grains that are resistant to disease, fruit trees that defy frost, bacteria that eat oil spills, vaccines for the cure of animal and human diseases—all these things and more are promised by genetic engineers. Then what is the source of my uneasiness? Certainly, genetic engineering is not the first breakthrough in science that harbored potential for danger as well as good: The discovery of radium comes too quickly to mind. Radium beckoned us forward with the promise of cures for disease and inexhaustible energy resources. Then Janus turned to reveal his other face—terrible weapons of destruction, a plague of nuclear waste, cancers caused, not cured. In many ways, the fruitful promise of genetic engineering is greater than that of radioactivity, but so is the potential danger. A gene reproduces. A gene copies itself into the fabric of life. Nuclear waste remains radioactive for thousands of years; a gene is potentially immortal. The soft phosphorescent light of the genetically altered tobacco plant beckons us toward a future bright with health and plenty, but it also has a spooky Frankensteinian quality that warns us to proceed with caution. "For Beauty's nothing but the beginning of Terror," wrote the poet Rilke, and all too often his words might describe the enterprise of science.

On those sultry nights in Tennessee we caught glowworms in our hands. Sometimes we pinched their tiny bodies to set their gene-activated fires alight. But we squeezed gently, and then released the insects to take their place again among the live constellations of the summer night. We recognized, if only in a childlike way, an integrity and balance within nature that demands of earth's dominant species a judicious self-restraint. The unexamined quest for knowledge is hemmed with peril.

"Scientific curiosity is not an unbounded good." One does not often hear those words, especially uttered by a scientist. I quote them from an essay addressed to scientists by the octogenarian biochemist Erwin Chargaff. Chargaff's cautionary comment was prompted by developments in genetics, molecular biology, and embryology, and particularly in the tech-

nology of human reproduction. In effect, he charges researchers with knowing *too much* about the molecular machinery of life, and with using that knowledge to "stick our fingers into the incredibly fine web of human fate." Research on human embryos especially arouses Chargaff's disapproval. He fiercely condemns *in vitro* fertilization, the freezing of embryos for later implantation into a mother's womb, surrogate motherhood (especially for a fee), and various forms of transgenic tinkering.

Chargaff dismisses as so much quibbling the question of when an embryo becomes "human"; the life of the embryo begins, he believes, with the fertilized egg, and deserves the same respect from researchers as any other human life. He takes note of the human benefits that are put forward to justify embryonic research—the correction of genetic defects, helping childless couples have children, and so forth. But with lofty defiance, he dismisses the idea that the end might justify the means. Even more disturbing, Chargaff suggests that the proffered "justifications" for embryonic research sometimes mask the real motives—the avarice and ambition of researchers. It is a serious charge, and one that in my view is largely unjustified. It is a charge that raises the hackles, even the anger, of those involved in reproductive research. But Chargaff's stern challenge carries the weight of a fruitful life in science. He is emeritus professor of biochemistry of Columbia University and is best known for his demonstration in the late 1940s that certain chemical components of DNA molecules always occur in constant ratios, a result that was crucial to the discovery of the structure of the DNA double helix by Watson and Crick. Chargaff was among the first to recognize that the chemical composition of DNA was species specific. He has won many international awards for a lifetime of pioneering work in biochemistry.

Chargaff has made himself something of a career as a scientific gadfly. His prescriptive moralizing is dismissed by many scientists as sour sentimentality and antiprogressive romanticism, but his words fall upon other ears with a kind of Jehovian thunder—and rightly so. Whether Chargaff's castigation of contemporary embryonic research is philosophically or morally correct is debatable; but that science should value its Chargaffs—thundering from on high—is beyond dispute. Sometimes it is necessary for the grand old men of science, no longer caught up with the self-serving activities of making a career, to question the moral implications of what we do. In setting himself up as the judge of science, Chargaff wins few plaudits; there are no Nobel prizes for curmudgeons. But as Chargaff himself once wrote, "Philosophy is one of the hazards of old age."

Erwin Chargaff spent his childhood in Austria, in what seemed to him the last golden rays of a more civilized era. He was watching the younger sons of Kaiser Wilhelm II play tennis when news came of the assassination of the Austrian archduke Franz Ferdinand, an event that plunged all Europe into darkness. The years between the wars were spent in Vienna, where Chargaff took his degrees. Torn between science and the study of literature, he drifted into chemistry, as later he drifted into biochemistry. He was forced to leave Europe by the rise of the Nazis. Again darkness descended. His mother was deported from Vienna into oblivion. In his autobiography, Chargaff says of his life: "In the Sistine Chapel, where Michelangelo depicts the creation of man, God's finger and that of Adam are separated by a short space. That distance I called eternity; and there, I felt, I was sent to travel." He has been at every moment of his life aware of the immensity of the darkness that is nature. As a scientist, he lessened the darkness with the light of his own genius. Now, as a respected professor emeritus surrounded by solved riddles, he remains struck by how *little* we understand—and made anxious by how *much* we understand. The darkness of ignorance and the light of knowledge equally seem to frighten him. In certain contemporary research, Chargaff apparently feels that science comes dangerously close to bridging the gap between God's finger and the finger of man. In asking us to hold back he gives voice to widely popular concerns, and throws into sharp relief our unsettling ambivalence toward science. "Restraint in asking necessary questions," he wrote, "is one of the sacrifices that even the scientist ought to be willing to make to human dignity."

Self-luminous children dancing in the tropic night, the glowworm light of radium issuing from glass vials in a darkened lab, tobacco plants chandeliered with firefly light—all friar's lanterns beckoning us to bridge the gap between God's finger and the finger of man. Many scientists hold that knowledge is an absolute good, to be pursued at any risk. Light is invariably better than darkness, they say; we must not forget that the glowworm light of the Brazilian children was stolen from an instrument of healing, and the glowworm light of the transgenic tobacco plant illuminates the darkness of ignorance and superstition.

Erwin Chargaff's challenge disturbs the sleep of reason. What he says about embryonic research applies with equal (perhaps greater) force to transgenic experimentation, nuclear research, and many other areas of contemporary science: The unshuttered light of knowledge threatens moral conflagration, and the unconstrained exploitation of nature holds the potential for shattering annihilation; the source of our power is also the source of our wounds. Chargaff believes humans cannot live without mysteries, and yet he has devoted his life to unraveling the greatest mystery of all, the mystery of human life. He contributed mightily to discovering the secret of DNA, and yet damns the use to which that knowledge has been put. He is a man of reason who agrees with Goya that "the dream of reason brings forth monsters." Struck by these apparent inconsistencies between Chargaff's life and words, many scientists dismiss his critique of contemporary research as cantankerous obfuscation. Unbounded scientific curiosity, they say, has proved its worth, and whatever are the dangers implicit in knowledge, they are far outweighed by good. Indeed, they say, in turning his back on contemporary research, Chargaff would have us return to a time when human life was the helpless plaything of poverty, disease, and death. Chargaff answers in a voice honed to a fine sharp edge on the whetstone of paradox: "A balance that does not tremble cannot weigh. A man who does not tremble cannot live."

Let's Eat Stars

NANAO SAKAKI

Believe me, children!

God made
Sky for airplanes
Coral reefs for tourists
Farms for agrichemicals
Rivers for dams
Forests for golf courses
Mountains for ski resorts
Wild animals for zoos
Trucks and cars for traffic tragedies
Nuclear power plants for ghost dance.

Don't worry, children!
The well never dries up.

Look at the evening glow!
Sunflowers in the garden.
Red dragonflies in the air.

A small child starts singing:
    "Let's eat stars!
        Let's eat stars!"

Roll Call

WILLIAM STAFFORD

Red Wolf came, and Passenger Pigeon,
the Dodo Bird, all the gone or endangered
came and crowded around in a circle,
the Bison, the Irish Elk, waited
silent, the Great White Bear, fluid and strong,
sliding from the sea, streaming and creeping
in the gathering darkness, nose down,
bowing to earth its tapered head,
where the Black-footed Ferret, paws folded,
stood in the center surveying the multitude
and spoke for us all: "Dearly beloved," it said.

Animisto Manifesto

DAVID GRIMES

POETRY AND MUSIC are my trusty ways of keeping a journal when I travel. Haiku, with its traditional seventeen syllables and a reference to the season, makes it easy for me to be a poet. A blank page is not nearly so daunting when seventeen syllables is the limit; there's liberty in the restriction. Plus I get to work out the poems on my fingers.

Poems are my shorthand record of memories, a picture that, in this case, might be worth seventeen syllables instead of a thousand words. Sometimes I link several haiku together to tell the story, not unlike the old Japanese game wherein two or more poets carry on a witty, spontaneous conversation in haiku form. A friend and I played this game for hours one evening as our train climbed a steep river valley into the Japanese Alps. While I can't recall much of the night's poetry now, I know the event took place in spring, that there were plastic flowers on the wall near the compartment door, and that we could hear a happy chorus of frogs through the open window whenever the train slowed to enter a station. I know these things because the Japanese word for frog, *kaeru,* is pronounced with three syllables, a fact useful to one haiku I do remember from that night:

> springtime—I can hear
> kaeru singing but I
> can't smell the flowers

Traveling in Papua New Guinea a half-year later, I found I couldn't use my camera much. Landscapes were okay, but I wasn't comfortable photographing people I'd only just met. I don't think I was afraid of stealing someone's soul, unless perhaps it were my own; the technology just seemed for me out of place. Anyway, the times I did take portraits—mostly of the ragtag laughing children who followed me and my tin whistle in search of adventure—the photos almost always were hopelessly underexposed due to a malfunction of the portrait lens.

Better exposed were a few beautiful tunes I learned from the children, who sing like birds while they paddle their dugout canoes or pound sago palm pith to produce flour. I learned, as well, melodies from birds that whistle and sing like children—the brush cuckoo, the pied butcher bird, and one of the birds of paradise. As with the camera, I think I would have been uncomfortable using a tape recorder to capture the music. The tin whistle was a simple technology and, requiring breath, more akin to the original. I remember the tunes reasonably well now with the whistle, and by having interacted with the music in its native place, maybe I feel more connected to it. I don't know, I didn't have a tape recorder. But I'm superstitious enough to imagine that tape recordings might have been erased by magnetic storms on the airplane home. Poetry and the whistle survive.

Here, then, a poem on a subject that is neither haiku nor from New Guinea, but it's true enough and concerns Turlough O'Carolan, blind eighteenth-century harper and father of Irish music:

My friend Bo is a stout lad, sure,
and the whistle fine he's playing;
A pilgrim he, to O'Carolan's grave
and the day it had been raining.

Now O'Carolan's skull, as well you may know,
once hung upon the garland,
'Til an Orangeman took his pistol to the bone,
and this to spite all Ireland.

The scoundrel's deed was long ago
and the skull Bo could not worship,
But a tooth lay gleaming in the mud
where rain on the grave unearthed it.

Says Bo, "I'm off this very day,
I must leave Roscommon entirely;
And O'Carolan's tooth in this matchbox strong,
to Amerikay beside me."

New York he landed, the immigrant's dream
and like millions before, he found it;
But likewise free was O'Carolan's tooth
and the empty matchbox confounded.

Now Turlough's music will travel the world
and fit like the clothes you're wearin',
But O'Carolan's teeth will never leave
the green, green groves of Erin.

*In those fabled days it was said that mushrooms along the Elwha grew as
big as rocking chairs, or at least, golden foot stools. And autumn in the Olym-
pic mountains brought forth many fruits and berries to keep the travelers
merry and give their cheeks and chins color. All day they rambled the deep forest ways, placing mushrooms in one sack, berries and succulent salad herbs in
another, an occasional silver trout wrapped in moss and placed atop their
packs, until at day's end they halted, amazed to see the feast spread out before
them, gathered by their own hands. The fire crackled and the stars sparkled
and many smiles grew deep in their bellies and thence spread to their hearts.*

In order to secure a spot on the natural history and wild mushroom
expedition to Alaska, you had to send in a sample of haiku to the guides,
and a lock of hair. I think the hair, sealed in wax with a mushroom
stamp, wound up on the diplomas we passed out at the end of the trip.
We called our fledgling business Bedlam and Breakfast Adventures and,
following the advice on two bottles of Japanese whiskey, our mottoes
were "Too wild to get the blues" and "Be tender like you used to be."
Shannon, our head chef, after a day foraging for blueberries and boletes
above treeline, changed the one motto to "Be tundra like you used to
be."

For three weeks we journeyed through south-central Alaska on foot, in van and boat, feasting on cloudberries, chanterelles, and wild cucumber greens. We traded our surplus salmon for caribou, danced to the guitar and accordion, and hung out together around the fire just like there ain't been no hard times. Our tribe, as tribes do, encompassed a wide range of age and experience, so the haiku created along the path of our migration reflected this diversity. If haiku holds up a mirror to nature, we were a diversity of mirrors.

A few folks found it hard to get the seventeen-syllable knack at first. They were in sympathy with my friend in Ireland who once passed on the following, perhaps my favorite haiku:

> to express oneself
> in seventeen syllables
> is very diffic

It can be like that, trying to find certain mushrooms for the first time, like morels. Until you get the right search image in your brain, they're damn nigh invisible: you crawl, for some time, the forest floor on all fours, until finally you *see* one, right in front of you, and then they're everywhere right in front of you. Well, some experts say the problem is that morels *move* to where you just looked, the longer to escape detection. But those folks who found haiku elusive in the beginning, by bedlam and breakfast's end had mushroom baskets full of poems.

Haiku at its best, which is often, reminds me of the clapping of hands in Shinto shrines to summon the gods, I imagine, from their divine sleep so they may hear a mortal's prayers. The brevity and clarity of haiku is like those hand claps, awakening me from *my* sleep to the sudden beauty and poignancy of the world, the moon of ripe berries, the season of falling leaves. During late summer and the beginning of autumn in Alaska our tribe managed to find, for a little while at least, grace in the wilderness. And each person's haiku, like the breath that is remembered, served to awaken us to the countless moments that stitch our lives to the fabric of the earth.

SOME BEDLAM AND BREAKFAST HAIKU

like a tiny wild raspberry, the Nagoon berry:

> *Rubus arcticus*
> magenta flower green leaf
> taste small wet autumn

with its last blossoms, fireweed marks the end of summer:

> one day green one day
> not green but scarlet we see
> fireweed bloom at top

solving the age-old question of who got who:

> stalk of cow parsnip
> dry and hollow, perfect for
> launching cranberries

on the hazards of autumn:

> night wind sets things free
> fat persimmon in a tree
> almost lands on me

I reckon I was born native to this planet, just like the rest of the animals who stepped down the gangplank when ole man Noah beached the Ark. Somewhere thereafter my friends and I started hanging with the wrong crowd. First off, we started smoking fossil fuel and inhaling. Next we began throwing plutonium in the river where the banana peels used to float. Then the doctors among us thought it would be a good trick to tell mothers not to hold or breast-feed their children. Man, we was delinquent! The children wouldn't mind their mamas or their papas and watched TV all day long, even on Sunday. The garden was looking mighty neglected. I don't know what might of come of it if the Lord hadn't finally stepped in and tossed the television out the tall window to prove the vertical hold didn't work.

Modern times, and our hunting and gathering, our musical souls hurl down the freeway where we visit upon ourselves the neuroses of animals caged at eighty-eight feet per second. One automobile is a work of art; a hundred million and I'm with my man on obscenity, Jesse Helms. I better warn you, I brake for blackberries six lanes over where the flute player beckons beyond the green Ferrari.

I celebrate my return from alien to native on March 24, 1989, date of the Good Friday Exxon *Valdez* oil spill in my home of Prince William Sound. Water has enchanted, nourished, and frightened me all the days of my life. But until the oil spill, it had not occurred to me that water was really *alive*, not in the way I felt a sycamore alive or, say, my brother. True, I have spilled wine on numerous occasions to Poseidon before setting sail in a rickety boat, and I have floated garlands of flowers above river rapids, spilling wine on myself, before descending the abyss. I have fallen, sunstruck in the desert, into a god-sent stream and opened my undeserving mouth for eternity. I suppose if we speed up the film of our lives enough, our bodies appear as droplets of water sucked into momentary shape before soon enough sliding back into the multitude of water's flowing forms. Well, I have respected water, but even so, my love has been repressed. I didn't know water was alive until I feared for its death.

The flood of oil that swept down the Sound was caught in arms of islands I felt as the most beautiful in all the world. It swallowed otters and murrelets and loons and whales. I knew no one who could sleep, and normal people instinctively took up the normal heroic work of those defending a home. The day the killing began in earnest, forty miles away my skin turned ashen under the inescapable weight of death. By the eve of the fourth day we were no longer scientists but children frightened out of our minds. That night, when countless animals were dying in the dark, we found a bottle of Irish whiskey and drank until we cried. We sang, and we read poetry. Through our shock, guilt, and profound grief, at last we arrived to touch the love beyond knowing that is the native's love for this beautiful blue planet. And I think then I actually began at last to have faith, to recognize the venerable truth in the Good Friday story, and I prayed that after sacrifice indeed would come resurrection. I needed to believe that.

> The tiding old sea is still taking and giving and shaping
> The gentians and violets break in the spring from the stone.
> The world and his mother go reeling and jigging forever,
> In answer to something that troubles the blood and the bone . . .
>
> > from a poem by
> > Michael Coady, on the wall of
> > O'Connor's Pub, Doolin, County Clare

Gaia est ergo sum. My beingness, my thought, is every bit all contingent on constant nourishment from a generous earth's air, water, and flesh, from first suck, sip, and sup to last. The earth is, and therefore I am. And my joy is discovering that water lives, and therefore I love. It's great being native. The earth, spinning on its tilted axis, revolves around the sun. We're the third stone out—the water planet—and once around is called a year. I think I was a fish in my last life. The season of descending leaves is called . . . fall. The season of sudden greenery we name spring, and when a thin shroud of clouds covers the full moon like a woman's slip, we clearly see the glowing round symbol of yin and yang.

Now I believe we in the Sound were lucky to have the oil spill come as an overnight disaster, an immediate, unavoidable crisis that forced us to stand up. Los Angeles' air quality was destroyed incrementally, over thirty years. Had it happened overnight, you may be sure everyone would have been in the streets long before Rodney King. It would have been unthinkable that our children could not go play outside one morning because breathing would injure them.

The story making the rounds goes that a frog thrown into a pot of boiling water will jump out. A frog who begins by swimming in a pot of cool water can be heated to boiling and will be cooked. The trick is to see if we humans, as the water around us approaches the lethal temperature, can be the one frog that climbs out. The crisis approaches, on all fronts simultaneously; the healing dose will be dangerously near the lethal dose. The word *crisis,* in Chinese, is composed of the characters for *danger* and *opportunity.* Crisis as opportunity. Opportunity to be native again. Prepare to stand up out of the steaming pot and defend yourself.

In the Southern Highlands of Papua New Guinea is remote Lake Kutubu, twenty miles long and nestled like a thick blue snake in the mountain jungle. Maybe two thousand people, in several villages, live scattered around the shore. This is about the population of the fishing village of Cordova, my home in Prince William Sound. The inhabitants of Lake Kutubu, save for the presence of two outboard motors, live pretty much as they have for millennia—fishing, hunting, gardening, bartering, and singing. In the long-houses and huts people sleep beside the fire, hypnotized by the glowing coals; they worship animals.

The day is lazy and still. Offshore a mother patiently fishes from her dugout, murmuring now and then to her child as it plays. I'm wet from swimming, drying in the sun. In a while I shall join my friend Kamoga up in his garden. A moment of peace. Afternoon cumuli build toward showers. The green forest extends its arms over the hills in all directions. Butterflies drift through the trees flashing sunlight from their wings in the most vivid experience of blue I've ever imagined; they seem to be fluttering shards of the portholes into paradise. Over the far mountain ridge I can see, like tiny dragonflies, and unheard, helicopters flying to a major oil discovery five miles away. The people on the lake have never worked for money. The oil companies want to employ them. There is talk of building a road to the lake.

I had spent the day before with a young man while crossing the lake to explore a river. He had a beautiful singing voice. At the edge of the river we found a brilliant green beetle on a flower and my companion anchored a blade of grass into one of its leg joints. He then held the flying beetle, tethered to the grass, in front of his mouth and sang through the droning wings, playing music with a living instrument. After a bit he set the beetle free and it lazily ballooned away up into the sky above the jungle. Some of the men in his village had decided to accept an oil company's offer of work. My companion asked me, "In your country do many people live with money?" I didn't understand, at first, his question, though it was simple and straight to the heart of the matter. Given the choice, do many people choose money? I think he was wondering, as I do now, how long a tribe can exist and not work directly for its food, water, shelter, happiness. We talked about the possible road. He told me his people are intelligent. They know there is great power in the world outside—Michael Jackson, Sylvester Stallone, automobiles, strange new music. A road connected to that world would bring some good. Then he shrugged his shoulders and said that once a road is built, now rascal he come long place bilong me bilong you, now he bugarumpim us.

I knew the man was my brother only a few months later when the oil hit Prince William Sound and it was my people who were asked to work for the oil companies, and my village that agonized over whether to build a road marrying Cordova with the outside world, a handsome groom with a chainsaw. Modern times, mon. Same all over, rascals all of us, as the last of the old world greets the new.

> don't know why I's born
> human mighta been a fish
> or bat or the big
>
> sycamore in the
> backyard that talked to me when
> I fell on my back

In 1933 two Australian brothers searching for gold first found a way up into the mountain highlands of New Guinea. It was believed that no one at all lived up in the clouds on this biggest island in the world after Greenland. The Leahy brothers discovered a million people living on the plateaus within the extraordinarily dissected topography of jagged green mountain walls and impassable rivers. It was the last large population of people on earth to be made aware of the rest of us.

Only after World War II could the gold miners return, and then joined by significant numbers and denominations of missionaries with a gold mine of souls to save. The first airfields were cleared, and when a plane landed, the indigenous folks would crawl under it and look for genitals to see what sex it was. I smile at the amusing childlike animism of these people who revere animals and dream by the fire. Then I smile more sheepishly, so to speak, when I remember it is we in Alaska who fly airplanes we ourselves name Goose, Otter and Beaver, we scientists of America who drive Broncos and Bugs, Foxes and Rams, Mustangs, Jaguars, Falcons and Thunderbirds. I have seen in Japan a car named a Parsley.

It's the truth I speak now, I don't know anyone who's not hypnotized by fire, and on the Sabbath, across the land, we slug down beers and worship football, baseball, and basketball teams with animal names. Eagles fan or Bulls fan? Killer Whale or Raven clan? To be human and healthy is to be animist, is to be and feel connected to a living earth and a sentient universe. My totem animals are hare, crow and dragonfly, Jiminy Cricket, tanuki and goshawk, harebell, spearmint, and watermelon rather than parsley. What artist among us has ever created a feather, a butterfly wing, a tiger's eye? To be human is to breathe clouds, drink rivers, climb forests, leap mountains, count moons, question stars, worship animals, become soil and ash. That bird in the tree could be my uncle. So could the tree.

Becoming Native to This Place

WES JACKSON

AT WORK ON my houses in Matfield Green, I've had great fun tearing off the porches and cleaning up the yards. But it has been sad, as well, going through the abandoned belongings of families who lived out their lives in this beautiful, well-watered, fertile setting. In an upstairs bedroom, I came across a dusty but beautiful blue padded box labeled "Old Programs—New Century Club." Most of the programs from 1923 to 1964 were there. Each listed the officers, the Club Flower (sweet pea), the Club Colors (pink and white), and the Club Motto ("Just Be Glad"). The programs for each year were gathered under one cover and nearly always dedicated to some local woman who was special in some way.

Each month the women were to comment on such subjects as canning, jokes, memory gems, a magazine article, guest poems, flower culture, misused words, birds, and so on. The May 1936 program was a debate: "Resolved that movies are detrimental to the young generation." The August 1936 program was dedicated to coping with the heat. Roll call was "Hot Weather Drinks"; next came "Suggestions for Hot Weather Lunches"; a Mrs. Rogler offered "Ways of Keeping Cool."

The June roll call in 1929 was "The Disease I Fear Most." That was eleven years after the great flu epidemic. Children were still dying in those days of diphtheria, whooping cough, scarlet fever, pneumonia. On August 20, the roll call question was "What do you consider the most essential to good citizenship?" In September that year it was "Birds of Our Country." The program was on the mourning dove.

What became of it all?

From 1923 to 1930 the program covers were beautiful, done at a print shop. From 1930 until 1937, the effects of the Depression are apparent; programs were either typed or mimeographed and had no cover. The programs for two years are now missing. In 1940, the covers reappeared, this time typed on construction paper. The printshop printing never came back.

The last program in the box was in 1964. I don't know the last year Mrs. Florence Johnson attended the club. I do know that Mrs. Johnson and her husband, Turk, celebrated their fiftieth wedding anniversary, for in the same box are some beautiful white fiftieth anniversary napkins with golden bells and the names Florence and Turk between the years "1920" and "1970." A neighbor told me that Mrs. Johnson died in 1981. The high school had closed in 1967. The lumberyard and hardware store closed about the same time but no one knows when for sure. The last gas station went after that.

Back to those programs. The motto never changed. The sweet pea kept its standing. So did the pink and white club colors. The club collect that follows persisted month after month, year after year:

A COLLECT FOR CLUB WOMEN

Keep us, O God, from pettiness;
Let us be large in thought, in word,
in deed.

Let us be done with fault-finding
and leave off self-seeking.

May we put away all pretense and
meet each other face to face, without
self-pity and without prejudice.

May we never be hasty in judgment
and always generous.

Let us take time for all things;
make us grow calm, serene, gentle.

Teach us to put into action our
better impulses; straightforward
and unafraid.

Grant that we may realize it is
the little things that create differences;
that in the big things of life
we are as one.

And may we strive to touch and
to know the great common woman's
heart of us all, and oh, Lord God,
let us not forget to be kind.

—Mary Stewart

By modern standards, these people were poor. There was a kind of naivete among these relatively unschooled women. Some of their poetry
was not good. Some of their ideas about the way the world works seem
silly. Some of their club programs don't sound very interesting. Some
sound tedious. But their monthly agendas were filled with decency, with
efforts to learn about everything from the birds to our government, and
with coping with their problems, the weather, diseases. Here is the
irony: they were living up to a far broader spectrum of their potential
than most of us today!

I am not suggesting that we go back to 1923 or even to 1964. But I
will say that those people in that particular generation, in places like
Matfield Green, were farther along in the necessary journey to become
native to their places, even as they were losing ground, than we are.

Why was their way of life so vulnerable to the industrial economy?
What can we do to protect such attempts to be good and decent, to live
out modest lives responsibly? I don't know. This is the discussion we
need to have, for it is particularly problematic. Even most intellectuals
who have come out of such places as Matfield Green have not felt that
their early lives prepared them adequately for the "official" culture.

I want to quote from two writers. The first is Paul Gruchow, who
grew up on a farm in southern Minnesota:

> I was born at mid-century. My parents, who were poor and rural, had
> never amounted to anything, and never would, and never expected to.
> They were rather glad for the inconsequence of their lives. They got up
> with the sun and retired with it. Their routines were dictated by the sea-
> sons. In summer they tended; in fall they harvested; in winter they re-
> paired; in spring they planted. It had always been so; so it would always
> be.
> The farmstead we occupied was on a hilltop overlooking a marshy river
> bottom that stretched from horizon to horizon. It was half a mile from

any road and an eternity from any connection with the rest of the culture. There were no books there; there was no music; there was no television; for a long time, no telephone. Only on the rarest of occasions—a time or two a year—was there a social visitor other than the pastor. There was no conversation in that house.[1]

Similarly, Wallace Stegner, the great historian and novelist, confesses to his feeling of inadequacy coming from a small prairie town in the Cypress Hills of Saskatchewan. In *Wolf Willow* he writes:

Once, in a self-pitying frame of mind, I was comparing my background with that of an English novelist friend. Where he had been brought up in London, taken from the age of four onward to the Tate and the National Gallery, sent traveling on the Continent in every school holiday, taught French and German and Italian, given access to bookstores, libraries, and British Museums, made familiar from infancy on with the conversation of the eloquent and the great. I had grown up in this dung-heeled sagebrush town on the disappearing edge of nowhere, utterly without painting, without sculpture, without architecture, almost without music or theater, without conversation or languages or travel or stimulating instruction, without libraries or museums or bookstores, almost without books. I was charged with getting in a single lifetime, from scratch, what some people inherit as naturally as they breathe air.

How, I asked this Englishman, could anyone from so deprived a background ever catch up? How was one expected to compete, as a cultivated man, with people like himself? He looked at me and said dryly, "Perhaps you got something else in place of all that."

He meant, I suppose that there are certain advantages to growing up a sensuous little savage, and to tell the truth I am not sure I would trade my childhood of freedom and the outdoors and the senses for a childhood of being led by the hand past all the Turners in the National Gallery. And also, he may have meant that anyone starting from deprivation is spared getting bored. You may not get a good start, but you may get up a considerable head of steam.

Countless writers and artists have been vulnerable to the "official" culture, as vulnerable as the people of Matfield Green. Stegner comments:

1. Paul Gruchow in *Townships,* edited by Michael Martome (Iowa State University Press, 1991).

I am reminded of Willa Cather, that bright girl from Nebraska, memoriz-
ing long passages from the *Aeneid* and spurning the dust of Red Cloud
and Lincoln with her culture-bound feet. She tried, and her education encouraged her, to be a good European. Nevertheless she was a first-rate
novelist only when she dealt with what she knew from Red Cloud and the
things she had "in place of all that." Nebraska was what she was born to
write; the rest of it was got up. Eventually, when education had won and
nurture had conquered nature and she had recognized Red Cloud as a vul-
gar little hold, she embraced the foreign tradition totally and ended by being neither quite a good American nor quite a true European nor quite a
whole artist.[2]

It seems that we still blunt ourselves with the likes of learning long
passages from the *Aeneid* while wanting to shake from us the dust of
Red Cloud or Matfield Green. The extractive economy cares for neither
Virgil nor Mary Stewart. It lures just about all of us to its shopping centers on the edge of Lincoln or Wichita, Louisville or Lexington. And
yet, for us, the *Aeneid* is as essential to becoming native to the Matfield
Greens as the bow and arrow were to the Paleolithic Asians who walked
here across the Bering land bridge of the Pleistocene.

Our task is to build cultural fortresses to protect our emerging nativeness. They must be strong enough to hold at bay the powers of consum-
erism; the powers of greed and envy and pride. One of the most effective
ways for this to come about would be for our universities to assume the
awesome responsibility to both validate and educate those who want to
be homecomers—not necessarily to go home but to go someplace and
dig in and begin the long search and experiment to become native.

It will be a struggle, but a worthy one. Taking Virgil as more than just
the ribband of a good liberal arts education, he could be worn back by
this new breed not as an adornment, like a patch on a shirt, but as part of
the shirt itself, and eventually as a tool.

We can then hope for a resurrection of the likes of Mrs. Florence
Johnson and her women friends who took their collect seriously. Unless
we can validate and promote the sort of "cultural-information-in-the-

2. Wallace Stegner, *Wolf Willow,* (University of Nebraska Press, 1980).

making" that the New Century Club featured, we are doomed. An entire club program devoted to coping with the heat of August is being native to a place. That club was more than a support group; it was cultural information in the making, keyed to place. The alternative, one might suggest, is mere air conditioning—not only yielding greenhouse gases but contributing to global warming and the ozone hole as well, and, if powered with nuclear power, to future Chernobyls.

Becoming native to this place means that the creatures we bring with us—our domesticated creatures—must become native, too. Long ago they were removed from the original relationships they had with their ecosystems and pressed into our service. Our interdependency has now become so complete that, if proprietorship is the subject, we must acknowledge that in some respects, they own us. We humans honor knowledge of where we came from, counting that as baseline information, essential to our journey toward nativeness. Similarly we must acknowledge that our domesticated creatures are descendants of wild things that were shaped in an ecological context *not* of our making when we found them. The fence we built to keep their relatively tame and curious wild ancestors out of our Early Neolithic gardens eventually became the barbed wire that would contain them. At the moment of first containment, those fences must have enlarged our idea of property and property lines. When we brought that notion of property lines with us to this distant and magnificent continent, it was a short step to the invisible grid that in turn created the tens of thousands of hard and alien lines that dominate our thoughts today. Did the natives at Lone Tree Massacre foresee this? Those lines will be with us forever, probably. But we can soften them. We'll have to, for the hardness of those lines is proportional to our sense of the extent to which we own what we use. Our becoming native will depend on our emerging consciousness of how we are to use the gifts of the creation. We must think in terms of different relationships. Perhaps we *will* come to think of the chicken as fundamentally a jungle fowl. The hog will once again be regarded as a descendant of a roaming and rooting forest animal. Bovines will be seen as savanna grazers.

An extractive economic system to a large degree is a derivative of our perceptions and values. But it also controls our behavior. We have to loosen its hard grip on us, finger by finger. I am hopeful that a new economic system can emerge from the homecomer's effort—as a derivative of right livelihood rather than of purposeful design. It will result from our becoming better ecological accountants at the community level. If we must as a future necessity recycle essentially all materials and run on sunlight, then our future will depend on accounting as the most important and interesting discipline. Because accountants are students of boundaries, we are talking about educating a generation of students who will know how to set up the books for their ecological community accounting, to use three-dimensional spreadsheets. But classroom work alone won't do. They will need a lifetime of field experience besides, and the sacrifices they must make, by our modern standards, will be huge. They won't be regarded as heroic, at least not in the short run. Nevertheless, that will be their real work. Despite the daily decency of the women in the Matfield Greens, decency could not stand up against the economic imperialism that swiftly and ruthlessly plowed them and their communities under.

The agenda of our homecoming majors is already beyond comprehensive vision. They will have to be prepared to think about such problems as balances between efficiency and sufficiency. This will require informed judgment across our entire great ecological mosaic. These graduates in homecoming will be unable to hide in bureaucratic niches within the major program initiatives of public policy that big government likes to sponsor. Those grand solutions are inherently anti-native because they are unable to vary across the mosaic of our ecosystems, from the cold deserts of eastern Washington to the deciduous forests of the East, with the Nebraska prairie in between. The need is for each community to be coherent. Knowing this, we must offer our homecomers the most rigorous curriculum and the best possible faculty, the most demanding faculty of all time.

III

The Family Is All There Is

Let's sit near each other and
Remember, remember . . .

—Martha Demientieff

BLOODLINES are among the strongest human connections. They are the stories that place us in history, that delineate our relationship to a clan, to a community, to a landscape. Our inheritance spreads out to include a web of people and places and circumstances. We find ourselves bound not only to immediate kinfolk, but to our kind in ways that require us to balance tolerance and principle, compassion and dignity.

The family provides a context for a range of understanding that stretches from the intimate to the infinite. Within the human bounds of that context, we come to know fundamental aspects of ourselves as people. Our lives are central to our knowledge of the world. Beyond those bounds, the lineage extends out into a context that encompasses more than we can comprehend. The paradox inherent in this range of understanding is at the heart of our existence.

Do You Hear Your Mother Talking?

WILLIAM KITTREDGE

THEY OFFERED me work in the mill when the woods closed down, but we had enough money and I hate the cold and ringing of the night-shift, everything wet and the saws howling. So I stayed home with Ruth.

This is one of those company towns the logging industry builds on its second-growth hillsides. You can stand at our big window and not see anything but the dripping roofs of green frame houses below us in the brush and piles of split wood covered with plastic tarps and old swing sets and wrecked cars, most of them without glass or tires, which are bright and washed in the rain and stained with rust, and you can watch the rain dimple the puddles showing black and wet on the asphalt, and you can wonder.

The place where Ruth parked her Desoto was empty, and I figured she must have gone down to be at the Mercantile when it opened. My Chevy four-by-four was on blocks in the shed behind the house. I thought about spending the afternoon getting it ready to ship south again.

It surprises me even now. I let the idea go through my mind with the taste of the coffee because I had wondered when I would come to feel that way. It just came to my head. I could feel myself leaving.

It was a dream in which Ruth was staying behind forever. For a long moment I couldn't even get myself to see her face, or understand how I had come to this yellow-painted kitchen in Alaska. The idea of leaving just fell into me like a visitor. I blew my breath on the window, and rubbed my initials in the steamy place.

It was light as it was going to get. The coffee was heavy and sweet, so

I poured another cup and lit up another cigarette. Some days nothing moves. You can look out at the evening and see the fog that was there in the morning, feathering off into the canyon where the river cuts toward the ocean.

What saved it was Ruth's old Desoto. She had the headlights glowing. Ruth drives slow and careful.

Outside you could hear the water in the river. I stood on the porch, holding the coffee cup, and watched her park.

Ruth got a paper sack in her arms, and stepped around the puddles until she was beside me. Her hair was wet on her forehead and the shoulders of her cloth coat were soaked. She grinned and shoved the sack at me, and I knew I wasn't going anywhere.

During the winter Ruth can look blotched and strange. Some nights she will go alone to a movie and come back after I am sleeping. But she was smiling, and I could read myself, and I had to smile.

"Turn off the headlights," I said, and I took her sack.

Ruth ran back through the rain and stuck her head inside the car door and fumbled at the switch. Her skirt was pulled high and it stuck to the backs of her legs, and I could see the dark net of veins behind her knees.

In the summer when we met, Ruth was deep brown from the sun and her legs looked like something out of pictures. She was working nights as a cocktail waitress in Brownie's, and sleeping away her days on the beach. I caught her there early one morning and spoke only a few words to her that first time. I'd seen her lots of times, since she was working at Brownie's. I woke her, not so much to start something with her as interested in why these runaway women act like they do. You see them in the mill, dirty and wet and working too hard and determined to be single as possible. And this one was a flirt at Brownie's, which was the other thing.

She told me she could always sleep if she was listening to the ocean, and she smiled and didn't look unhappy with me at all. I wonder how long it had been since I saw her naked in the light? Her hair was long and yellow and she was hard and tight enough, even after two kids, but she was a little too easy.

That was the first thing they told me about her. That she had two kids living with her first husband, but she was eager and not bad. She never talks of her other life and has never hinted at going to see those kids.

She slammed the car door and came back.

"I got bacon and eggs and juice," she said, taking the sack. "I'm going to cook a regular breakfast."

The fields smelled of fire. You could imagine little runs of fire burning behind the combines. My father would shred the heads of the ripe barley between his calloused hands, and blow away the chaff and bite down on the kernels, chewing like they were something to eat. I would lay on my back, hidden down in the barley, breathing the smell of burning while the stalks rattled in the breezes.

All I could see was the sky. Ruth might have been with me, listening and quiet. That would have been a fine childhood thing, me and Ruth.

Ruth smiles when she looks away to the window where the rain runs in streaks. You have to wonder who she sees in her reflection, and what kind of family she sees in me and her.

We live on a big cedar-forest island at the edge of Japanese Current, where it never snows. Everything comes in by boat or floatplane. Ruth and I do not tell each other much of what we came from, letting it go at the fact that we are lucky, and here.

The first morning, after we woke up in her bed, she came along to spend the day with me. It was her funeral. Before noon we were down in the tavern, which is a dark old barn built of cedar planking and shakes, called Brownie's since it was built in the early days of this town. No one knows who it was named for. Big smoky windows look out to the street, if you want to look.

All winter while it rains people gather to sit around a barrel stove welded together from sections of culvert, looking at the little isinglass window in the door, where you can see in at the fire. The shadows run up the walls and over our faces.

"We can give them something to talk about," Ruth said that first morning. That's when I said it was her funeral. I should have told her I was proud to walk in with her.

That was October, and I was already done falling timber for another winter. The low clouds hung down into the fog coming off the seawater. That afternoon we sat outside Brownie's under the veranda, on the wood bench where everybody has carved their initials. We had our cans of beer and we were out of the rain as we watched the two nuns go along with their tiny steps on the board sidewalk. You could see the trouble they had taken to make themselves precious in the world.

"They think it's something," Ruth said.

I'll give myself some credit. Right then I knew this wasn't just some woman from the night before.

The dark red bedsheets are part of Ruth, and her saving graces. She changes them every day. She says winter is underwater enough without damp sheets.

The rain was flushing through the galvanized gutter above the window. Ruth would be in close beside the oil stove and reading. I could see her, wrapped in one of the Hudson Bay blankets I bought in Victoria. She keeps a pile of magazines on the floor beside the new platform rocker that was supposed to be mine after we moved in together.

Turned out I like to sit at the kitchen table, under the bare bulb. Ruth wanted to put a shade on the bulb, but I said no. There is a big window in the kitchen. I can see out into the canyon through the mirror of my face on the inside of the window and imagine the runs of salmon, and the old Tlingit fishermen in their round cedar hats.

My father and my mother were sleeping and I stood in the doorway and watched them sleep in the square of moonlight from the window. I walked away beside the shadows of the long row of poplar trees that ran between the irrigation ditch and the road from the house. Over on the highway at daybreak, while the sprinklers turned their arcs over the al-

falfa, I hooked a ride on the back of a stake-bed truck. The last thing I
saw was the trees along the high irrigation ditch; I can still see them clear
as yesterday. My father was just like me. But Ruth is nothing like my
mother. I wonder what a kid will remember from this place we live in
Alaska.

The cardboard patches Ruth nailed over the knot holes are already turning green. At least we didn't buy the house. I was right about buying the
house. This is not the house we want. We want to build a house of cedar
logs.

Ruth always keeps a big jug of orange juice in the refrigerator. It
burns away the taste of my cigarettes. That first night, in one of the cabins by the beach, where she lived by herself, saying she had only come
north for the summer, while I was still living in the logging-camp bar-
racks, Ruth said she had grown up learning to sleep naked. I can almost
taste the feel of her.

All this winter my boots sat over by the wall, ready and oiled for the
day when I can go back into the timber. You have to wonder what there
is to like about falling those virgin-growth cedar trees, and what kind of
man would stay with timber-falling long as I have. The cedars are the
most beautiful trees in the world.

The red-grained back-wedge comes falling out, and I shut down my
long-bladed Stihl, and I sit there letting the quiet settle in. I work alone,
which is dangerous, but I want silence when I shut down the saw. The
sawdust smells like some proper medicine. Right then I have enough of
everything.

The first-growth trees fall true as angels, with the whoosh of their needles through the air, and they are dead. Like the natives I have learned to
tell the trees I am sorry, but not so sorry I won't cut another in the afternoon. You kill to fill your belly, and then you tell them it was necessary.

You have to smile at such things.

It is my best life, out in the woods, and this winter there have been
times I ache for it as I sit through the rainy afternoon in Brownie's and

listen to the talk of fish. I wonder if falling trees is a true work. But I forget such worries as Ruth and I walk downhill through the dripping early darkness to the movie house, and we are saying hello to everybody and Ruth is excited like a girl.

"I walked in the rain," Ruth said. "After you went to sleep I walked in the rain."

"You got to tell me what was wrong with you," she said, and she ran her cool fingers down the long scar on my inner arm.

Each step of it seemed right at the time. I can see the pale tender skin along the inner arm separating as the blade traced toward the wrist, my flesh parting along the length of my wound in a perfect clean way, and the tough white sheath and the deeper seeping meat before it is all drowned in blood.

I am telling you about craziness. I lay in those beds and I thought I heard my mother's voice and never slept until I came to believe there was some tiny thing wired into my arm, and electrical circuits flashing along with their messages, right at the core of my arm like a little machine, and all of it a trick. Then I could sleep, because I knew someone could cut it out with a surgeon's blade.

The idea got me in trouble. I found out about doctors, and I went into the office of the best doctor in Klamath Falls, I asked him to cut the wiring out of my arm, and the crazy part was cutting on myself when he refused.

It seemed like a good idea to think my troubles could be solved by the touch of what they call micro-sharpened knives. It was the kind of thing you come to believe, like babies believe the things they learn before they are born. It was like knowing which way is up. But the trouble with me is over. I sit in our kitchen and read hunting magazines, and I imagine stalking waterbirds like they were my friends.

I am telling you about craziness, but I wouldn't tell Ruth. "We all been born with too much time on our hands." That is what I said.

We have nights to think about our earliest memories. In mine there is a red dog resting in the dust beside a stunted little lawn juniper and the crumbling concrete walkway.

There is a thunderstorm breaking.

That was out front of the apartment building where we lived when I was a little child in the farm-hand town of Malin, on the northern fringes of the potato land that drops toward Tule Lake and California. My mother walked me on the sidewalks, in and out of the stores, and to the barber shop where they smiled when I climbed up to the board across the arms of the chair.

That red dog barked in the night, but usually he was sleeping and wrinkled in the dust. What I see are heavy drops of rain. I can still count them as they puff into the dust. I can close my eyes and call up those raindrops striking each by each.

Like my mother would say, "Each thing in its place." I can hear her voice clear as my own.

My father had his two hundred acres of barley farming property out south of the Klamath Falls airfield, he was hiring winos to herd his few hundred head of turkeys, and he always had my mother. I would ride out with him in the gray pickup truck, gone to check on the well-being of his turkeys, and then home to my mother.

Him and my mother, in those good years after the war, they called themselves the free world. But they were playing it like a joke, at parties, with other men and women.

Men would come to the kitchen while my father was gone, and my mother would pour whiskey. They would sit at the kitchen table with their whiskey in a tumbler, and my mother would laugh and stand beside them, and those men would hug her around the waist and smile at me while they did it.

"You better go outside," my mother would tell me, and she would already be untying her apron.

"We was late with our lives," my father told me. "Me and your mother, so we just stayed with our playground." He told me there was too much room for running with your mind when he was growing up in Tule Lake during the Great Depression. He said he went crazy during those years, and that I should be careful if I got my imagination from him.

My father told me this when I was thirteen, maybe as a way to explain his lifetime. That was the first time I left, wishing I could hear my mother say good-bye.

"If you won't answer me," Ruth said, "I was only going to tell you what happened." She was at the stove, tending the eggs and bacon.

"You were feeling bad," I said, "and you had a few beers and you walked in the rain and felt better. Like nobody ever did."

"I drove down to the ocean," Ruth said, "and walked on the beach. Before daylight." Her back was to me. She was turning the eggs. "It was nothing but that and I felt better."

Ruth colors her hair golden and it was running with seawater when she came walking up from the summer ocean. Ruth shook her head, and I knew her face would taste of salt. Right there was the first time she reminded me of my mother. My mother was young, and her bare arms were red in the summer rain. The drops stood in her dark hair as she was laughing in the yellow light under the thunder.

It was just before the 4th of July and hot and clear and still when I came north. The low fog was banked far out over the ocean. After some drinking I would see the gray summer tide coming cold over the sand, and think about the Lombardy poplar trees you could see for twenty miles over the fields of alfalfa on the right sunny day around Tule Lake. If you imagined them clear enough those trees would come closer until their leaves were real, like they could be touched.

Crazy is really a place you could learn to stay. You could learn to live there forever. It was a reason for drinking. I never imagined myself into somewhere else when I was drinking; it was only afterwards.

Down in Victoria I bought myself a whole set of Alaska clothes as if that would turn me into an Alaska man, got me a barbershop shave, and rode the Alaska ferry north. It wasn't the right way to travel into such a place, but it was easy at hand and it was the season for seeing sea birds and all the fishes from whales on down.

The days were warm and sunlighted and you could smell the evergreen trees over the diesel exhaust as we came to dock in midafternoon. I walked out over the sandy flats to the ocean, a wind was coming off the fog on the horizon, and I found a stone fireplace where fish had been cooked. The sand was littered with red berry boxes, and there were torn newspapers in the brush. You had to wonder who had been there.

By nightfall I was sitting on the bench outside Brownie's, listening to some men who talk about the salmon run and lumbering. The inside of Brownie's looked hammered out as a cave. I thought of the mills where I have worked, the howl of saws and wet sawdust, and I wondered if I had come to another wrong place as I sat there being a stranger in the side-angle lights outside Brownie's.

Give it a summer, I thought. There was nobody to notify. I had my clothes folded into a canvas warbag and a half-dozen one-thousand-dollar bills. My chainsaw pays me a hundred and fifty dollars on a good day. Only a fool does things without money.

"We ought to be married," Ruth said. She was washing the few dishes and stacking them in the openfaced shelves above the sink. She went on placing the dishes carefully atop one another, then dried her hands and went to stand before the oil stove. "I could have another baby," she said. "It's not too late. That could be my calling." She smiled like that was going to be funny.

I got up and walked away from her and went into the bedroom. After closing the door, I sat on the bed. *That could be my calling.* I couldn't hear a thing from the other room, not even Ruth moving around. After a while I pulled my worn old black suitcase from under the bed. With the suitcase open the next move was easy. Ruth could come and stand in the doorway and watch while I packed.

"I'll take a little money to travel on," I would say.

She would look down a moment, and her face would show no sign of anything, and I would think it was going to be easy to get out of here with no trouble. "Watch me," I would say. "I'm gone."

When the suitcase was packed I would head past her into the other room, pull on my slicker and leather cap and go out to the shed where my Chevy four-by-four was up on blocks. It would be dry inside, with the rainwater splattering from the cedar eaves. The dirt is like dust mixed with pine needles.

There is a pint of whiskey hidden under the seat in the Chevy. Two long swallows and I would think about laughing, and sit in the dirt with my back against the wall and whistle *ring-dang-do, now what is that.*

My mother beat my ass for that song, and washed my mouth in the irrigation ditch. It's a song I think about when I want to remember my mother and the way she laughed and hugged me as we sat on the grass with water coming from her hair in little streams. Now that is not crazy, thoughts of the water streaming through the little redwood weir in that irrigation ditch and my mother knowing some joke I didn't understand.

Ruth came and sat beside me and my black suitcase on the bed, her elbows on her knees and her head down and her hair hanging forward like she was a wrecked woman with nothing to do but study her hands while some man made up his mind about her life. "My mother told me a joke about times like this," I said.

Ruth didn't answer.

"My mother told me everything you got is like a China cup," I said. "Because it never came from China, and you always got to worry if it's going to break."

"Some joke," Ruth said, and her face was an old woman's face when she looked up at me.

Not that Ruth was crying. Her eyes had just gone old, and the strength in her flesh had lost some of its hold on her bones. Her lower lip fell down, and her teeth were stained by so many cigarettes. I could see the years to come, both of us old in some house where she looked like my mother and the radio was always playing in the other room.

Out at the Klamath Falls hospital, a nurse unlocked the door and I walked into my mother's care, a man thirty-four years old and unable to even trust his own brain.

My mother's hands were cold. What could I tell her? That I had lived too long watching my father turn hermit in the house he built on the corner of his property out by the airfield where the air force pilots flew jet planes every hour or so like a clock. Could I tell her jet airplanes will make you crazy for answers to everything?

She showed me an old photograph of my father: a young man with just the tip of his tongue between his white teeth, and his hands deep in his pockets and the brim of his city-man hat snapped down over one eye, like the picture-taking was going to stop everything for all time at this moment in his schoolyard. Behind him you can see the painted sign: *Turkeys*. "He was the best man they ever had," my mother said. "Now he's made you crazy."

You could take the same picture of me, deep in my forest beside some fallen cedar tree, and you might think, *Who the hell does he think he is?* We've all seen pictures of men who are dead now, with their long saws crossed in front of some great stumpage, and their sleeves rolled up over their elbows.

My mother puckered her soft mouth as she eyed me and didn't talk any more, as if her tongue had locked and she had lost her speech. Then she shook her head. "I'll tell you the joke," she said. "This is the joke of it." She looked around at the house where she was making her stand; expensive hardwood furniture and a mantle decorated with half a hundred engraved stock-show trophies. Silver spires with imitation silver Angus bulls on the top.

She didn't look like anything was a joke.

"Things changed," she said. "Things will change." She was trying to make it sound like a hopeful notion. I imagine the first lie, and a time when they came to know there was nobody to trust. I imagine them coming to want every Goddamned thing they could get their hands on. It's simple. You are going to die, so you better get in on the money and the screwing.

One afternoon she took off in a Lincoln Continental with a heavy-built man nicknamed Cutty. "Cutty had this house left over from the time he was married," she said. "Your father wouldn't even take me to bed. Cutty knew better, right from the start."

She took off those frameless eyeglasses, and cleaned them. There was a box of Kleenex on every table in that house. I picked up one of those trophies with the little silver Angus bull on top, and I thought like a child, "So this is the way to be rich."

The fall-of-the-year sunlight percolated into my mother's house through layers of gauzy curtains, and she never went outside. Twice a week there was a cleaning lady, and every day there was a boy delivering things. My mother just cooked me meals, and waited for me to make my peace.

There was nothing to know. Maybe it is true about my mother and Cutty. Maybe they are a great love. Over the years Cutty has worked himself up from auctioneer to purebred cattle breeder. He was always sending flowers from Bakersfield or some show town. She said it was his busy season.

For nine years I worked my summers in the woods and batched through the winters with my father in his house. On winter afternoons I would drive over to the Suburban Tavern and shoot some pool, and come home to stir up some tuna and noodles for the microwave oven. Nobody, my father or me, ever really cleaned up the kitchen, and more and more I started to feel tuned to the trembling of those microwaves, all the time closer to discovering I had been wired for other people's ideas.

Just a quarter-mile south of my father's house there's a barroom built from a Quonset hut back in World War II, with gas pumps out front. My father is still eager for a walk down to the bar and some drinking and talk first thing in the morning. It's just that you can learn to live in some of those stories. But that is enough about craziness. It's a place you swim like deep in the black ocean with strange fishes. You might never want to come up. It's a country where I could go visit and find a home.

Ruth refolded each thing I owned, her hands trembling as she filled that black suitcase. The unshaded overhead light was on bright in our bedroom, and she moved like an underwater creature. "Fine," Ruth said. "Just Goddamned fine."

Her face was flushed with that fallen look you might imagine as secret to animals, her eyes glazed like stones and this way and that, quick as lizards. I remember my mother late in the night when she was drunk in our kitchen where the windows were glazed with ice. I would come awake from hearing her laugh, and ease from my bedroom where the people's coats were piled on the other bed, and she wouldn't even see me with those eyes.

"Just fucking wonderful," Ruth said.

"You pitiful son of a bitch," Ruth said, and I didn't know if she meant me or her.

Ruth unfolded my stiff canvas Carhart timber-falling pants with the red suspenders, the cuffs jagged off and the knees slick with pitch, and she stepped into them, and pulled them up and hooked the suspenders over her shoulders, her dress wadded up inside, and she stood there like a circus girl. "How do you think?" she said. "You think I could work in the woods?"

"You ought to have a baby," she said. "You ought to lay down on your back and come split apart and smell your own blood in the room."

"But you never can," she said. "What can you do?"

This is what I could do. I could lace my boots, and I could get the blocks out from under my Chevy and spend the afternoon cleaning the plugs until she idles like your perfect sewing machine. It would be twilight and the white Alaskan ferry boat would be rolling in the long ocean troughs as I stood at the rail with a pint of whiskey in my hand and watched the cedar tree mountains turn to night under the snowy mountains beyond to the east. I could go anywhere in America. But Ruth was smiling, and it wasn't her sweetheart smile. "You better get me," she said, and she dropped those suspenders and stepped out of my canvas Carhart pants.

"You know what I can do?" she said. "I am going to lay down and come unseamed for a baby."

You wonder what the difference is between me and women, and if women really like to think there is some hidden thing inside them which is growing and will one day be someone else, some hidden thing telling them what to do. There was Ruth at thirty-nine years old, with her babies behind her in another end of the world, too old for what she said she wanted, standing there with her hands open and willing to look at the possibility of dying for some baby.

You think of the old explorers. You have to know there was a time when they smelled their land from out to sea and the clouds blew away, and it came to them that this coastline they had found was a seashore where nobody exactly like them was ever given a chance to walk before.

"I'm going to say, Baby," Ruth said, "do you hear your mother talking? Baby, are you listening?"

Me and Ruth were there in the glare off the glass, I could see us, and I had to wonder what our children would see if they were watching and looking for hints about who they should come to be. Ruth looked mottled white like the blood was gone out of her. "Either that," she said, "or you can get the hell out of here."

Those old explorers must have studied their mountains, trying to think this was what they had always wanted, this place they didn't know about. You try to control the shaking of your hands, and you want to say, all right, this will be all right, this is what I'll take, I'll stay here.

"We'll split some shakes," I said. Teetering around that room, picking up my stuff and storing it back into where it belonged, refolding those stiff canvas Carhart pants along the seams, carefully as they could be folded, I felt like a child on a slippery floor and Ruth eyed my moves like all of a sudden she wasn't quite sure what she wanted after all. Ruth could see I wasn't going anywhere, and the rest was up to her. There was no one thing to say, and I still cannot name the good fortune I saw except as things to do.

"You coming with me?" I said. In this country they roof their houses with shakes split from pure cedar. We went out that afternoon and bought a straight-grain cedar-tree log, and had it hauled to us. Ruth wouldn't hardly look at me or say anything, but she went along.

That night Ruth slept in her chair with her magazines. By late in the next day we had built a canopy of clear plastic to keep our work dry from the rain, and we started splitting the shakes, side by side. We will build a house where our things to do can be thick with time on our hands.

People will watch us build, and we will be the ones who know the secret. We'll watch strangers on the sand flats. We'll know they envy us our house built of cedar logs. We will live with one garden that grows nothing but red and yellow flowers, and we'll have another garden with cabbages. Our dogs and our cats will sleep on the beds, and me and Ruth will carve faces into the cedar-log walls, and those faces will smile back at us in our dreams and be our friends and warn us of trouble, looking back at us like we were the world, and watching what we do like we watch the sea birds picking on the rocks at low tide.

There will be cabins with covered walkways to the house. My father could live in one, and my mother could come visit, and Ruth and I and my father and my mother could all go down to the movie house and over to Brownie's after the show.

Your mind is sometimes full of little animals and you have to trick them with things to see. We will live in our house like the old people lived in their houses. Maybe we will come to know what it is like to lie awake in the night while our children listen for our talking and laughing as we listen for theirs.

Dressing Out and Barking Knuckles

KEN DOLA

i.

You'll have to watch your knuckles today
in the narrow valley air.
The cold silver of last night's rain bites.
It'll make you numb and stiff.
But you warm up with the work of it all.

A limber crown flicks a last mark
against the watching sky
and commits to the fall.
The spruce is small and doesn't look old:
sixteen, eighteen inches across the stump
and tapers fast to sixty feet.

But run fingers across the tight-grain
there's bands of rings squeezed so tight
I can't count them.
The bark feels warm
as trees do.

The bark spud slides under the red bottom bark
popping off round flakes as I work it up the trunk.
Cambium still covers the bright, wet wood
it is silvery, elastic and tight.
Like membrane around venison.

166

ii.

A scruffy hemlock won't let go the sky.
Make a wedge and mallet out of a sapling.
Wood-hollow echoes in the see-your-breath air
warming the chill with pounding's work.
The top wobbles,
the hemmie goes down slow and quiet,
hardly bounces on the spongy muskeg.
The grain is tight enough for a wood engraver's block.

Limb it and buck it.
Take an axe to the thickest south-side bark.
The cambium turns brown
like an apple missing bites.

Whatever it is that collects light
from the eyes of the dying
is here now.
Light fades up the length of each log
following the progress of the axe.

Limbs have a peculiar look about them
after being cut from the trunk.
They look like ribs around the backbone
of a gutted animal.
Maybe the real value is in the slash:
the millions of small, dead green lungs.

It's something to consider
breathing as we do for each other.

Between the Steens, the Trout Creeks, the Rising of the Sun

KEN DOLA

Owen Mink is singing to Buster his dog,
one great horned owl and four ravens
while raking leaves in the desert.
The ranch has just enough cottonwoods
to dapple the cranky desert grass
and make the stream bottom glimmer pale yellow
between the barn and machine shop.

He's singing "Home on the range . . ."
in the same sincere way he eats steaming dinner rolls
that kind of days-work-done thoughtful indulgence,
and I can't believe it.
But I do as I listen to the deep wandering voice
ebbing and flowing with each new wave of leaves
brought into the harbor with his rake.
Buster listens too, lying in the grass
squinting at the warm day, mouth open, tongue rolled out.
His herding days are over in the Oregon high desert
he's just waiting to ride in the old white pickup with Owen
and finish the rest of their chores.

———

This is a brawny sea-like land
whose rawboned, badger-pawed body
can hold the most delicate plant, forever.
If the law were around, it would arrest the wind
for carrying a knife.
Clocks balk and get confused by skittish howls of memory
and dreams.
The second hand is sun glinting on harness silver
the jingle of tug chains tick off the hours.
Colors come here to grow up
to be apprenticed to winter light.
And humans are only a skillet of grease and gristle.
There's a relentless beauty that will burst you
with a longing for your life to come back
without any pain.
There's so many hungers seeping inside you
it makes you sad and quiet
until you want to hide your clay body
from the land itself.

On these freezing nights when we gather in the dogs
who go off to gnaw on bones
in the closet or under the bed,
we hug the pains of liquor and wait
for morning's quiet smell of horse and harness leather—
the morphine of work and animal energy.

———————

From out there by the coyotes,
out in the free grass,
soft as tines in hay
some nights, tight, it seems like a voice is calling:

Ollie Ollie in come free . . .
Ollie Ollie in come free . . .

calling me home, raking me in.
Singing with inhuman gentleness,
songs for one dog, one owl and four ravens
taking me far into the hills beyond this life.

Zeta's House

JOHN KEEBLE

—for David Grimes & the Orca II

IT WAS LATE afternoon when I arrived, but as usual I wondered at the last minute if I had taken a wrong turn. The color of the house was like the coat of a coyote that took up the red, brown, pale yellow, and silver of the earth, as changeable as that. One could look at such a coyote standing in a field, and look away, and look back and not see it, then look away and look back again and find it there just where it was. It was so with the house. Although it was hardly a small place, it could seem invisible until one came right upon it. Suddenly it was there, rising from amongst the rock and tree and bush.

I got out of my car. On the deck, I had to maneuver around a large food dryer and several bushel baskets filled with unhusked corn. I found the front door thrown open. A wasp flew in. I had seen the nests of the mud daubers cemented to the eaves, as well as openings made by swallows. I peered through the doorway and discovered my friend, Zeta, and one of his sons sitting at a large table in the living room. The table was heaped with corn. The large room was filled with light. The light was filled with motes. The two gazed expectantly at me, and then my friend motioned to me to come in. I went and sat with them.

Zeta explained that Nona, his wife, and the other children were pressing cider at a neighbor's place. The apples had come in early. It was hot. Zeta's house was located at the edge of a long valley that ran northward across the Canadian border. Even here, near the border, a curious, seemingly displaced microclimate allowed for the cultivation of apples, plums, peaches, and apricots. Heavy snows fell during the winter, but the summers were desert-like. Water for irrigation came from a nearby river and drinking water from deep, expensive wells. The kitchen was open to the living room and in it I could see a glass pitcher filled with water and ice. The pitcher stood on a counter. It glittered in a shaft of sunlight. Nona had put it there, I thought, in a place of honor.

Not long ago a daughter in the family had died. I had come to visit, to be with my friend, to comfort him by my presence. We did not speak of this yet, but of our families otherwise, our work, the pennant races, the weather. As we spoke, Zeta's son, a fifteen-year-old, moved his eyes watchfully from one of us to the other.

The two of them were shelling corn. They took up the corn from the center of the table, husked it, dropped the husks onto a pile on the floor, and stripped the kernels from the cobs with knives. The kernels went into a large basin that rested on the floor between them. It was a field corn with hard, dark yellow seeds. Several wasps buzzed above the table, but the steady movement of hands kept them at bay. I had understood from the start what Zeta and his son were doing, and had insisted upon helping. It was always good to mix work with pleasure and talk. Zeta brought me a knife and small basin. When I filled my basin with kernels I emptied it into theirs. From here the corn would be carted out to the dryer. Later, it would be ground into flour. Nona and Zeta would then make tamales on special occasions throughout the year.

I had eaten their tamales. Late last March my family had brought a pig's head to them. We boiled it over a fire in the yard. It was cold. A cloud of steam suffused the air. We drew out the brain of the pig for soup and stripped the cheeks of meat. In the kitchen, we stewed the meat in broth with peppers, made a cornmeal mush, and spooned the mush into corn husks, and then the meat, folded the husks into envelopes, and cooked the tamales in a steamer. The delicate smell of the corn on the table before us now brought it all back to me: beans, rice, soup, tamales, the people laughing and working, our children running back and forth from the house to the snow that still lay in patches under the trees, or to the coals of the fire, and my wife there, and Nona in her dark blue skirt moving quickly from one thing to the next.

The daughter the family would lose was in the kitchen, seated on the end of a counter. She was six years old, and pale. Her eyes looked unnaturally large, too bright, and her hands seemed too long, too thin. She was dying. Her family treated her with deference, but not so much so as to force her into herself. She observed everything closely and at times her face brightened at the antics of the other children. Once, she forgot herself and slid down from the counter in an effort to join the children who flooded by on their way to the living room. She lost her balance and nearly fell, but caught hold of the edge of the counter, and turned, tottering weakly.

A hush moved from those of us who had seen her to the others. The children stopped and came back toward her. The daughter smiled shyly, and said, "Don't worry." One of her brothers—this one, the stripling who sat shucking corn with his father—moved to her and placed his arm gently around her. She put her head against his waist. "It sounds like it's raining," she said. Everyone listened. In fact, it was clear outside. The stars were brilliant in a black sky, but in the quiet of the kitchen the refrigerator made a ticking noise like the sound of water dripping from an eave, and a bubbling pot on the stove sounded exactly like a spring rain driven against the roof. For a moment we all entered the phantasm. Having her there seemed a gift. It was as if she'd been sent to us to stand watch for a time at the avenue to the other, adjacent world.

Here at the table, I selected an ear of corn and pulled back the husk, then glanced upwards at the heavy timbers that bound the walls together, and said, "This is a fine house." It was the best I could manage.

"Yes," Zeta said. "It holds all the things we leave behind, the marks and gouges, the wear." He smiled and as if he'd read my thoughts, added, "It holds the grief for us."

We fell silent and continued working. Not far from our table lay a large black dog with a grizzled muzzle. The dog grunted occasionally in its sleep. Next to it lay the shadow of a branch from a fir tree, elongated and yet precisely articulated. At the far side of the kitchen was a doorway that led into other rooms. The door was open and through it I could see a cage that hung from a rafter. In the cage were two parakeets. Every once in a while, magpies could be heard chattering outside, and each time they did the parakeets talked back from the other end of the house. This exchange became an irregular measure of our wordlessness and our work. The sound of the shucking, of knives tearing softly along the cobs, and the papery whisper of leaves falling to the floor measured the work. The heap on the floor was a measure. Every so often, Zeta or his son would carry the basin of kernels out to the dryer, or cart in more corn, or get up to sharpen a knife. Those were measures.

The son had an electric gluegun at the table. He was making a construction out of scraps of metal: screws, bolts, spokes, little gearwheels, and small engine parts. Every so often he paused in his work with the corn, fished through his box of parts and glued on another piece. The strong scent of epoxy snaked through the air. The construction had begun compactly. At first it looked like a mechanical root, then a human form, a large animal, and then it grew abstract. The son was tied to the work we shared, but at the same time the construction asserted his separateness. This was another measure, one of his own time and of his relation to his father.

At dusk, when the last of the corn dwindled on the table, the shadow of something large flitted by a window. The son went out the door, then reappeared with a crow perched on his wrist. He took the bird to a corner of the living room and set it gently on a peeled limb that had been screwed to the wall. The crow cawed once and the dog snapped up its head. Its collar jangled. The parakeets answered from the other room. Zeta and his son looked across at each other and laughed. The crow preened its wings. A white cat appeared and stalked the crow. The crow glared at the cat with its black eyes. The cat stopped and began to roll in the dust.

Zeta told me how they had insulated the north wall of the loft with old books. He liked that, the wall loaded with words. It made him think of all the words afloat in the house, the talking, the murmuring in the night, the cries of children waking in their trouble, the moans, the laughter. Sometimes he heard his lost daughter calling him, her voice as clear as if she were here. The house held every word spoken in it, and the softness of hands, the weariness of legs, the terror. It held the pain, and every bit of the decomposable, flimsy, true substance of life.

I wanted to say something, but could not. I felt I had unexpectedly tumbled to an obscure ledge within myself, a place of hazard. It struck me that I was here seeking Zeta's comfort for something that had yet to happen to me, and not he mine for what had happened.

At that moment a bat flew through the doorway. It circled the living room again and again in the characteristic, ragged flight of its kind. Our work was complete and we watched the bat. Soon, Nona and the children would arrive, and I wished to greet them before setting out on my journey home, to see the flurry when they all came in, the way their energy would change everything. The son had gone off. He came back with a tennis racquet, closed the front door, and stood up on a chair. Each time the bat circled he swung. Outside were more bats, and swallows gliding in graceful loops, eating the twilight insects. Finally, the son hit this bat and sent it hurtling way across the kitchen and through the open doorway to the other room. We heard it ping against something hard. The son went to retrieve it.

Zeta leaned toward me. A button on his vest clinked against the table edge, and he nodded in the direction his son had taken. "That one was most affected by his sister's death. He was her companion." He explained that in his daughter's pain, through the long trial of being carted in and out of hospitals, she came to believe in reasons. He said, "She told her brother that God was taking her for a reason she would soon learn." Between us was the son's construction, which had grown increasingly abstract. It had exploded into pure geometry. It shimmered in the fading light like a constellation afloat in space. "It's true, our house is a refuge," Zeta said, "but it's as permeable as skin. The world comes in. We are never safe here, but we are never alone."

Memorial Day in Kiev (May 30, 1990)

NORA MARKS DAUENHAUER

—for Lydia Black

The rain:
a mother's tears
for her children
falling on blossoms,

umbrellas
brightly colored
lining streets of Kiev
through steamy bus
and streetcar windows
from St. Sophia's
to cemetery,

and flowers
we carry for you
to your mother.

Endurance

MELINDA MUELLER

In a household of daughters
and their mothers—grandmother, mother,
my aunt, and I—there could be secrets
but not privacy. No one knows a daughter the way
her mother does.

       And so the childshape
who went to school, came home,
came to the table, was not the child.
I was

   elsewhere, in another life, outside
the guarded life of childhood. I lived
in my mother's books.

       Here is the photograph
of Shackleton's ship *Endurance*—
more like an after-image than a photograph;
the rigging, furled sails, the spars, masts,
all of it burned white with frost
against the absolute black sky.

       The seas
thrown against her sides are ice. The timbers shrieked
in the press of it, you couldn't sleep;
there'd be cannon-shots—snapped beams or

sheering ice, you didn't know—
the lanterns shivering. I knew it,
I knew it all and still know it; I know the thick
damp fur that lined my hood; the diamond,
lacerating air.

       By the time I read about it, it was
planes, half-tracks, shortwaves—*anyone*
could go and it wasn't what I wanted.
What I wanted was gone before I was born,
though I lived it every night, thinking
I can't get there. I can't get back
to my real life.

       I didn't care
that there weren't women on the expeditions.
If I couldn't have any of it, I'd have it
all. And I had seen her, in the dark—her level eyes
above the heavy muffler.

       On Shackleton's expedition,
during the brutal trek toward rescue,
all of them had, without telling
one another, the same obsessive illusion—
that there was one more person in the party
than was there. They kept counting,
and getting one short.

       Not every
landscape was full, not every life
taken. Yet how could I discover such a place
if all I could imagine had already
left me out?

From the house of friends
I have a memory, like a photograph:
their grandmother (not the crippled one who lived
with them, but the other, rarely seen)
looking in at us from the hall. Grandma
Shackleton. His daughter-in-law.
I was too late.

As for men,
my first crush was an actor who played
a Western scout. He was beautiful and self-
reliant, high-humored—nothing
fazed him much.

And so I began
and went on falling in love with the men
I wanted to be,

falling in love, finally,
with a man sympathetic as a woman, a complete
surprise, and wholly lucky.

Among my students I read,
as my mother read in me, a child's inhalation
or quick averted glance: *So that's how it is with you today. All right.*
I never meant to teach, never meant
to marry. Shackleton meant

to reach the South Pole
and wasn't equipped at all for that task he'd set himself.
But he was born and bred for the task he got instead:
his ship carried far off course, first
crushed by the ice pack—the same, in my child's mind
as wolf pack, but with ice—
then swallowed down.

Standing on the floes, with the masts
sinking out of sight, he turned to his men and said, "Well boys.
Now we go home." And so they did, across the ice, the open
ocean, a frozen island never crossed before—every man alive
of them got home.

One late afternoon not long ago
I climbed with the man I married to a deep cleft
in a limestone outcrop; a look-out with a satiny floor
from 20,000 years of use. Dingo tracks
were painted overhead—a ghost-dog who walked
across the ceiling.

On the plain below were eucalypts,
termite gnomons, great demonic black cockatoos flapping
to roost—and the old, real,
long-waiting child looked out

in sudden recognition—
When did I escape into this life?

My Auntie Jennie's Bed

NORA MARKS DAUENHAUER

She always slept on a bed
with many pillows,
small ones, large ones,
old and new.
Once in a while
she made me sit among them
and made me play rag dolls
with dolls made of old rags
from whatever she decided
was good for dolls.
My dolls would always smell
of raisins and seal oil
because I kept them
in a Sun Maid raisin box.
She would help me make the dolls
talk to each other.
On occasion
she would have the dolls go fishing
or picking berries.
Each doll would have a Tlingit name
and the families would have names too.
She taught me how to give names
to Tlingit dolls.
I now give names to my grandchildren
and nieces and nephews.

—September 19, 1988

Burying the Tongue Bone

SETH KANTNER

IN THE STORIES I grew up on there were no spelling-bee winners, no inventors or rich men. Those would have been pale unheroes. The stories were the old Eskimo ones of hardships and hunts, lost dogteams and snowed-in trails, told by travelers spending stormy nights around our stove.

"Yep. Lotta barking and my dogs run away in the night. I had nuthin'. Not even rifle." Old Stoney Williams would laugh as if it were the funniest thing that could have happened to him. I'd bend close to the kerosene lamp, waiting for more, picturing him on the wide dark tundra and wondering if I'd ever be old enough to have those stories to tell, dreaming of being tough and able to laugh into storms like the old-timers. Stoney called me by my Inupiaq name and talked slow as if it were important that I understand.

But on rare trips to the village thirty miles upriver, ready fists reminded me that I was a white kid, an uncommon sight, not a native species of the Arctic. I couldn't claim the oldest stories, the mystical ones cloaked in nativeness and the past that I longed to be linked to, the ones about caribou with long teeth and the pike head out there in some lake swimming with only its guts trailing behind, the little strong-armed *inukuns* trying to strangle sleeping hunters. Those stories, I learned, could not be my own, even though they were hung before me like wonderful tempting objects in a native store where white people weren't allowed credit.

In the village I heard from Outside schoolteachers that money was very important, and I learned from their pupils that no amount of dirt on my face and in my hair would make me Eskimo. And that a thirty-word English vocabulary was more admirable than a hundred-word one that evoked responses of "Sure always try to be smart," and "Whachew try ta prove, honky?"

Classics like *The Scarlet Letter,* about Pilgrims, meant nothing to me. Those weren't my grandparents, not my ancestors. I never learned "The National Anthem." It belonged to the country of America.

Now for years high-top tennis shoes, basketballs, and TV have been covering over the old stories, the old reasons for hunting, the reasons for making heroes out of hunters who laughed at the cold. I searched for new stories to own in the alleys of wet concrete, between the tall close skyscrapers that squeeze you in a city. I learned to drive cars and talk about them. "Yeah, '65 Mustang. Cool ragtop." And to call random 800-numbers from payphones when I was lonely to hear a woman's voice that wasn't frightened of me. The world of malls and movies and K Mart was sometimes fun, but always like a science fiction movie, never real. So it was easy to laugh at the hard city-times like a bad storm. But cement is harder and colder than any ice, to me, anyway.

I went home. To the tundra; that is still the same. I'm lucky it hasn't changed. And in the village I returned to the people who were often hard on me for being white, but they were the same elders who told me the old stories, showed me how to bury a bear's tongue bone to let the spirit come back. And the same kids that once pounded me for being white were the ones who had also laughed and showed me how to open easily the tough plastic on a bag of potato chips. "Come on Apikiilik, you don't need knife. Been in camp too long?"

Now enough years have finally passed, or maybe just change has left us all stunned, like a gun going off too close to your ear. But we share stories now. Not all of them. Not way back where we're from. We share what we know of our own past and this strange present, maybe because we see we're going to share the future now. *Adiga,* it's good.

Ayagumagalha, the Wanderer

JAMES MUMIGANA NAGEAK

THE STORY first became evident when the Simon Paneak Memorial Museum was built at Anaktuvuk Pass. I was at Anaktuvuk Pass and helped with the construction of the only museum on the North Slope. When the construction was finished and the contents of the museum were put in place, the first display was a statue of Ayagumagalha. The display explains that this was the person who created the Nunamiut, the inland people. You see, I am married to a Nunamiu, Anna.

Pursuing the interest pricked by the statue and the synopsis of the story, I asked Justus Usisana Mekiana to tell the story. Over the years I have had contact with the Nunamiut, I have found Justus to be the best storyteller. Justus Usisana Mekiana is a man of sixty-three years and he first told this story of Ayagumagalha to me in the summer of 1991. The spoken word was in the Inupiaq language. My translation is quite literal to keep the Inupiaq language flavor in the English translation. The structure and vocabulary as presented here are characteristic of ordinary Inupiaq usage.

Some words and concepts need explanation:

blubber. This is the insulating fat between the outer skin and the meat of
a seal or whale, which is sometimes rendered into oil.

pingo. This is a growth or blemish on the tundra. It is a result of water
becoming ice and pushing the top layer of soil and making a rounded
blemish like a pimple on the tundra.

hole to the house. In the subterranean houses there is an outer entrance
and a passageway to the center of the floor of the inner house, where

there is a hole that is used to enter the dwelling. That is the katak—a place where you fall to get out.

qargi. This is the community house, but in the old days it was where the men of the community would gather and work on their equipment and a place where the young men would gather and learn from the older men. This is usually the place where the dancing would take place.

maktak. This is the outer layer of the whale. It consists of the black outer layer, which is about half an inch thick, and then the blubber, which is about a foot or sixteen inches thick.

The elders and the people of the North Slope Borough got together and began to think and say things—that there is a need to get the Messenger Feast back. And because the elders of the villages have never been to one of these things, the only way they can give you the story, the beginning, is the way that they have heard about the Messenger Feast. And this is where the oral history comes in, that what you hear, and sometimes what you hear is something that does not really make any sense at all, or it is something that is, ah, like he say that something is hard for him to remember the good words. Sometimes it's easier to remember words that doesn't make any sense at all. And those are the kinds of things that he remembers the most and that is one of the things that they are trying to remember, the story of the Messenger Feast.

This is the story. There is a man named Ayagumagalha. His name is Ayagumagalha and this Ayagumagalha lives where the Alatna River starts. That is where Ayagumagalha lives.

He is living alone and Ayagumagalha is of a much bigger stature than we are. And because he is living by himself, he begins to think, should he make people? He begins to think; through the thinking, it becomes a reality. And so he created these people that could live with him.

And because these people are living there, after Ayagumagalha created the people, they begin to multiply. Just like Anaktuvuk Pass today. Just like, when he was a young man, there were only sixty-two people at Anaktuvuk Pass. And as he is growing older and older there are close to three hundred in that village of Anaktuvuk Pass. And so it is the same kind of process that when Ayagumagalha created these people they began to multiply.

Because he has created these people, he is taking care of the people. He is able to call any kind of animal that the people want to eat. Ayagumagalha is able to say "Come." Maybe it is not just the way that a human being of today does; he had some other power, what the people understand, in the English language, as shamanistic power. This person, Ayagumagalha, had that particular power, to be able to care for his people, by calling whatever is needed for his people.

And because he is able to care for his people by calling the animals of the land, he knows that these people do not know nothing, anything about blubber. Because he is concerned that they should begin to know something about the workings of the blubber and the seal and all of these things, he began to think maybe I better go down and see if I could get some blubber. Maybe he went downriver through the Killik River and went into the Colville River and followed the Colville River and just this side of Nuiqsat is a place called Puviqsuq. It is a pingo. It is flat land all around the pingo, but all of a sudden there is a mount. And this particular place is where Ayagumagalha camped on his travels down to see if he could get some blubber for his people and the name of that particular place is Puviqsuq. And if you look at Puviqsuq today, this side of Nuiqsat, there's a pingo, but it's flat on the top. That was Ayagumagalha's snowhouse. The reason why it is flat on the top is because he put his backpack on top of it. Being a big person and there is a lot of weight on his backpack and that flattened the top of the snowhouse.

Ayagumagalha left his first camp and headed toward Barrow; this is where he was intending to go. If the people of Anaktuvuk Pass had stayed in one place they would have probably been as numerous as those people in Barrow. But because the ships came and they were beginning to have less food in that area and trapping was good, the people from Anaktuvuk Pass area traveled with boats and ended up in Canada. They dispersed and some of them are starting to come back now. And that is the reason why there's not as many people here. That is the way it has always been. There were people in that area and Ayagumagalha arrived at Barrow.

The people in the community center, the qargi, the community house, heard something outside of their community house. Somebody or something is out there so they send two of their young men out, out of the community center to check to see what was going on out there.

And when they went out of the community center they saw a man that was bigger than they were; because they were curious as to why this particular big person is there, they asked him, "Who are you? What are you doing here?"

When they began to ask Ayagumagalha, Ayagumagalha, of course, understood those two men. "Who are you?" "I am Ayagumagalha. The reason they call me Ayagumagalha is because I'm a wanderer. I travel from one place to another. And that is the name they have given me, Ayagumagalha." The two men, of course, are trying to remember, Ayagumagalha, Ayagumagalha . . . , as they are going into the community house they keep trying to remember the name by repeating it to themselves, Ayagumagalha . . . , but they couldn't go all the way into the community center without forgetting the name.

The third time, trying to remember the name Ayagumagalha while walking into the community center, on the third time they finally made it through the hole to the house to announce to the people inside the community house, "His name is Ayagumagalha and the reason why they call him Ayagumagalha is because he travels a lot. He's a wanderer."

They found out that he was a friendly person, so everybody went outside and greeted Ayagumagalha, outside of the community center. And, of course, after they greeted him they want him to come in with them, but Ayagumagalha is much bigger than they are. He couldn't fit in through the doorway; so they had to make room, so they had to rearrange the community house, because Ayagumagalha could not get into the community center. They removed some supports of the doorway so Ayagumagalha could enter the community center.

They began to question him, "What is the purpose of your travels? Why did you come here?"

He told the people. "I am living where the Alatna River begins. That is where I am living. And there are some other people that I have created there and because they don't know anything about blubber I'm here to see if I could get some blubber from you so that I could share it with my people."

And the people in the qargi, the community center, responded, "Sure, we'll provide you with blubber." And Ayagumagalha said, "Well, you give me blubber, I'm going to be able to somehow repay for what you have given me."

"Tomorrow, the men of the community should stand on either side of the Ukkuqsiq Creek there with their bows and arrows ready. That is what they should do tomorrow and I will call for the animal."

When the men were ready with bows and arrows on either side of the Ukkuqsiq Creek Ayagumagalha began to look toward the land and began to call for the caribou. And when he called for the caribou the caribou came in between the men and as the caribou are running, the men are shooting them.

And after the men and the people from the community have removed the caribou that have been killed right alongside of the Ukkuqsiq Creek, Ayagumagalha told the men to get ready again on either side of the creek. "Get ready again because I haven't finished repaying you for the blubber that you have given me. Get ready and I will call in some other animal again, but if one of you runs out of arrows, don't holler 'I'm out of arrows,' don't holler that." This time he gave them instructions on what not to do. "Don't call out 'I'm out of arrows,' if you run out of arrows."

After the men have gotten ready on either side of Ukkuqsiq Creek, he raised his hands so they pointed inland and called. This time he called for the wolves, and the men on either side of the creek are shooting the wolves. As they were shooting them, someone hollered, "I'm out of arrows!" This made the wolves turn around because Ayagumagalha had told them not to mention that they were out of arrows, but one of them had disregarded the order that they shouldn't holler, "I'm out of arrows!"

"I would have been able to call in some other animals, like the wolverine, but because of the statement that you made, when I told you not to make that particular statement, I could have gotten you some other animals, but because you did not follow my instructions, that is all I'm going to be able to provide for you."

Ayagumagalha is ready to leave and puts all the blubber into his backpack. There is a story that maybe every time that he grabs a piece of blubber and maktak and puts it into his backpack, they would get small, because he was able to put all of the blubber, a big pile of blubber, into his backpack. He told the people of Barrow that they should follow his tracks back to where he is from, "Because if you come and follow me, we will have sheep skins, wolf skins, wolverine skins, all of these skins you can get from inland, we will pile them up for you at our village and if you come and follow me we will all have our young men come and meet you. And from where they meet you, you will have a race back to the village. And if you win, if a young man from Barrow wins the race, then you will be able to come back with all the skins that have been piled up in our village for this particular price. But if you lose, then, of course, the inland people will keep the skins and use them for themselves. But, of course, even though you don't win the skins, we will provide for you to come back with some grub, like dried meat and anything else the inland people use for themselves."

When he was ready to go back to Alatna River, he did not go the way that he came to Barrow, by way of Nuiqsat. This time he began to travel by way of Ikpikpak River. He began to follow that Ikpikpak River. And on his way, of course, he had to rest for a while and made camp. And on the east side of Ikpikpak River, there's a mount or some high place there; this particular place where Ayagumagalha had camped is still there. The name of the place where he camped on his way back to the Alatna River is Ugvik.

So this is the beginning of the introduction of the blubber to the

Nunamiut, the inland people, by Ayagumagalha. He wanted them to be able to associate themselves to things they did not know about. They did not know it was maktak or blubber until Ayagumagalha came back with them from Barrow. When the Barrow people got into this certain area, it was like the time they had a race from Qalutaq, which is south of the village of Anaktuvuk Pass, to a place called Tulugaq, north of the village of Anaktuvuk Pass. The distance of the race that these people have to go as they are coming into the Messenger Feast is probably over twenty miles, compared to the distance from Qalutaq to Tulugaq. That is probably the same distance from the village in Alatna where the men of Alatna are meeting the men of Barrow and that is where they began the foot race.

They began the race, and as the race is going on, the slow ones are beginning to be left behind. But there were four men from the village of Barrow keeping up with the two men from Alatna River. So there they are, six of them running, the Alatna men running as fast and hard as they can because they want to keep the skins that they have piled in the middle of the village, because if the winner is from Ayagumagalha's people, they will keep the skins. And if the winner is a man from Barrow, then he will be responsible for getting all the skins back to Barrow. That is the reason why, as they are running, other runners give them the encouragement to go on. But as they are going along three of the Barrow men fall back and there are only two of them running, one running for the skins, and one of them running because he wants to keep the skins in the village.

And as if they are running for their lives, one running for the skins and one to keep the skins, they gave all of themselves. The man that Ayagumagalha has made wasn't able to go any faster, but luckily for him the man from Barrow was not able to get any faster also, and so the man from Alatna won the race and kept the skins.

As they were staying there for a while the people from Barrow decided to leave and Ayagumagalha's people made dried meat for them, as much as they can carry back to Barrow. So they traded with them like that and this is the beginning of the story. And this is the way that the Nunamiut people have been able to tell and remember it.

And because of the way that the story is told and the way that Ayagumagalha has created these people, I reminded him, this is the way you are going to remember Ayagumagalha. Ayagumagalha had mittens, a pair of mittens. He said, "As I am leaving I am going to set my mittens on the side over here and my mittens, when you see them you will remember me." And this is after he had taught the people from Kivalina, Noatak, the people from the Kobuk area, after he had taught them the race, and today if you look far into the horizon sometimes you see the peaks, these peaks that are sticking up like a glove, just on this side of the Alatna.

And when Ayagumagalha left, he never returned and they don't know where he went. That is how the story of Ayagumagalha ends.

Mental Health Meeting

MARTHA DEMIENTIEFF

Can we sit at meetings and talk
Endlessly, endlessly
About pain and death?
Which way will words lead us?

Can we read the signs of despair?
Words, words.
Sorrow talks without words.
What does the hurt one *do?*

Mind our brother here.
Watch, watch.
His clothes are new because
He needs no food now.

He's buying clothes to travel in.
Walk, walk
With him, or he'll slip away
And we'll cry with his relatives.

This meeting's to talk about living.
"Why, why
Do they want to die?"
They'll show us how to stop it?

Let's sit near each other and
Remember, remember
How to live in an altered world
Bearing our pain over and over.

Let's mind each other
Always. Always
Things happen when there's no help.
And then they call meetings.

The Family Is All There Is

PATTIANN ROGERS

Think of those old, enduring connections
found in all flesh—the channeling
wires and threads, vacuoles, granules,
plasma and pods, purple veins, ascending
boles and coral sapwood (sugar-
and light-filled), those common ligaments,
filaments, fibers and canals.

Seminal to all kin also is the open
mouth—in heart urchin and octopus belly,
in catfish, moonfish, forest lily,
and rugosa rose, in thirsty magpie,
wailing cat cub, barker, yodeler,
yawning coati.

And there is a pervasive clasping
common to the clan—the hard nails
of lichen and ivy sucker
on the church wall, the bean tendril
and the taproot, the bolted coupling
of crane flies, the hold of the shearwater
on its morning squid, guanine
to cytosine, adenine to thymine,
fingers around fingers, the grip

of the voice on presence, the grasp
of the self on place.

Remember the same hair on pygmy
dormouse and yellow-necked caterpillar,
covering red baboon, thistle seed
and willow herb? Remember the similar
snorts of warthog, walrus, male moose
and sumo wrestler? Remember the familiar
whinny and shimmer found in river birches,
bay mares and bullfrog tadpoles,
in children playing at shoulder tag
on a summer lawn?

The family—weavers, reachers, winders
and connivers, pumpers, runners, air
and bubble riders, rock-sitters, wave-gliders,
wire-wobblers, soothers, flagellators—all
brothers, sisters, all there is.

Name something else.

Lullaby for Lloyd

JENNIFER BRICE

IN MY IMAGINATION, Frances lurches slightly as she walks the one-lane, windblown streets of Barrow, an Eskimo village on the Arctic coast of Alaska. Darkness and swirling snow swallow the plywood-and-tarpaper shacks that line the narrow streets. In my imagination, Frances is not alone. She carries her baby boy in the Inupiaq way, his body cocooned in the hood of her fur parka, his face framed by her wolf ruff. With Lloyd snuggled against her back, Frances sways down the streets. She doesn't know where she's going, only what she's looking for: a place to sleep, a hot meal, her next drink.

My picture of Frances is drawn from newspaper articles beginning in 1971. They recount how, one night during the subarctic spring, when the sun lingers just below the horizon, Frances left a bar with a white soldier. They must have argued. He shot her, then he threw her body out of his truck.

Lloyd's name is missing from articles about the killer's arrest and trial. Did the men who pulled Frances's frozen body from the snowbank find the little boy in her hood? Had he been somewhere else on the violent night when his mother died, might he have grown up happy? The answer is, "Probably not." Long before Frances became a victim of a white man, she fell victim to a white man's disease; her son was born a victim of her disease. Even if a drug existed to cure the brain damage caused by drinking during pregnancy, no medicine, no amount of love, could heal the hurt of an alcoholic mother's rejection, neglect, and, in Lloyd's case, physical abuse.

For the first few months after Frances's murder, social workers shuffled Lloyd between foster homes in Barrow and Fairbanks. A four-year-old ball of fury, Lloyd terrorized classmates at Head Start, a government-funded preschool for children from low-income homes. His first complete sentence was, "Fuck you."

Lloyd Henry Nukatpiaq is my brother.

My parents adopted him in June 1971, bringing the total number of kids in our family to five. I was eight, Tobe seven, Hallie six, and Ramona, the baby, only two. Dad ran a fledgling construction company and Mom worked as health director for Head Start, which is how she found out about Lloyd. Social workers were looking for a foster home with connections to the preschool, and ours fit the bill.

At Lloyd's adoption hearing, the judge asked us kids if we wanted to say anything about our new brother. My brothers and sisters looked at me, the eldest and usually the most outspoken. I swung my legs beneath the courtroom bench, squirmed on the slippery wood, and forgot every word of my prepared speech.

For the first few months we were enamored with our new baby brother. He looked different from us: we were all gangly legs and arms, freckles, curly hair, and blue eyes. Lloyd was small for his age, encased in baby fat, brown-skinned, pink-cheeked, with thick black hair that defied Mom's home haircuts. We older kids treated him like a life-size doll; my baby sister toddled worshipfully after him. Dimly aware of unhappiness in his past, my parents put him on a regime of hugs and figure-skating lessons, as well as green vegetables and visits to the dentist. Lloyd acted fine during the day. At bedtime, though, he cried for his mother until his eyes swelled shut and snot drenched the front of his flannel pajamas. The rest of us lay in bed listening to his chest-wracking sobs. After a couple of hours, he always climbed out of bed, lifted the toy box out of the corner, emptied it onto his bunkbed, and, clutching Matchbox cars and Tonka trucks, Lloyd slept.

The Christmas of Lloyd's first year with us, I asked Santa for a Barbie beauty kit. Tobe wanted a banana-seat bicycle, Hallie a horse, and Ramona a Baby Dear. Lloyd wanted to be a cowboy. Mom and Dad bought him a Stetson, pointy-toed boots, a bandanna, and toy six-shooters. On Christmas morning, Dad photographed Lloyd in front of the tree: a bow-legged, brown-skinned, Eskimo John Wayne.

Buying Lloyd the cowboy get-up might have been a mistake. It didn't occur to my parents until years later that Lloyd might like costumes too much. He and Ramona started playing dress-up in the afternoons when the rest of us were in school. Ramona wore Mom's lipstick and a cousin's cast-off prom gowns. Lloyd mimicked her in high heels and flesh-colored negligees from Grandma's trunk. At the time, it seemed like normal brother-sister play. Looking back, I realize that Lloyd's self-image was too fragile for costumes. He didn't understand where the play-acting left off and real life began.

Virtually from the beginning, life with Lloyd was anything but normal. The first signs of just how different he was from the rest of us were barely noticeable. TV bored him; he couldn't see it. He didn't come when we called him for dinner; he couldn't hear us. At meals, he ate until Mom took his plate away; he'd never had enough. My parents took him to a pediatrician, who recommended specialists. It turned out that Lloyd was nearly blind, with a drifting eye too far gone to corral. Chronic infections had eroded his eardrums, and an early diet of candy bars, soda pop, and potato chips had rotted his teeth. What concerned the doctors even more was Lloyd's inability to use words, even Inupiat ones, to describe how he felt. When he was happy, he kissed and cuddled. When he was frustrated, he lashed out with teeth and fists. He lived in a haze of un-seeing, un-hearing, un-speaking, uncomprehending.

By the time Lloyd started elementary school, my parents suspected that his deficiencies ran deeper, beyond the purely physical. A school psychologist diagnosed him as suffering from Minimal Brain Dysfunction. Nothing serious, it meant that learning would probably be more difficult for him than for other kids his age. Next, when the behavior problems started, school counselors stuck him with a new, even more unwieldy label: Attention Deficit Hyperactivity Disorder. Finally, after ten years on Ritalin, a drug that slowed his reactions and stunted his growth, Lloyd was diagnosed with Fetal Alcohol Syndrome, a label just coming into vogue in the mid-1970s.

Twenty years later, researchers differentiate between Fetal Alcohol *Syndrome* and Fetal Alcohol *Effect*. Some children born to mothers who drank heavily during pregnancy show no visible signs of damage. Of those affected, however, only 20 percent suffer from Fetal Alcohol Syndrome, the remaining 80 from Fetal Alcohol Effect. Lloyd's mother, Frances, could not have foreseen the devastation her drinking would wreak on her unborn son. A few drinks more, a few drinks less, and his life might have been dramatically different. A cynic might say that Frances was lucky to have borne a child who suffered only from Fetal Alcohol Effect.

Children with Fetal Alcohol Syndrome tend to be severely malformed and profoundly retarded, registering IQs between 40 and 60. In most cases, they live out their short lives in mental institutions or nursing homes. Kids with Fetal Alcohol Effect usually end up in different institutions. Like Lloyd, during their early school years they suffer from language deficits, poor social skills, and hyperactivity. Like Lloyd, their symptoms as adolescents range from below-average intelligence to low self-esteem to violent behavior. Depression, broken relationships, alcohol and drug abuse mar their adulthood. Like Lloyd, they slide between minimum-wage jobs and rescue missions, between detox units and jail. Victims of Fetal Alcohol Effect don't live: they survive.

If my family had known two decades ago what they now know about Lloyd's disease, growing up with him might have been easier. Instead, his anti-social behaviors always preceded the research by four or five years. It is now widely accepted that many alcoholic mothers unwittingly abandon their babies from the time of conception. Children like Lloyd who have been abandoned by their mothers typically grow up to be sociopaths, their fear of further abandonment driving them to sever bonds, often violently, before they can form. Their problems defy '80s-style psycho-jargon. Unconditional love, nurturing, empowerment—my parents thought these things could fill the gap left by Lloyd's mother. They were wrong. It's possible to change the environment for a child with Fetal Alcohol Effect, but not his life.

Approaching adolescence, Lloyd acted out more and more. On the swing set one day, he casually asked the neighbors' four-year-old daughter to have sex with him. On car rides and camping trips he played our teenage emotions as expertly as a symphony conductor. My weak spot was my looks. I had sprouted braces, breasts, glasses, and pimples all in the same year. Lloyd would jump in the back seat of the station wagon and inch closer and closer to me until his grubby brown thigh stuck to mine like Saran Wrap. Then he'd chant under his breath, "Jennifer is ugly. Jennifer is ugly."

One night at the end of an excruciating family vacation, I slammed his head into a hotel room wall over and over. Mom and Dad quit leaving the house at night, even to go to the movies. For one thing, they were unable to cajole any babysitter back a second time. For another, they were honestly afraid one of us kids would kill Lloyd while they were gone. Not that they didn't sympathize. One time Lloyd experimented with a magnifying glass and the winter sun to burn holes in Mom's brand-new sofa set.

In the long run, though, Lloyd didn't need help mutilating himself. Swimming in a gravel pit one summer day, he nearly cut off his left foot on a piece of glass. Not long after, he teased a neighbor's German shepherd until the dog turned on him, mauling his face. In total, he ended up with more than 150 stitches that year. It seemed like sometimes Lloyd's body acted before his brain thought.

When he was nine or ten, his fascination with the abyss nearly killed him. We were on a family trip to Georgia. One minute he was playing alone at the end of a dock; the next, his otter-brown head was bobbing down the muddy Savannah River. Dad ran to the end of the dock, ripped off his watch, kicked off his sneakers, and dove in. Five minutes later, Lloyd sat on the bumper of the car, soaked, shocked, and—for once—subdued. He looked so small and scared I pulled him onto my lap and rocked him like a baby. Of all my memories of Lloyd, that one stands out most. Not because I came closest to loving him at that moment, which I did. But because, the second I saw his head drifting downstream, I thought in a horrifyingly detached way, "Now we'll be a normal family again." I cried as I rocked him. I was a strong swimmer then as now. I saw him first. I could have jumped in the river to save him, but I didn't.

By the time Lloyd turned fourteen, living with him was like listening to a stuck recording of the Chipmunks twenty-four hours a day. He pilfered from stores when Mom took him shopping, beat up on special-ed kids at school, conducted guerrilla warfare at the dinner table. Our family disintegrated into factions: Lloyd and my parents against the rest of us. Desperate, Mom telephoned the commissioner of the Department of Health and Social Services. She said that if the state couldn't help with Lloyd, she and my father might have to nullify the adoption. A few days later the commissioner called back. She said that if my parents could locate an appropriate facility for Lloyd, the state would pay.

A year later, during spring break from college, I drove up to Spokane, Washington, to visit Lloyd. He was attending Excelsior, a school that taught basic skills such as getting a job and cleaning an apartment to emotionally disturbed teenagers. Tuition at Excelsior was $30,000 a year, far more than my parents could have afforded. In exchange for paying, the State of Alaska required my parents temporarily give up custody of Lloyd. When I learned that, legally, he was no longer my brother, I felt the familiar mixture of guilt and relief that, since the afternoon by the Savannah River, I had begun to associate with the possibility of losing Lloyd.

In the Fairbanks public schools he'd come off less smart and less popular than the other pupils. At Excelsior his classmates were prostitutes and pushers. There, for the first time in his life, Lloyd became a role model: the only one in his class who'd never done time. Someone took a picture of me and Lloyd, arm in arm, one afternoon in Spokane. At fifteen, he stood taller than me. He'd lost his baby fat and outgrown Mom's crew cut. Looking at the picture, I saw him for the first time as a stranger might. And I realized he was handsome.

My family knew it was only a matter of time until the newness wore off and Lloyd was expelled from Excelsior, the same way he'd been asked to leave the Boy Scouts, KO'd from the Five & Dime, suspended indefinitely from high school. When he telephoned, Excelsior's principal seemed sincerely apologetic but said he just couldn't keep a student who kept trying to burn down the dormitory.

Lloyd flew home smoldering with interest in and resentment toward hadn't wanted him after his mother died. My parents had always been open about Lloyd's adoption but they'd refrained from telling him how his mother had died. Now he wanted to know. Then he wondered why the space for a father's name on his birth certificate was blank. My parents didn't know the answers to all of his questions but they knew where he could look for them. The day Lloyd left for Barrow, Mom carefully wrote out his full birth name, birthdate, and mother's name on a piece of paper, which he tucked into his jeans pocket.

In Barrow, Lloyd met a younger brother who had been adopted by an aunt and uncle. The brother introduced him to a toothless old Inupiaq woman who had taken care of both of them as babies. She gave Lloyd a photo of three women sitting side by side on a bench, dressed in colorful cotton *qaspeqs*. The woman in the middle is Frances. The solemn-faced baby on her lap is Lloyd.

Lloyd flew back to Fairbanks exhilarated about finding his brother, grieving for his mother, angry at the father who never acknowledged him, and more confused than ever about which world he belonged in. Was it the Inupiaq one or the white one? These are my words for his feelings, not his. Lloyd never expressed his emotions, he just acted on them.

After Barrow, he got fired from a succession of jobs at fast-food restaurants for laziness, rudeness, stealing. One morning after he left for work Mom lifted a sagging ceiling panel in his bedroom and got hit by an avalanche of *Hustler* magazines and burned-up matches. Pornography my parents could handle; pyromania they couldn't. They moved him into a rooming house. When he lost his job again and couldn't pay the rent, they paid it for him. He went to a psychiatrist. My parents went to a psychiatrist. He wanted a snowmachine. He wanted a car. He wanted a girlfriend.

Mom called Delilah "jail bait." Lloyd was twenty-two and she was sixteen, underweight, and pale except for the hickey-blotched skin on her neck. Her parents spent winters traveling in their Winnebago, watching cable TV, and living off welfare checks a friend forwarded to post offices in the Lower Forty-Eight. They took Lloyd with them in the fall of 1989.

He called collect from a truck stop a week before Christmas. Delilah's parents had kicked him out of the motor home with no money, no clothes, nothing. He didn't know what state he was in, let alone which side of the Mason-Dixon Line he was on. By that time my mother had earned a master's degree in education and started a business teaching, among other things, tough love to other parents. There was no way she was wiring him money for a plane ticket home. She and Dad told him to make his way north as well as he could and to call collect every day.

On Christmas Eve, Lloyd phoned from Seattle. It turned out he'd hitched rides with truckers all the way from South Carolina. Mom cracked. She gripped the phone, tears dripping down her face. "I can't bear for my son to spend Christmas on the streets of a strange city," she sobbed. Dad wired Lloyd $100 for a hotel room and food. An hour later Lloyd called again. This time Dad arranged for a plane ticket home. Early Christmas morning Lloyd strutted off the jetway at Fairbanks International Airport wearing a new leather jacket and Sony Walkman. After we opened our stockings, he called Alaska Airlines to ask about his "missing" suitcase of presents for the family.

Twenty-four years old now, Frances's son is still trapped in adolescence. In his mind the line between right and wrong, good and evil, love and hate, is blurred, distorted like the world he sees when he loses his glasses, which is often. He exists on the fringes of our family. Last New Year's Eve when my sister got married he skipped the receiving line and headed straight for the reception to start drinking early. Nine months ago my mother was hooked up to life-support in the intensive care unit at the hospital. Lloyd never called, never visited.

Now that all five of us kids have left home, Lloyd no longer pits us against our parents. Instead he plays Mom and Dad off each other. When government or Native corporation checks arrive at the house, Mom tucks them in a drawer for Lloyd to pick up when he's willing to use part of them to pay back what he owes for rent. So Lloyd calls Dad at his office and asks him to drop off the checks, which Dad does.

When my parents adopted him that June day in 1971 they swore to raise him like one of their own children. They've never given up on him, never stopped feeling responsible for his well-being, never stopped hoping one day he'll be happy. These days Lloyd blames his troubles on being trapped between two cultures. My parents have contacted Inupiaq leaders in Barrow to arrange for him to live there for a while, but their phone calls have gone unanswered. At a conference recently I told an old Eskimo woman about Lloyd. She shook her head and said, "There's no hope for those children. No hope at all. They're lost to us." Perhaps the biggest problem with FAE kids is they make themselves so unlovable, only saints can love them. I cannot speak for my parents, but I am no saint.

Lloyd and I are so disconnected I don't know his latest phone number. On the rare occasion when he comes to my house for dinner, I hide my purse on the top shelf of the closet. When he came to the hospital last fall after my first child was born, he filled the room with alcohol fumes. Sometimes when I rock my baby in my arms, I think of holding Lloyd that day by the Savannah River. And I feel strangely empty. Maybe I should have tried harder to save him. But most likely I would have failed, and I might have drowned too.

Frances's son is technically an adult now, old enough to drink, drive, and serve in the army. He holds a high-school diploma but he can't multiply nine times six or fill out a food-stamps application. He lives in a rooming house until he sets fire to it, holds a job until he gets demoted, works at a relationship until someone works back. Fine white lines crisscross the undersides of his wrists. The last time someone from the emergency room called the house in the middle of the night, my sister said she wished that next time Lloyd would cut a little deeper, like he really meant it. Someday he probably will.

Keeping Watch

JANE LEER

I

The sky's dark palms, pricked by starlight,
hold no moon, just a milky plate
of stars seen edge-on. On the porch
in parka and boots, hands curled around a warm cup
I watch Rigel ride Orion's instep
above the horizon. Five hundred years
since this blue light first slipped
past molecules so sparse it shines
seventh brightest; light older
than the plagues of Europe, from a time
before parallax separated
the Hunter and his foot,
before the transience of light sliding
into the heaviness of some black hole or blossoming
in one last burst of power was known.
I want to feel that distal brightness burn my retinas,
want my brain to know what was once there
before it fades, each night becoming small
witness to events unfolded.

II

The man in the coma, my husband, lost
in a reflux of memory, is unable to find the smallest
key to wakening. The nurses leave me
alone with him, and I sit warming his small
square hand in mine, put it to my face
and try to draw him back, but all he can do
is let thin tears slip from closed eyes,
a steady stream as long as I talk and when I finally stop
he is taken away for a different kind
of torment, for knives and lasers to open his eyes,
changing him into someone I can't recognize.

III

If I could appear to rise and turn like Orion's feet,
if I could travel five hundred years,
riding like Einstein's idea, on a beam of light,
I could make it to Rigel,
and I would know, I mean *really* know,
if it still blazed; and maybe
where the soul goes when the brain slides
past the weight of some event-horizon;
and how far you have to go before
there is no catching you.
Each night I await Orion's step,
tea cooling while I drink,
as the old starlight plays out its rope,
before the winter sky breaks
and spring's running sunset
catches the Hunter by his heel.

IV
A Certain Attention

The mind is a replica of what we see out there and in its order and disorder, its capacity for expressive forms and its incapacity for any final understanding, is a reflection of that world, the only one we have.

—John Haines

MINDFULNESS encourages us to be most fully ourselves. It requires that we both take notice and take care, that we use perception, imagination, and memory to render a complete and honest description of what we know, and to explore what we don't know. By default, that rendering and exploration is grounded in the human experience. By necessity, it must also extend beyond.

A simple transposition of letters in two words provides the spectrum: egocentric and geocentric. What's there to be fathomed asks of us both the simplest observation and the utmost extension of our minds. Neither is more important than the other. What matters is that we stay alert, that we cultivate our capacity for wonder.

Bringing in the Storm

RICHARD K. NELSON

I'M AWAKENED during the night by wind rattling the bedside window. Then it starts to rain and the house begins creaking in sudden gusts. Each hour, the storm increases, measured by the moaning and whining of its voice. At dawn, a southeasterly gale rumbles down the mountainside, sets the forest waving like a field of grain, roars and pummels against the house, howls in the whipping, slacking wires. Shungnak comes upstairs and lies next to the bed, frightened by the banging and shuddering of unknown things.

No longer able to contain my excitement, I crawl out at 5:00 A.M., take a front-row seat by the living-room window, and watch the oncoming storm. The marine forecast warns of an intense weather front lying just off the coast, its center a tight spiral of low pressure in the north Pacific. As it comes toward us, walls of cloud smother the mountains and reduce the islands beyond Windy Channel to silhouettes between dark water and ashen sky. The gale increases, as if the storm's entire strength is focusing against this part of the coast. Bubbles of wind cascade from the slopes of Antler Mountain and burst on the surface of Anchor Bay, sprawling outward in dark, rippled crescents, raising sheets of spray that fling themselves against the far shore. Windy Channel is a mass of black water and torn whitecaps, driven seaward by the gale, only half visible through squalls and torrents and milky sheets of rain. Leaves and twigs fly past the window. Pink and violet rhododendron petals tumble across the lawn. I wish I could soar up into the gale like an air-dancing gull. But I can only dream the wind, and imagine the gusts that rush invisibly above the bay.

The world never seems more alive than during a storm. I can almost sense the storm looking down at us, throwing its arms out and bursting with raucous laughter, at play in the tossing sea and the trembling forests. It has all the power and beauty of a wild animal—a bear in the backyard—unbridled, tempestuous, feral, petulant.

Koyukon elders treat storms as conscious things, soothed or angered by the way people behave toward them. Not surprisingly, they say that when someone dreams of a bear it can mean a storm is on the way. Along this coast, each storm has its own personality. Some whisper like cats, wrap themselves around the islands and stalk into the mainland valleys, purring and soft and wet. Some are quick and feathery as birds, dancing over the peaks in airy wisps, spraying rain across the water like droplets flicked from wingtips. Some are ponderous and dark, wallowing ashore and resting heavily against the land, heaving thick, saturated breaths that hang in the air for days. And some, like this one, charge in swift and strong from the Pacific, throwing dagger winds, scattering the waters before them, bearing down vehemently against the coast, shouting and celebrating. I love to look into the throats of storms, feel their wet breath, their tension and strength. Being out in a good storm is like standing on the back of a living whale or running under a trumpeting elephant.

But today, I watch from inside, sitting at my desk, trying to work in spite of the distraction. Gusts fret and jostle against the walls, shaking window panes, clicking door latches, creeping through seams and cracks. From time to time, I feel a draft against my skin, as if the storm is looking for a way into the house, trying to put some life into the still, imprisoned air. I feel like an animal hiding inside its den while a predator digs at the entrance. I should run outside and let the wind take hold of me, wrestle with my clothes and toss my hair, pitch me down and roll me across the yard. Suddenly it seems all wrong—the storm on the outside and me on the inside, each of us wanting a little taste of the other.

So I run through the upstairs and downstairs, open every door and window, and welcome in the storm.

The first gusts push through the front door and into the hallway, shaking coats on their hangers, scattering piled newspapers, spewing raindrops across the floor. Curtains flap wildly in the kitchen and living room, as a thousand chilly feathers tickle through every nook. The house fills with frenzied, exuberant energy, like a bunch of puppies fresh from the outdoors, wagging tails and shaking off, sniffing and licking and rubbing against the rugs and furniture. Wind tumbles through the upstairs and downstairs, runs in the front door and out the back, spatters rain on beds and tables and dressers, stirs little balls of dust from secret places, hisses and whistles and whispers, dances through this crannied space and spangles it with delight. How many years has it been since a good gust of wind touched the wood inside this house and brought to life its faded memories of the forest? I may not be the only one who celebrates here.

As the storm runs through the house, it's as if I've been encircled by a great, rollicking beast. I feel its playful fingers touching my skin, its wet lips pressing against mine, its chill breath rushing across my face. But while the storm is something outside me, it also expresses itself through me, just as the sighing boughs are its voice and the pounding waves are its fists. I move within the storm and the storm moves within me. I *become* the storm. Even these words, like swells rolling against the island's shore after the wind has passed, are the storm's echoes, given life through it and becoming a part of its life. I am a tunnel the wind blows through.

After I close the doors and windows, the whole house seems renewed, as if the wind has left it tingling. And there's a wonderful familiarity about the gusts cavorting outside my window. We've touched each other and shared a moment in the intimacy of home.

On a Certain Attention to the World

JOHN HAINES

It's some time now since the river,
the nightingale, the paths through the fields,
have disappeared from man's mind.
No one needs them now. When nature disappears
from the planet tomorrow, who will notice? . . .
There may be nothing so quiet as the end.

—Milan Kundera

I AM LOOKING at a photograph of the Milky Way, at an arrow pointing to our Sun, a microdot in all of that interstellar dust; and attached to the Sun, though we cannot see it, a small planet we call Earth. "You Are Here," reads a caption fixed at the top of the arrow.

And this is nature, so much of it that we will never know but the tiniest fraction of it. The star closest to our sun is 4.5 million light-years away. Our sun is 30,000 light-years from the center of the Milky Way. Each galaxy contains at least 100 billion stars, and the universe contains at least 100 billion additional galaxies. To speak, then, as some do now, of the "death of nature" is merely, in the context, but another instance of our unrepentant arrogance.

This small item in the universe called Earth, with all of its manifestations and seasons: the flowering and dying away of species, the shifting of continents, prevailing dynasties, wars and decimations—so important and yet they are nothing. Nothing and everything.

I think of the poet Robinson Jeffers, of some of his more passionate

Note: the lines I have quoted from Kundera are taken from an interview with the writer and transposed by me from their original sentence form into verse lines, in keeping with their poetic character.

evocations of the night sky; of the stars and planets as he watched them wheel and pass over the Western ocean; and of his instinctive placing of human crimes and passions in that context—one poet among us who felt deeply and actually the immensity of things, of our own relative insignificance, and who found a place for this in his poems.

I think too of the painter Richard Possette-Dart, some of whose later paintings, abstract as they may appear, have in them something of the substance and impression of this photograph I am looking at—myriad points of colored light, swirls and galaxies—a reflection, whether intended or not, of that immense ring of light in the sky; as on another scale, some of his later work seems in its black and white simplicity a reflection of a snowy field marked with stubble.

Last spring, while in Washington, D.C., I spent some time in the Museum of American Art. And there, among other impressions, I was once again struck by the consistent accuracy of those towering landscapes of the early American frontier and the Far West, with their complexity of details, their space and solidity, their record of things seen and felt: water and woodland, soaring peak and quiet pool. Hardly modernism, yet in its own way the art is compelling, and gives rise to the thought: how close and necessary was that relation then to the physical world, which the observation that went into the work bears witness to. Clearly, on the evidence, something has been lost in the art-of-nature study in this century; not simply curiosity, or even excitement, but a better word: *rapture*. It is an emotion that comes, not merely from looking at things, but from seeing them with a kind of veneration, as if within these objects, these vistas of water and mountain, something of the impenetrable mystery might be sensed and named, and before which one might be, not designing or dominating, but quietly attentive.

While it would seem that enormous attention is being given to the world, to nature, in recent decades, as witnessed in numerous studies and reports, and by the many calls for action to rescue what is left of wild nature from the abuses of humankind, few of us now see the world as they who painted these works must have looked at it, long and patiently, and with the utmost affection—that which alone sees to the heart of things. It is there in the ordered details of their work, down to the last feather of a loon or a duck, to the last wave-break on the shore of a mountain lake.

For this art one needed, at the least, a conception of reality, of light and shadow, distance and detail, depth and rising plain, that could only have come from having lived acutely in a physical world, and from which one might escape only at great cost. Today, with all the technical means available, that escape is possible on all fronts, but again at cost and only for a time.

I am thinking too of a book I have recently looked into, *Pathway Icons: The Wayside Art of India,* which evokes in its carved stones and painted objects, its abundant folkloric imagery, something of the incredible richness of ancient religions, with their manifold deities; the gods and demons, male or female, principle and manifestation; and which answered in the most apparent and profound way to the variety of nature in the outside world. Here, as in all of the old religions, each of the elements, or what we now call by that name, are represented by actual beings. In the heavenly bodies could be seen, and sometimes spoken to, actual people, gods and heroes, all of whom might figure in some symbolic and instructive story, or who ruled in some significant way a part of the cosmos. And this view of things, animated and filled with human drama, can be said to have been as true as any of our later explanations of phenomena, whether scientific or otherwise.

The images shown in this small book are referred to as "pathway icons"—images that accompany and make easier for the pilgrim his path from village to village and through life itself; as once similar images performed a like purpose for devout Christians on their way to a shrine or holy place.

A few phrases and descriptions from the introduction to this book seem to me to illuminate the nature of our subject, and I would like to quote or paraphrase a few of them here.

"Trees are anointed and worshipped, for they symbolize the cycle of growth and regeneration. Each tree has a spirit, and a large tree is always revered by the village community." We are told that "nature is a mirror reflecting the divine," and we learn that artistic creation is "a means to carry the individual consciousness into the universal." "The artist invoking the images gives form to the formless. . . . " And of particular importance here: "Images are not made as art objects, but as channels of communication with the divine, generating a power not often felt in images placed in a museum."

Here, as in all of that memorable art of the past, life, art, and religion are one. "The creation of a work of art is an act of worship in the true sense, in which the invisible becomes visible."

Nature and Art: forms and objects, representations that are the embodiment of emotions, of will and personality, in the things of nature, its plants, insects and creatures, wind and water. To turn to art, to make art of this, is "an act of discovery that unites the human spirit with the divine."

Life, art, and religion are one. Behind the art forms and within nature stand the gods, the forest deities and indwelling spirits; the divine embodiment of earth and its weather, stars and planets—all of it, and without which it is impossible to imagine *art* in any form. The true sign and proof of this is to be found in the artifacts of the past, in those richly articulated representations in stone, metal, and wood, of reptiles and insects, animals, fish, and birds; and in the intimacy these display, and which is so far removed from our own semidetached curiosity and sentimental descriptiveness. These objects, but they are more than mere objects, were alive in ways that we have all but forgotten, and the voices within them are seldom heard now.

Here as nowhere else we encounter the varied personality of the world, which embodies, among other things, the principle of conflict in nature, in the opposing forces of good and evil, light and dark. "Duality is intrinsic to nature. Creation and destruction are two faces of the same coin."

Much of our problem, I feel, lies here, in this difference between the attitude of worship, with its implied humility toward the resident spirits, a humility that encouraged at once a confident familiarity with those spirits, together with a necessary respect for their evident powers and in which the art participated; and our own modern attitude and practice of reducing everything to its particular function and direct usefulness to us. In this difference lies a whole world of time and loss.

To turn from that ancient sensibility to its characteristic modern counterpart is to measure the abstraction and dissociation we have fallen into. This subtle change, whose effects and full significance have in many respects gone unnoticed, can be verified in a late remark by C. G. Jung that "the gods have become neuroses." The import in this remark can be compared with a comment by the psychoanalyst James Hillman: "In the absence of the gods everything becomes huge." These observations, as brief as they are, give us, among other things, insight into our obsession with power and bigness; and to which we can add the universal use of the word "super" to preface or describe nearly everything from games to markets.

We are involved here with a subtle and ancient paradox: while we talk at greater and greater length about *nature,* nature itself, in its assumed sense, has retreated from us and before our very eyes. Meanwhile, nature in other and less attractive forms reasserts itself: violence, irrationality, aberrant forms of social behavior—aren't these also nature, returned with a particular force?

In this context, and as beguiling as it may seem, the idea that we can somehow "fix" the planet, repair what we think has gone wrong with it, is so absurd and self-referential as to resemble one of those panic periods in history, when all kinds of normally sane people begin to see signs and omens in every manifestation of nature and human behavior, and to believe in radical remedies, seeking scapegoats and sacrificial victims.

It is worth remarking on, too, in respect to the loss of that ancient richness of the many gods and companionable spirits, each ruling some manifestation of nature, that all of this multiplicity, and the art that came of it, should have degenerated into the *One,* the all-demanding, righteous and vengeful Father, with the withering injunction to "subdue the earth"; that in this idea of the one god lies the origin of the totalitarian spirit, or at least its final justification.

If we turn for a moment to the English literary landscape, to the descriptions of the countryside to be found in Wordsworth and Clare, in Keats, Hardy, Lawrence, and others, we find again this vital and affectionate closeness to things, as from a deep historical past, and which has only recently lost its hold on imagination. What I refer to can be felt, for example, in a few characteristic lines, from William Collins's "Ode to Evening":

> Or where the beetle winds
> His small but sullen horn
> As oft he rises 'midst the twilight path
> Against the pilgrim born in heedless hum

There is little that resembles this fluent familiarity in modern English and American poetry.

But how potent was that influence, that familiarity and affection in the past, from Chaucer on to Edward Thomas; and even in Eliot, whose subtle evocations of places in England have not been equaled in subsequent poetry. In contrast, much verse in recent years has been almost entirely concerned with subjective states of mind. We are given, characteristically, little more than a kind of baffled personality, intent on imposing itself on the reader. The words, rather than revealing the world, tend to obscure it and become an end in themselves.

It would follow from this impression that poets now do not see things clearly, or see them, perhaps, through a screen of words and books. A lack of precision and appropriateness shows itself in the use of that ubiquitous term "like," where the likeness, more often than not, is forced and unconvincing, as if mere use of the word were enough. The simile, that ancient device of comparison, has lost the better part of its accuracy.

But not only have we stopped looking, we have stopped listening also, if the lines I have quoted from Collins can be said to be representative of a certain acuteness of sensibility. It is apparent to me, at least, that the cadence of such verses, and of innumerable poems from the tradition to which they belong, must have derived from centuries of foot travel, from walking in the land, not driving through it or flying over it. Once more, it seems to me, we are faced with that indivisible connection between the way we live and the art we must make of that living.

It is just here, I think, that Kundera's insight, in the passage I quoted at the beginning, becomes tangible and can be verified. That is, even while we talk more heatedly about nature and wilderness, and about saving the planet, and about all related topics, as necessary as that attention is, nature in its ancient and spiritually flourishing sense is passing from our lives. We are, as Kundera remarks in a closely related text, already looking elsewhere.

Reality has assumed a form we hadn't anticipated. But it is always so; as when the conduct of empire has lurched onto a downward track, and society begins to show unmistakable signs of instability, statesmen and political people continue to talk as if matters were still as they were just yesterday. Meanwhile, nature, that baffled and refuted thing, has taken up residence within us, in our very household, and we become, not the masters of nature, but its prey.

The relation between art and nature can be demonstrated in so oblique and mundane an instance as the behavior of the stock market, in the surges and rallies, deficits and episodes of panic buying and selling, etc. And the point here, surely, is that once a system, whether economic or political, is put into place, it soon assumes a life, a vitality, and direction of its own; becomes in fact a natural force only slightly and erratically subject to control. The illusion of control, of course, is much a part of the attending problem. Hence the eternal surprise of investors and experts over market behavior, its ups and downs. Nothing is more obvious in reading the business page of a newspaper than the fact that no one, in a moment of crisis, is really in charge, or has, typically, much understanding of what is happening. And the greater the illusion of control, the more drastic the consequences when matters really begin to deteriorate.

But a real artist, and there are such in the economic and political spheres, will comprehend the energies at work, and be able at times to make of the situation a more positive and creative force. Such an art, in the field of politics, in business and warfare, is not after all so far removed from the field of art itself. The principles of selection and imitation, of precedents and their usefulness, are in many ways alike. Which is to say that human creativity can be understood in a much broader sense than we mostly admit.

Are these things of which I have been speaking in any direct or essential way related to our assigned topic, Art and Nature? I believe so. They are, after all, a sign of the way we see the world, of the kind of attention we bestow on nature, on the things of nature, and on people. For all of this too is nature, is a part of nature and its processes, if the corruption and decay of societies and civilizations tell us anything beyond being a lasting and dismal chronicle, and from which we seem to learn almost nothing.

I am thinking here of the cattle trucks I passed or was passed by on the interstate last summer: those horrendous metal cells, boxes on wheels, whether empty or filled with captive beasts, going to market or returning from it. And it occurs to me that this passion for capture and imprisonment, for what must seem at times to be a total domestication of the world, must pursue humankind with its consequences forever. For it is not far from the stockyard, with its animals penned and waiting for slaughter, to cattle cars and death camps for people. We may think otherwise, but history, that relentless ghost, tells us it is so.

The way we see and experience the world is inescapably determined by our attitude toward it, by the use to which we put nature and the things of nature, whether this means diverting the flow of a river, removing a hillside to make room for a highway, or otherwise converting land, bird, and beast to our specialized purposes. With increased technological means, and the sense of power and mastery that these seem to instill in us, the world has become radically changed. A field or a woodland, a rose or a lark, with all of their gloom and light, their vibrancy and color, are not for us what they were for Wordsworth, for Keats, for Yeats, or Thomas Hardy, emblematic of more than mere stem and leaf, feather and petal. From being places and creatures of mystery and fear, of myth and local tale, they become something else: objects of concern, of examination and analysis, perhaps, but not of enchantment.

What is missing, and for some time now, is delight, that sense of delight in discovery that renews everything and keeps the world fresh. Without it, poetry dies, art dies; the heart and the spirit die, and in the end we die. Which is to say, perhaps, that the more we know the less we truly know. And in our terrible world the original beauty, the instinctive awe and mystery, become in time a matter of nostalgia and of scenic views.

I think of the blackbirds I saw this past spring in downtown Minneapolis, hopping up from the pavement and the nearby benches with straws in their bills, and flying off to a nest they were building somewhere close by; making for themselves a life in all of that street noise, among shops, walls, and windows. The city may disappear one day, but these will go on, picking straws for a nest from the debris of an empty street.

A sudden flight of birds, rising from a tree in alarm, scattering and re-forming in a flock; and I know in that image the scattering of my own thoughts disturbed by a sudden interruption, and then once more composed. And with that image in mind, it occurs to me to say: we have no thoughts that do not come from nature.

It should be obvious to us by now that we have invented nothing. Of all that can be pointed to as human accomplishment—whether it be an electronic contrivance, the wheel as a mode of transport, a dance figure, a composition in line and color, or even a line of poetry—it can be said that the model exists in nature. The same can be asserted in reference to any field of human thought and action, no matter how apparently abstract, if we were able to trace it back to its source. And to use the figure, "field of thought" in itself evokes a certain truth.

One can say further that there is nothing in this *mind*, this imagination, this capacity for thought, that does not find its source, its example and inspiration, in the natural world. To forget this is to account for the confusion and chaos that every society is prone to sooner or later, as is surely the case with our own at this time.

To Nature, writ large, we owe every art and skill. It is, to say it yet another way, the great book we have been reading, and writing, from the beginning. Signs, clues, tracks and traces, vocabulary and syntax: it is all there. Yet we do not live solely in nature, but in history also, which is our own story and itself a part of nature. What was said in reference to the Swiss historian Jacob Burckhardt seems appropriate here:

> The significance of history is . . . not the undeniable rise and fall of civilizations, but the enduring and permanent tradition of those values created by men in a thousand situations and carried onward in the collective memory of the race as a guide and inspiration. The "soul" of the Greeks, for example, lives in *us*. And historical tradition . . . meant especially the body of the aspirations of men, a summation of the intrusions of the eternal into time, as delineated in art and literature in every generation. And here, he would say, in this strange land, half reality and half the intimation of an ideal world, is our true home.
>
> —James Hastings Nichols

It seems to me that the eternal task of the artist and the poet, the historian and the scholar (to use what are inadequate terms) is to find the means to reconcile what are two separate and yet inseparable histories, Nature and Culture. To the extent that we can do this, the "world" makes sense to us and can be lived in.

It would follow, and for many reasons implicit here, that no subsequent art has ever surpassed in power and expression the Paleolithic art of the caves, or that unsigned art of rockfaces and burial artifacts, and little has equaled it or the tribal arts surviving today. In art, certainly, if not elsewhere in human affairs, there is no progress, only change and alteration in the rise and degeneration of forms, techniques, and materials. Picasso understood this; Delacroix and Michelangelo knew it; Arp knew it; Brancusi and Giacometti knew it. All true artists have known it, and in principle and in practice have paid instinctive respect to it, in their re-invention of the very thing that is always about to be lost.

You Are Here. And in the night sky, whether obscured by clouds or brilliant with stars and a full moon, light and shadow come and go on the fields of life and death. On that ground, with its perpetual alternation between emptiness and depth, are enacted and endlessly repeated the histories of men and beasts, whether they are actual or imagined, and perhaps the two cannot be finally distinguished. The mind is a replica of what we see out there, and in its order and disorder, its capacity for expressive forms and its incapacity for any final understanding, is a reflection of that world, the only one we have.

REFERENCES

Kundera, Milan. *The Art of the Novel*. New York: Harper & Row, 1988.

Mookerjee, Priya. *Pathway Icons: The Wayside Art of India*. New York/London: Thames & Hudson Ltd., 1978.

Burckhardt, Jacob. *Force and Freedom: Reflections on History*. Ed. James Hastings Nichols. Boston: Pantheon Books, Beacon Press, 1943.

Emissaries

PATTIANN ROGERS

How will we convince them,
when we return, of the beating crimson
of the honeycreeper's body, the quaking
violet rump of the velvet cuckoo wasp,
or simply of an easy night rain
over hills, that dizzy falling, grains
of moisture the size and multitude
of stars, a rain not lull and loop
alone but a perfect elucidation
of sleep? How can we describe it to them?

How will they understand the scaffold
of logic or the shape of mercy,
with neither the informing patterns
of the swallow's nest nor the radiating
structure of needles on a slash pine
in their memories to help them, without
even the razzling of poplar leaves
in an evening wind or the intensity
of spotted trout braced against clear
currents in their speech to help them?

How will they know how to perceive
without ever having witnessed

the grasping talents of the moon snail,
the salt-marsh snail?

Maybe they won't be able to attend
to us at all, not realizing how the sooty
owl attends, how the black-tailed jack
and the hoary cress and coyote thistle
of the grasslands rise alert and still
to listen, as if listening were a place
with boundaries each created.

And when we tell our stories,
can they follow the plots, never having seen
the spreading revelation, word by word,
of the wood lily, or the unfolding
revelation of a fruit bat's skin wings?
Can they recognize resolution,
never having watched the constellations
completing their circles around Polaris,
never having studied the rising
and sinking vortexes of a sharp-shinned
hawk circling above a gorge?

Be sure to remember the surprise
among the ashy leaves, that ashy flick
of five-lined skink, living slizzard,
and the surprise of burnished mushrooms
sprouting in a ring through black forest
trash. Take notes on the spotted cleaning
shrimp at work with its silver wands
on the mouth of a great reef fish. Assimilate
each polished prick and sun-sharpened claw
of the jumping cholla and learn now
to imitate the bask of the seal,

the sleight of willows in a storm,
to recite the rigid blue illumination
of ice shelves under pressure.

We'll need all these, everything, when we return
to that place after death to tell them, back
to the silent, uniform darknesses we were
before being born on earth.

Making Amends to
the Myriad Creatures

STEPHANIE MILLS

A FEW WEEKS AGO, a friend of mine, Lowell Cate, invited me over to his place, a couple of miles northeast of my home, to have a look at his woods. He's an older man, living near land his great-grandfather homesteaded in 1868. A lot of Lowell's acreage had been farmed, much to its detriment, and was recuperating under straight, evenly spaced rows of white pine. The hardwood groves where we walked were on hillsides steep enough that the stout maples, beeches, basswood, birches, and hemlock had escaped being cleared. Over the years the slopes had been cut selectively, for firewood. Here and there stood some quite substantial trees, beeches mostly. My friend Lowell seemed familiar with them all, and recalled the years and storms in which others had blown down to await the arrival of the chainsaw and the service of the flame. In Lowell there's no dearth of feeling for the woodland and no want of lore of local land use. He's got knowledge of his home place.

As we were emerging from the leafy shadows to a spot where he'd had a commercial pulpwood harvester clear a stand of popples, I noted a burdock on the sunny margin and asked if he minded if I pulled it up, because it's a weed ("just a plant out of place," by one definition). I explained that I'd just learned a new rule of thumb to justify this act. Every alien species that establishes itself in a new surrounding displaces about ten natives. This was news to Lowell, something that he immediately began to ponder.

My point is that most of us, even people like Lowell who know and love and daily walk bits of land presumed to have been well and carefully used, usually don't see the non sequiturs or gaps in those ecosystems. It's quite understandable. The tendency of our civilization from its beginnings has been to simplify the natural world in the process of taking it over for human occupancy. In the modern era, this human tendency to transform landscapes for short-term advantage has, with the accelerations provided by rapid population growth, global transportation, and the juggernaut of industrialization, annihilated hundreds of thousands of species and made lonely relics of countless others in their dwindling habitats. Absent some special interest in botany or ecology, we haven't much sense of all that is lost in the domestication of wild places.

The difference between the whole world and one's own home, or settlement, is a fairly recent concept in our life as a species, along with the human self-concept of existing in a transcendent category, apart from and superior to rude nature. For traditional peoples, we are told, nature and human habitat were one big, if not always happy, family wherein the two-leggeds were just folks, along with coyote, raven, old doctor loon, fox, deer, and waterbug, and it was only polite to beg the pardon of the grass people upon whom you slept in the course of your journeys. Now, because our upstart civilization's insensitivity to the personhood of each member of an ecosystem threatens to bring the whole domicile down, we're being forced to remember how to belong and how to cherish. It may not be too late to begin to cultivate what culture historian Thomas Berry has phrased, with apt simplicity, as a *courtesy* toward the other beings of the living world.

Today a practice of such courtesy is developing—a discipline of learning how to beg the pardon of damaged and decimated landscapes. It is work called "ecological restoration." Barry Lopez, who writes with a sense of the solemnity of the relations of humans and nature, extolls it as "so rich in the desire to make amends!"

Ecological restoration is an experimental science, seeking the ways and means of healing damaged landscapes, attempting to reinstate their orig-

Delivered at the Eleventh Annual E. F. Schumacher Lectures, October 19, 1991.

inal plant and animal communities and revive their chartless web of interactions. Restoration ecology recognizes that habitat is complex, distinct, and essential to the preservation of diverse species. Conceding that nature is unsurpassed in its genius at evolving niches, creatures, and adaptations beyond counting, this science cares to be faithful to its ways. By stoop labor, painstaking observation, and much applied intelligence, ecological restoration pays more than lip service to the sacredness of Earth's phenomenal—and threatened—biodiversity.

Beyond that, I would say, it is work that has the potential to engender true love with the land; not romantic love, not blind love, nor possessive attachment, but a love that declares, "I want thee to be." Not platonic but erotic, it is a love that increases one's knowledge of the beloved—the myriad creatures—and of the self, through deeds.

Part of the work is in gaining eyes to see the detail of the natural world. It's finding eyes to see an ecosystem's past, to notice significant events in the course of its recovery, and to see a time of future thriving. Restoration ecology demands ingenious historic research and a little bit of schooled inference.

The motives for ecological restoration are several: Some restoration is required by law, as in mine spoils reclamation or the trade-offs implied in the "no net loss of wetlands doctrine." Mandating and bureaucratizing restoration projects can lead to low-bid jobs and very crude approximation of original conditions, vastly inferior by any measure. Satisfaction of minimum requirements is the wrong philosophical context for the mission.

It remains to be seen whether even the most exacting restoration ecology will succeed in its aspiration to restore successional processes and cradle evolution's continuity. From 1936 to 1941 Theodore Sperry oversaw the pioneering restoration of the Curtis Prairie at the University of Wisconsin's Arboretum at Madison. He is perhaps restoration ecology's most venerable practitioner. Asked how long it would take to restore the prairie, Sperry replied, "Roughly . . . a thousand years."

However appropriate a millennium is as a time frame for work of evolutionary dimensions, it is a rather longer while than engineers and agencies generally accept or abide waiting for permission to dredge, or approval of a satisfactory result. Despite this fundamental mismatch of frames of reference, a legal requirement for some kind of restoration or mitigation of damage to ecosystems marks a positive turn.

Some ecological restoration is ostensibly altruistic. (Although given our absolute dependence on the functioning of the biosphere, nothing that we do to maintain its diversity and health fails to benefit our species.) If we employ a narrower definition of self-interest, though, spending your weekends in pursuits like lopping European buckthorn saplings, scything weeds, torching grassfires, gathering, threshing, labelling, storing, then sowing and raking seed from hundreds of different varieties of rare plants is altruistic. In Chicago, and many other venues, hundreds of volunteers do this work, for the sake of the plants' survival and for gaining a new sense of relatedness with the wild plant, insect, and vertebrate communities they serve.

In the Chicago region, in a scattered group of sites called the North Branch Prairies, this seasonal round of restoration activity is conducted under the knowing eyes of volunteer preserve managers. All are engaged in stewardship of lands that are either publicly owned or held in trust by nonprofit organizations. Chief among these is the Illinois Nature Conservancy, whose basic mission is ecosystem preservation. In northern Illinois, the keynote endangered ecosystems are prairies and savannas, or oak woodlands.

One of the greatest threats to ecosystems, and a subtler menace than the omnipresent bulldozers, backhoes, and paving machines, is biological pollution, invasion by exotic plants or animals. When botanical immigrants find themselves in a happy land where no predators or pests have co-evolved with them, they proceed to outcompete the natives and simplify and generalize the landscape. Damage to the natural community offers invaders advantages, as the scruffy plant gangs crowding vacant lots and edges of woods and fields demonstrate.

Hence much of the work of ecological restoration is plain old weeding—removing exotics, restoring enough of the original structure and function that earlier, more diverse communities can regain their

ground and stand resilient against future incursions. Restoration is inescapably labor-intensive. Sometimes this tending involves the application
of herbicides or mowing. Often it entails just going into the thickets and
weed-whipping the garlic mustard, or girdling the soft maples in an oak
woodland so that they will die and admit the light that the understory
natives have been dying without.

Another, and far more spectacular, part of ecological restoration is
"ritual pyromania." The prairies and oak woodlands of Illinois are particularly fire-dependent ecosystems, communities that require periodic
burning of grasses and leaf litter for a reduction of thatch, a release of
nutrients, for the killing of invading brush. If left to their own vegetal
devices these few species of weedy herbs and woody perennials rise up
and shade out the natives—scores of grasses, sedges, rushes, and forbs
that make a dappled tapestry of life in which no single color or thread
predominates. Only recently have we grasped that fire was the evolutionary force that maintained that original richness.

When the plow broke the soil in the Upper Midwest, prairies and savannas began to vanish in favor of the relentless order of agriculture,
which depends on planting lots of the same damn thing and then defending it from all the plagues that assail even-aged monocultures. Years
later, the advance of suburban residences guaranteed that wild prairie
fires would occur no more. Thus if the rare plant communities lurking in
the shadows on preserves and parks are to be revived, there have to be
fires, and the fires must be managed with exceeding care. Benign neglect
will not suffice to ensure a future for these species.

In the summer of '91, through meeting John and Jane Balaban, who
are stewards of the Harm's Woods and Bunker Hill Prairie, I was able to
learn a little about the spirit of restoration as practiced in Chicago land.
That same day, touring a savanna restoration site with Steve Packard,
who is the science director of the Illinois Nature Conservancy, I caught a
sense of the entrancement in the work. There's a mutuality in stewardship. It begins with a desire to know the plants, to be able to name them,
and to get a sense of their ethology. Plants live as any organism must—
within ecosystems. Now, since there's been a whole lot of ecosystem

degradation goin' on, we've reached a turning point in evolutionary history when the plants need us.

The "idea that these sites can't exist without our help anymore" convinced the Balabans of the importance of their stewardship. "You can't just preserve something by building a fence around it," as John Balaban put it, remarking, "how dependent that [ecosystem's] structure is on our interference."

As volunteers like the Balabans deepen their involvement in prairie and savanna restoration, they may wind up propagating rare plants, like the threatened small sundrops or pale Indian plantain, in their gardens, a few beds away from the tomatoes. It is a further invitation to dedicated amateurs to share in a crucial botanical endeavor, and the beginning of a postmodern interpenetration of human habitat and the natural world. For restoration ecology is scientific work, involving thousands of people in what is certainly the most critical array of biological experiments now under way.

With Packard, I visited the Somme Woods Preserve near Chicago that not so long before had been a suburban wasteland. In 1913, a generous and farsighted act established the Cook County Forest Preserves for the people of the Chicago region and their posterity. But ecological ignorance and neglect led to the degeneration of these lands. In their weedy, brushy overgrown state, they were used and abused the way vacant lots generally are—for kids' rendezvous, party spots, offhand trash heaps. Therefore, thirteen years ago, a preliminary step in restoring the site was hauling away soggy car seats and quantities of broken bottles. The earlier, commonplace desolation was not hard to imagine, which made the present, resurrected beauty all the more miraculous.

Accustomed as we are to seeing rare plants and animals only in the confines of botanical gardens and zoos, it's quite a wonder to be able to tread careful trails past healthy populations of these plants in natural communities. That was my experience that day in the Somme Woods Preserve. It was marvelous to gaze across a pelt of dozens of rare, and some endangered plant species, lifting their faces to the same sky that arched over their ancestors' arrival on the empty loess plains, left 10,000 years ago after the glacier's retreat. In these open settings, restoration has become liberation.

The knowledge and ethic that had to be arrived at to effect these prairie and savanna restorations is of a peculiarly contemporary sort. It could only have been called forth in, and by, this unprecedented moment of life's peril. Most of the people who engage in this hard work both love it, and have some very bad days. The stories of human ingenuity and dedication that characterize restoration work are heartening. They suggest the correct behavior vis-à-vis evolution's precious mystery of species. People who make an actionable commitment to their life-places are among my greatest heroines and heroes. I admire their relationship to the land, or what I am able to observe of and infer from it.

The only relationship to land I can claim intimate knowledge of, however, is my own. And so as not to limn an unqualified idea of what such tenure can feel like, I mean to let some of my own experience twine around the trunk here, like a bittersweet vine whose leaves also seek the light.

Thanks to very little forethought and no slaving on my part, I own thirty-five acres of Section 26, Kasson Township, Leelanau County, Michigan. The acreage is like a foster child, and at least one of us has post-traumatic stress syndrome. By the standards of my township it's a middling-sized parcel. According to the 1880 survey, the woods in Section 26 consisted of sugar maple, beech, elm, ash, basswood, and hemlock. Of their descendants there are only a couple of little patches of second- or third-growth trees remaining, huddled along my property's south boundary. Most of the county was clear-cut for timber that fueled Great Lakes steamer traffic. When the trees were gone, the land was farmed, with varying degrees of success, varying with what the glaciers had deposited where. Corrugations just faintly perceptible in the central clearing and as-yet undecomposed cornstalks suggest what the last crop growing on this land was before it came into the possession of certain feckless hippies. Four-fifths of my part of the holding is in teenaged Scotch pines planted straight and regular as corn to hold down the naked, sandy soil.

I must confess, to my shame, that at times my relationship to this land has been quite as judgmental as my relationship with some significant human others in my life. I have "known" it to be damaged, impoverished, manipulated, and not the best. I have coveted my neighbor's woods. I have felt mortally threatened by all these wretched, marginal pines, many of them sick and dying, rightfully fearing that in a drought year it wouldn't take much to kick off a conflagration. From time to time, I have resented the self-imposed obligation to do something about all these earth-afflictions, being in my essential character a sedentary type facing a grim thirty-five acres of yard work. I envy those whose love of their land is unalloyed. Maybe it's the curse of having as yet mainly restoration eyes, but no restoration skill, back, or upper body.

Despite watching the weeds encroach, sand blow, pines pine, and fire hazard mount, I love visiting the patchwork of places out back of the house. Spectral dead pines grizzled with lichen. Stemmy, deer-browsed young maples, nuzzling right up to the pines for shelter. Small, secret clearings. Blackberry thickets and popple copses. Every ramble through the property reminds me that there is a universe-a-plenty here, with not a square foot unworthy of respect. Affection returns and I'm forced to conclude that the whole community's got to be held sacred, even the nattering of my thoughts, or nothing on earth can be.

On a wet day one August, I bestirred myself to follow a suggestion from Malcolm Margolin's wonderful *Earth Manual,* which is a guide to restoration projects for individuals. He urges the would-be erosion battler "to try to forget everything your mother ever taught you about 'catching your death of cold'" and go out in the rain and see what the water is doing on the land. Despite a downpour, it was a mild day, so I figured I could risk a soaking.

I started threading my way back through the thicket, and soon was sopping wet, squelching around dreamily sans spectacles that had been rendered useless by fog and droplets. I looked up and watched the rain falling at me out of a blotter-flat sky; I saw it course in rivulets down the trunks of the chokecherry trees. And by and by I got my new name: Woman Who Rips Up Knapweed in the Rain. Knapweed is one of those nefarious Eurasian invaders. It is the compleat weed and has come to pervade the disturbed ground where I live. Periodically I engage in hysterical fits of knapweed pulling, but it's like trying to get rid of oxygen molecules. Every day I pray for a mutant virus to annihilate knapweed.

Emerging from the pines to the south slope of a little knoll whose north face I regard from my writing studio, I see the makings of gullies. These present a more urgent and slightly more manageable problem than biological pollution. White pine seedlings planted there a couple of years ago weren't quite able to hold the ground.

Periods of drought alternating with slashing summer rains ensured that until I figured out something to do about that raw hillside, the sound of rain on the roof would just be tributary to a Mississippi of eco-guilt.

A few mornings after the rain-soaked reconnaissance, some more of Margolin's advice registered and I concocted a way to build some brush dams with available materials. On either side of the incipient gullies I pounded in some sharp sticks. Then I lopped branches from the omnipresent pines, thanking the trees for their sacrifice to the cause. I wove the branches crossways against the stakes so as to impede the water's flow and catch the soil on its way down. For now my hope is simply to prevent a blowout, which is how great ugly gashes in the land are referred to in my part of the country. Ecological restoration is yet a ways away.

Henry David Thoreau, who in the mid-nineteenth century hadn't seen nothin' yet, wrote this about ecological loss and change:

> I take infinite pains to know the phenomena of the spring, for instance, thinking that I have here the entire poem, and then, to my chagrin, I hear that it is but an imperfect copy that I possess and have read, that my ancestors have torn out many of the first leaves and grandest passages, and mutilated it in many places. I should not like to think that some demigod had come before me and picked out some of the best of the stars. I wish to know an entire heaven and an entire earth.

I came into the ecological concern at a time when the valuing of wild over tame was the rock upon which conservationists built their church. Thoreau's saying, "In wildness is the preservation of the world," was a basic article of faith. I became, minus the hikes, a devotee. One of the most startling realizations of the present moment is that the living tissue of wildness—biodiversity—may no longer persist except by human sufferance.

The psychological and moral shock of simultaneously losing that myth, or holy ghost of entire wildness, and assuming custodial responsibility for the preservation of species is terrific. To me it seems as though the fundamental ground of mind, god and being are all shifting.

I am not unmindful of my privilege in having an extra large and rangy backyard peopled with deer, skunk, grouse, jay, knapweed, and revelations unexpected—a fox's skull, an indigo bunting. It is more land than I ever would have dreamed of knowing, but I will never not be cognizant of its woundedness or wondering whether my modest, homespun efforts at restoration won't be obviated by the geophysical and climatic change civilization is producing on the planet. How are *we* to evolve in a moment when the relation of humans to the natural world has become the hinge of life's history on Earth? Taking the bad days with the good, the people I know who work at healing land and saving species are satisfied by the endeavor in some fundamental ways. It may be that they have developed what some thinkers characterize as an "ecological self," an understanding of the soul as bedded in Nature. If all goes well, and it could, someday I imagine that humanity will be a lot like them.

Song of Returnings

WILLIAM PITT ROOT

All the bones of the horses rise in moonlight
on the flatlands, dropping
from trees, squeezing out from
under rocks, disengaging themselves
from the earth and things that live from the earth
and the scattered uniforms assemble
   to the sounds of bugling come back from the stars
and what has rotted into dust reforms with a furious sound
   of whirlwind tearing the faces from the astonished living
and gold flows molten from the mouth of Cortez
   and returns to the stones and the water and the air
and the redwoods collapse back into cones
and Christ is pried from the cross and flogged and spat upon
   and let loose among fishermen who scatter to their ships
   and enters his mother's womb and enters into the stars
and Babylon reassembles and Sodom and Gomorrah reassemble
and David sings then babbles in his mother's arms
and all living things return to their sources
and the waters return to their sources
and the sun returns to the source
and the vast darkness returns
and all things are
and are not.

Three Green Thoughts

PAUL SHEPARD

1. THE SHEEP AS CUSTODIAN

THE IDEA of an *Ovisian* sentry came to me as my wife and I stood on a large ring of earth in Southern England, trying to imagine the medieval castle keep of which it was the foundation ruin. Sheep grazed quietly in the center, and it was *their* turf that protected the relicts buried beneath from the erosion of the centuries. Their droppings fertilized the protective green shroud. Like a company of mild wardens they occupied the space, giving it an air of permanence.

But that air, like the static feel of a museum, is an illusion, for such places are the filters of old havoc, piles of the dismembered and disjointed. The unspoiled-looking site had long since been sliced through and the old mounds covered up again.

Why must one dig up the past? How and by what agency do all those fragments get buried in the first place? In the Western world in particular, our sense of history (and of evolution) is intimately related to exhumation. Of course graves are part of the explanation, and the walls of villages and cities from England to Teheran were built on top of the ruins of predecessors. Fallen ceilings became new floors in a hundred cities across the Mediterranean world. Our roots are down there and we—represented by archaeologists—are like moles, otherwise blind to our origins—tunneling and nibbling at them.

Any archaeologist will tell you that relatively little of the remains of 7,000 years of town and city life actually got buried. Most of the products and belongings of vanished peoples simply disappeared, not buried at all, just kicked around, worked on by weather and time, carried away, broken up, dissolved, disintegrated. Yet the fragments of old pottery, hardware, and masonry were not randomly buried. Much depended on the local drainage, the city's place in the watershed.

The mortality of those ancient cities was itself related to the impact of people and their animals on the terrain. Throughout the "cradle lands" of civilization, the agriculture upon which the city depended developed a tangled network of canals, reservoirs, gates, and channels presided over by specialist engineers and bureaucrats.

The elaboration of the state was dependent on making land usable, and it in turn supported greater populations. As irrigable land ran out, the tensions between neighboring tribes and chieftains escalated, and as human numbers overflowed the centers, the surplus went higher up in the watershed. There they cut timber and grazed their animals. They sent down wood, skins, wool, meat—and the soil.

Upstream denudation, valley floor saturation, and conflict: The debacle came when some war, famine, or epidemic combined with the weather to unman the hydraulic works.

The sheep in grassy places represent the whole tribe of "hoofed locusts" who have toppled so much of the highlands down upon doomed societies. They (the sheep, goats, asses, horses, cows, mules) administered the internment of eleven successive Mesopotamian empires. They were the barbers or scalpers of the Judean highlands, the Peloponnesians and the Syrian upper slopes, where their dextrous toothwork and footwork buried a hundred cities. King Solomon paved the way 3,000 years ago when he sent 80,000 axmen and 70,000 haulers to take cedar and cypress from Phoenicia. Two thousand square miles of forest was thereafter reduced to four tiny groves today, the largest of which has about 400 trees. The livestock followed on the loggers' heels and sent that forest humus into the sea—or into the valleys where it simply buried the pillaged and burned remains of whatever tribal clash happened to have swept through.

In such a series of debacles are many generations. The magnificent forests of the Mediterranean rim and islands were progressively demolished and their seedlings and root-shoots eaten and trampled by livestock. The relics of that vegetation, the *Maquis* (myrtle, box, oak, olive, and olean-der shrubbery) and the even more degraded *garique* (heath, juniper, pis-tachio, viburnum) cling to raw earth between the rocks, giving an appearance of timeless austerity. The blanket of soil, once the sponge for a million springs, vanished so long ago that even (perhaps especially) the educated traveler who finds the region so picturesque considers the rough, raw land as "natural."

Still the classicist writes of the "puzzle" of the demise of Minoan civili-zation. The historian calculates the political and military factors that de-stroyed Jerash, a village of 3,000 that was once a city of 250,000. The cities of Mesopotamia faded before bloody invaders and "natural" catas-trophes.

It is possible that in some places this cycle of buildup and collapse was run through relatively quickly, while in others there were periods of sta-bility when the downstream mainworks and the upstream plundering were not so intense and a stable ecological relationship prevailed. These places were, so to speak, in the process of not being buried. Having left us less to dig up they are less well known and, being unknown, are omit-ted from our archaeological and written history.

So we come to the inverse relation of land use and history: the worse the practices the more surely the "culture" was buried for our eventual delection. No wonder Western consciousness is an overheated drama of God's vengeance and catastrophe, preoccupation with sacrifice, portents and omens of punishment of a heavy-handed Jehovah. Like the dino-saurs who are known mainly for their vanishing, the ancestors we know best, and from whom we take our style, are those who seem to have lived mainly to call down calamity upon themselves.

The whole thing seen from the standpoint of the goat or sheep might seem to be utterly reasonable. First the centuries of teeth and hooves slowly cutting loose the sides of the mountains, and finally their silent presence in the lowlands, like woolly old museum docents, inane munch-ers, watchful angels over all that stuff filed away in the basement.

2. WHY THE GREEKS HAD NO LANDSCAPES

The lack of landscape does not mean that the ancient Greeks lived suspended in the sky with Apollo or spent all their time at sea with Poseidon. They, like ourselves, had their feet on the ground most of the time. It refers to a lack of description, to setting or scenery in literature, poetry, and painting. The Romans, for example, had whole walls covered with mosaic views and a tradition of pastoral poetry with images of the country retreat.

This seeming lack of attention to the details of the terrain or accounts of plants and animals as part of narrative or myth led scholars at one time to conclude that the Greeks were either not interested in nature or had no talent for exploring it. "The literary genius of Greece," wrote Walter Greg, "showed little aptitude for landscape, and seldom treated inanimate nature except as a background for human action and emotion." Together with the ancient relics of the sculpted human figure, pottery painting depicting figures but not place, and "classic" architecture, this absence of surroundings was seen as Greek narcissism, an interest only in the relation of man and God or man and man.

For Homeric man there was no "scene," no purely external description, no nature at all in our mode of portraits of place, picturesque settings, or charming atmosphere. The non-human context was not an esthetic container of the action. For him the events were not depicted against a background, neither starkly real as in the barren sets of a play by Samuel Beckett nor conjured scenery, as in Virgilian poetry. For Ulysses, objects were never only things. Hence things are not simply acted upon; they participate, standing out brightly for the sake of the relations among them, which are messages from mind to mind.

For the old Greeks, nature was never "treated" by the artist, but was for all consciousness part of the animation. Creatures, plants, rocks did not surrender their otherness to scenery. They abided in their own right and moved in relation to the psyche, converging without simile, a true kindred reality, never merely symbolic. All terrain was an extension of what men experienced mentally and metaphysically, occupying places of existence but not different parts of a dual reality.

Paolo Vivante says in *The Homeric Imagination* that we must imagine a consciousness in which there are no literary associations, but a reality in which all events, human and otherwise, derive from common vital principles. The human feelings are expressions or extensions of more profound commotions. Greek verbs combine human and natural action, which have both a psychic and physical meaning. The word for "melt" refers at once to a state of snow and human tears. Things are not "like" other things but express a shared process.

Although there is little reference to the features of particular places in Homer, each place is profoundly unique. Each is a presence. The sanctity of the earth is locally signified by the enclosed *(temenos,)* a place often defined by horizon lines in which the the sacred is immanent. Divinity resides, characterizes it; mind and feeling have worked upon it. Shrines are possessed by the God, not built for him or dedicated to him. Because of the universality of events, human action is never separate from its other forms. Thus intense human action, says Vivante, may stop while men attend to the glitter of bronze or the resounding sea, which are part of that action. In this the significance of one thing is heightened by the mutually responsive qualities in another.

Our modern perspective of space and time in which human action is located and described may also have some of its roots in later Greek thought, particularly in Plato, in Euclid, and in some aspects of Greek theatre with its scenes and its parabasis, in which the chorus removes its disguises to comment on the action. It is this detached observer for whom the pictorial view becomes possible.

Socrates scorned the old oral traditions. By the time of Periclean Athens the Greeks may have been philosophically capable of conceiving landscape. The Roman frescoes of the first century are Greek thought in picture; painted portraits involve a distancing and eventually a setting. In Flemish painting of the fourteenth century there appears beyond the faces of saints fragments of landscape, the harbingers of a new subject matter. The revolution in visual thought, keyed by mathematics, was first incorporated in panels painted by an architect, Filippo Brunelleschi. This perspective of distance was discussed theoretically by Alberti Leon Batista in 1435 and came to be called Euclidian, distance-point representation in which space was "mathematically homogenous," ruled by "laws" of convergence. From this, various other abstract rules developed for describing the "unity" of the pictures, hence of nature. Marshall McLuhan has been at pains to point out how the application of mathematics to space organized the visual world into perspective, isolating the seer from the seen and creating secular space and man's alienation from nature. "Civilization," he writes, "is founded upon the isolation and domination of society by the visual sense." The visual sense requires a kind of human identity that is extremely fragmented. Outside the picture, the participant becomes an onlooker, a spectator. He becomes connected to the picture itself, not what is shown, a part of a work of art. Life as a work of art was born. Its relationship to nature is *stasis*: a presentation of selected fragments of visual experience. Like literature and through literature the "scenes from a life" are connected by a story.

Panofsky has said that the painting—unlike its medieval predecessors—became a kind of window. The modern reader may find this idea confusing; as we now think of windows as *connecting* us to nature. What it connects us to, however, is landscape: the window makes real the wall as a separation, its fenestration a calculated visual portrayal of certain external, "symbolic" objects. An interior with no windows is a whole canvas. The window breaks the analogical separation of symbolic and real, just as pictorial perspective or the story-line breaks it. It seems odd to say that the continuous line of visual perspective disconnects the world. The unity that is achieved is of physical space while what is fractured is the continuity in time without which there is no life. The optic culture tries to repair this by an association of the scene with a literary idea or story, but the repair is purely intellectual. It is not lived. The multisensuousness, especially the auditory quality of the Homeric world, did continue in Medieval Europe as *participation,* in which speech and the word continued to be a shared principle in the whole of nature.

For most of Western history, these two different approaches to experience have both existed. One, evident in Homeric and primitive thought, the other, apparent in art in Athens as early as the fifth century and inseparable from Euclidean space, increased with phonetic literacy, and was essential to the idea of nature as distinct from men. A contrived picture of the world is a landscape, which in our time we have come to think of as synonymous with "nature."

3. VIRGIL IN WESTCHESTER COUNTY

The appeal of suburban (or exurban) life is that it provides a bucolic setting without the concomitant monotony and trash of agriculture. Its popularity implies that we share a pervasive, almost compulsive ideal, an ideal not hammered out of personal reflection or social dialogue, but one that the culture imparts. It is an adjustable ideal. Basically, it is composed of a large yard (from *jardin,* or garden) separating the house from the street, an extensive, unbroken but undulating meadow with scattered trees that sets the house off and yet blends it gracefully with the surrounding countryside. Subordinate buildings, pools, streams, rockwork, paths, are incidental to it. Its original theme was the association of hoofed animals and dogs in a tight symbiosis with people. What it does not include in its most perfect expression are naked wire and steel fences, cultivated ground, standing crops, farm machinery, fuel tanks, storage bins, loading docks, junk or garbage piles, woodpiles, manure heaps, old vehicles, wheelbarrows, wagons, a cordon of old barns, electric wires, washtubs and washlines, pigs, and any other of the paraphernalia of the working farm.

Yet the suburban concept is not derived from a tidied-up farm. It is not a sort of Puritan or Dutch housewife or modern sanitized version. It has wholly other sources that come not directly from agriculture but via an urban dream and its esthetic consequences, interposed between distant rural antecedents and middle-class taste. Without being aware of it, even the educated habitant knows little or nothing of the convoluted history of the Pastoral.

Modern writers often use the word "pastoral" to mean anything outside the city, from farmland to the wilderness. Actually they know better, for the pastoral is a literary genre. This slipshod use of the word is uttered deliberately to minimize the variety of non-urban landscape by those whose theme is the contrast between the city and the country. The genre has a long history. Its lineage includes Theocritus, certain Romans, and a number of poets and dramatists—Boethius, Jean de Meun, Boccaccio, Sannazaro, Spenser, Sidney, and Milton. Its best-known exponent is probably Virgil, whose name, for anyone with the least smattering of literature, conjures just such idyllic scenes of shepherds and their animals as the layout of the modern country-house is intended to imitate.

What is one to say today of a 2,000-year-old body of poetry that alone created the images of the idyllic and bucolic that still fill our heads? How are we to deal with the magisterial pronouncement of Johan Huizinga that "however artificial it might be, pastoral fancy still tended to bring the loving soul into touch with nature and its beauties. The pastoral genre was a school where a keener perception and a stronger affection towards nature were learned." What "loving souls" does he mean— shepherds themselves, urban people, naturalists, or just lovers? And what "nature" does he mean—the denuded slopes of a half-million square miles of Mediterranean watersheds?

Theocritus knew the real harshness of real Greek terrain so well he placed his poems in Sicily. The Roman, Virgil, no less aware of the gap between the Campagna and "nature," set his version in Arcady. Only if you put it far enough away could the illusion of goats scrounging sprouts among the rocks be accepted as "nature." Huizinga must mean educated loving souls whose "keener perception" of classical lands was that enhancement of landscapes through Virgil's spectacles, and those of the great "naturalists"—Petrarch, Boccaccio, and the rest who used it for tales of social intrigue, satires of prominent politicians of the day, nostalgia, allegory, escape, a model of the Christian paradise, or other metaphysical imagery.

The main connection between that ancestral body of mostly defunct literature and the modern expression is by way of landscape painting and, in turn, landscape architecture. This series of emulations, each removing the modern reality farther from its model in ancient Sicily

(Theocritus's boyhood home), has been written upon at length. It can be quickly reviewed in Elizabeth Mainwaring's work and its American extensions understood in the influence of nineteenth-century architects such as Andrew Jackson Downing and Frederick Law Olmstead. The point is that this ancient revery about pastures made its way through the arts steadily and perniciously, emerging as the stereotype of suburban dwelling and rural beauty.

It is ironic that the term has come to symbolize the whole of non-urban environment, for its antecedent has no equal for ecological destitution. Looking at the epitome of its type, the country house with its graceful horses and purebred dogs, it is difficult to believe that this pattern and style of the occupation of habitat is the product of a great ecological lie.

As for the social metaphor made from the relationship of man and sheep, Aldous Huxley makes the rueful observation, "We go on talking sentimentally about the shepherd of his people, about pastors and their flocks, about stray lambs and a Good Shepherd. We never pause to reflect that a shepherd is not in business for his health, still less for the health of his sheep. If he takes good care of his animals it is in order that he may rob them of their wool and milk, castrate their male offspring and finally cut their throats and convert them into mutton." How is it that an economic activity that, as much as any single factor, is one of the most destructive forces in the world, could be so beautified? Anyone who wishes to look at the evidence can satisfy himself that grazing and browsing animals have been an agent of the collapse of Mediterranean empires, nations, and city-states and the principal means of the impoverishment of equatorial lands more decisively than all the wars. On any slope at all the goat is simply the nemesis of the land that he sends rapidly off to deltas, estuaries, and lower river valleys around the sea.

The lie is that the goat and its fellow grazers and browsers and the denuded and impoverished lands are an enchantment. It might be imagined that the ancient Greeks and Romans, the Renaissance Spanish, or the modern Moroccans and Syrians are blind to it, but the record does not show it. On the contrary, there is written evidence of every age that

some people could see what was happening. It is not a question of ignorance.

Rather, I think, the pastoral fraud is based on a selective vision. Whatever the motivations for perpetuating the geological disasters of grazing,
that economy over the centuries evoked its own artistic expressions. The
most deceptive feature of such land systems is their stability. Indeed, pastoral art has often been criticized as "static," for nothing seems to
happen; things go on for centuries without apparent change. Large ecosystems do not vanish, but they do change, often imperceptibly. Their
productivity and composition diminish to a low equilibrium. So there is
built into this complex of flocks, fields, and herdsmen an image of endurance: the abiding earth. The city has often been sacked and burned,
redesigned and rebuilt and destroyed again. Even the farm was altered—
or disappeared as its fertility was exhausted. Against these rip-tides of
political turmoil and upheaval, the politician and merchant found unfail-
ing consolation in the peace of meadow and sylvan glens, murmuring
flocks and brooks, piping shepherds, sunshine and birds.

That the shepherd himself was usually brutal, hostile, stinking, and
stupid, that the order of magnitude of destruction was more like that of
glaciers and climatic change than of battles and plagues, that the potential of the land for human well-being was degraded under asses, sheep,
cattle, horses, and goats—these were not what the harassed bureaucrat,
military chief, or tradesman wanted to see. What they did see was physical evidence of Elysium, a land of leisure where drudgery was unneces-
sary and bribery and conniving unknown or innocent by comparison.
They needed respite from the stench of cities without sewers, from rats,
epidemics, assassins, noise, and the treadmills of survival. Compared to
all that, the dung of cattle is sweet and the vacancy behind the shepherd's
eyes a relief. Things could have been seen this way especially when the
magic of art could make it so.

Theocritus, roasting in Alexandria, was dreaming of his boyhood.
Virgil is not known ever to have held a hoe in his hand; he was a gentle-
man farmer. Spenser and Sannazaro were allegorists and Pope a dandy.
Bellini and Claude, the landscape painters, were not doing portraits of

place but imagined scenes from Greek Arcady or the biblical pastoral. The landscape architects like Capability Brown and Humphrey Repton, using plants instead of paint, mimicked scenes already twice-removed from the physical world, once by the poets, then by the "classical" landscape painters.

Theocritus had been interested in the balanced joy and sorrow in life, while Virgil is said to have "discovered the evening," that is, to have associated melancholy with certain landscape effects and with lateness or time-gone-by. Thus the past instead of the distance was associated with the elegiac sentiment: the twilight reminds us solemnly of the idyllic world of long ago.

The emphasis on images and vision tells us that what was sought was a picture of that eternal prospect in the mind's eye, a world made simple and endlessly comfortable. Since the world, naturally and socially, is not simple, what can one do to realize it? The goat, under our guidance, has solved it for us. It amounts to a kind of lobotomy on the land, done not with scalpel but with teeth and hooves. There is the victim, placidly like the ex-patient in his threadbare green robe, no longer full of primeval thunder and night creatures, but all sunny and sweet, or at least mild, and as they say, "spacious."

Singing the Fins

LAUREN DAVIS

FOUR MEN KNEEL over a huge topo map spread on the cabin floor like an area rug. The glow from a dusty lamp lights the scene. Carefully concealing their zeal, the faithful plan their pilgrimage. Canyonlands.

Reverently, their fingers trace the twisting blue lines of the Green and Colorado. Chanting a litany of remote canyons, creeks, and washes, they speculate with misanthropic glee on the inaccessibility of island mesas. A change comes over them. They belch. They spit. They scratch where they itch. One looks up, eyes gleaming, and says, "How about the Maze? We could look for Hayduke's route."

Ah, the Maze. On the map its canyons twine like night crawlers. Hayduke disappeared there at the end of *The Monkeywrench Gang*— evading the law. Wild country. Good place to get lost in a hurry; or forever. The four curmudgeons stare at the map, savoring the possibility.

Although curmudgeons will say they have no use for women, they're deluded. Without women, their journeys plummet into the picaresque. Deep down they know this. So, while outwardly maintaining their irascible image, the details of our trip are worked out. South of the Maze lie the Fins, ordering the tangle of canyons into neat rows of parallel ridges. At the south edge of the Fins is a large plateau called Ernie's Country (after a cowboy who ran cattle there). We circle a spring on the map and agree to meet in a week.

The day before they leave, the curmudgeons hear the news—Ed Abbey is dead. They head for Utah with heavy hearts, acutely aware of their own mortality.   248

Melanie and I arrive in Utah beneath an evening sky spitting snow. All night, wind snaps the rainfly like a wet dishrag. In the morning we load our enormous packs and stumble to the top of the Flint Trail—switchbacks fall off below our toes. Melanie manages a nonchalant yawn. According to the topo, we pummel down the Flint Train, cross a plateau, descend the Golden Stairs, and traverse a series of canyons until we reach a spring near the Fins. Nine miles by nightfall. Amid the contorted remains of old seabeds, nine miles can be grueling. Up, down, over, around. We climb through gullies, hand-over-hand with heavy packs full of fresh vegetables. We regret our culinary ambitions. Melanie says, "This is a grunt." In near darkness, we reach the spring but find no sign of curmudgeons. After a half-hearted supper, we bed down on a large boulder surrounded by cactus.

Morning breaks warm. The scattered tribe regroups to explore the country. That afternoon, we come upon an Anasazi pictograph panel of human-like figures. Featureless faces stare off the wall into the dry desert air. Their presence seems incongruous now. We've found little wildlife, only one pothole of water, and few edible plants. Each day reveals more bone-dry, parched country. The only flowing water is a thousand feet below Ernie's Country deep in Cataract Canyon—inaccessible.

Try as I might, the country doesn't excite me. I feel as though I'm a traitor to the cause—a naturalist bored by nature. But I am bored. The sandstone canyons are dramatic, but not beautiful. They are fractured and raw, not moist and sensuous like the curving washes of Glen Canyon or the Escalante. Ernie's Country has me feeling like a gnat on the old cowboy's hand. "Ernie can keep his country," I mutter to myself. There is no gentleness here, no grace.

Early one morning, Melanie returns from filling canteens at the pothole, eyes sparkling. "I went up the canyon to look at the pictograph people again. There a herd of bighorn pecked into the wall below them. You can only see them when the sun is low."

Melanie's discovery makes me realize that each morning I have been waking up alone and wanting to stay that way. Instead, I've gone off with the herd on yet another hike to see the sights. Maybe alone the rocks would speak to me too. I pack a lunch, watercolors, journal, and head into the heart of the Fins.

Piñon jays make their raucous rounds of the canyons. Their tumbling, streaming flight pulls the sky color down into the orange rock depths. Their screeching is as loud as the canyons are quiet.

In the heat of mid-morning I stop beneath a scruffy juniper in the main wash. Crawling into its shade, I inspect the skyline. Rows of walls rise perpendicular to the wash on both sides. The walls are striped with thin, horizontal layers, each representing an epoch of deposits in the ancient inland sea. The Fins dive into the wash like immense orca whales, tall dorsals silhouetted against the piñon-jay sky. Whole pods of ancient whales turned into wren homes and washes.

I climb onto the snout of a whale and get out my watercolors. As I paint, a raven glides between the rock walls, cawing. She weaves in and out of the narrow slots, riding the thermals. Watching her feels like twining a smooth blue ribbon between bare toes. With a last call, she's gone.

I continue my climb up the beached, stone whale. Standing in the shadow of the fin in front of me, my eyes follow the edge of each wall until the rock abruptly stops, leaving a deep cutting "V" of sky. That piece of sky is spacious, endless.

Something tells me to test the acoustics of the stone. At first I am shy. My voice squeaks. I keep trying, taking deeper breaths. Single notes float out and hang enticingly in the air. I begin to trust the walls with more. I try "Ave Maria" and some Irish airs. The notes linger and become purer as they reverberate in the slot. The sounds become a tangible presence that vibrates my body.

I am awed that a sound birthed from my scrawny frame can become full—filling the cleft between the Fins and launching out into that perfect sky. I begin to sing with my whole self into that blue void between the shadowy red cliffs. The notes hold on a grand scale. No longer dwarfed by the immensity of the Fins, I am empowered by them. The light and sound, depth and darkness, mingle to produce this aria—to involve the soul. The air I draw deep into my lungs is the same air Raven used to caw between these Fins, the same air that touches each rock and cleft. I abandon the formality of Bach and the Celts to sing the Fins themselves. Wandering melodies come to me out of the air, the light, the colors of the rocks. I've never heard music like it.

I let the sounds play through me for an hour. There's no need or desire to hold the tune any longer than the last haunting note, then it is gone. Silence flows over me. I make a little bow of thanks toward the notch and turn back—transformed.

Returning along the wash, the emotional thrill fades and my mind begins to analyze—a process I wish I could stall. Mulling the experience over, I realize this land is a gesture toward a deeper appreciation of place. Its churlish nature has pointed me to a dimension not at first apparent. I wheel in my tracks and gaze back at the Fins. They look like huge baffles now—obstructions that have angled me to something much larger than my self, than my perceptions. Sometimes, wild beauty isn't on the surface. It dwells deep within, like a shy nocturnal creature. Only a kind of mischievous grace lets you see it at all.

This cracked and broken land does have a feminine aspect. There are none of the fluid red clay curves of the Navajo sandstone, but there's something else. I haven't found it climbing all over this country with the frenetic curmudgeons, but when I sit alone and listen, the invisible music pours out.

I'm not prepared for the curmudgeons. They look up with full mouths, grunt, and indicate a spot for me around a ferocious-looking pot of beans. One of them swallows, belches, then wonders aloud, "Did Hayduke really jump off that cliff into the Maze or is there a route down?"

"It's just fiction," another huffs. "We looked at that cliff and there's no way down."

"We could have found a way if we didn't have to come over here to Ernie's cow country," a third one mutters.

The first curmudgeon stuffs another very-full-spoon of beans in his mouth and continues, "What's there to do here, anyway? We haven't done a good route since we got here. I'm tired of sitting around watching birds. Why'd I even bring the climbing rope?" He swallows his glob of beans with a grunt. "Lost in the Maze is where a man belongs."

Ain't that the truth.

The next morning is our last in the Fins. At sunrise, I walk up the canyon to the pictograph people. The bighorn sheep run out of the stone. Beside the sheep I discover more figures pecked into the rock—coyotes chasing the bighorns, trying to drive an individual out of the herd.

The little coyote figures glow within the patina of stone. They seem to have a life of their own. I've heard of mischievous coyote angels who bring divine guidance at inexplicable moments. Benevolence disguised as bad news. This whole trip has been like that—blessed backwards.

A loud belch echoes up the canyon from down by the pothole. The noise startles a canyon wren high up on the wall. Bell-like notes cascade down, glittering in the morning air. I laugh to myself as all around me, the Fins begin to sing.

Resonance of Place (Confessions of an Out-of-Town Composer)

JOHN LUTHER ADAMS

Landscape is the culture that contains all human cultures.

—Barry Lopez

THE ENVIRONMENTS in which we live exert deep and subtle influences on the music we make. The sounds around us—the rhythms of the seasons, the songs of birds, the cries of animals, and the resonances of the elements—are all echoed in the music of a place.

The rich diversity of musics around the world is largely a result of peoples living for centuries within the bounds of their own cultures and geographies. Today, even in highly urbanized areas where musicians have little or no intimate experience of the natural world, there are qualities of music unique to specific places. In large measure, those qualities arise from the vitality and persistence of ethnic traditions. But how did the music of the natural soundscape influence the birth of those traditions? How does where we are influence the music we make? And how might closer listening to the rhythms of place contribute to a renewal of contemporary musics and cultures?

Since the eary 1970s, I have lived and worked in out-of-the-way places: rural Georgia, the Nez Perce country of north-central Idaho, and, for almost fifteen years now, in the interior of Alaska. Not surprisingly, I have given some thought to these questions and to the question of what it means, at the dawn of the next millennium, to be a composer so far removed from the cultural capitals of contemporary society. These questions are of continuing relevance to my work, and although I have not arrived at any conclusive answers, I have affirmed for myself some convictions about why I choose to live and work where I do.

MUSIC IN THE COLD

The natural soundscape and a strong sense of place are deep and enduring sources for my music. Like many of my generation of middle-class North Americans, I grew up in several different places, amid relatively homogenous urban and suburban surroundings. In my twenties, I sought and found my spiritual home in Alaska and made a commitment to pursue my life's work here. Through deep and sustained listening to the resonances of the far north, I hope to make music that belongs here like the plants and the birds; music informed by worldwide traditions but that can best, perhaps *only*, be made here.

As a composer in the far north, I have come to feel increasingly detached from urban attitudes and fashions. After all, the only music that has been here for very long is that which grew here—the dance songs and chants of the Yup'ik, Inupiat, Aleut, Athabaskan, Tlingit, and Haida peoples. There is a sense (illusory perhaps, but exciting nonetheless) that one just might make a new kind of music here that somehow resonates with all this space and silence, cold and stone, wind, fire and ice.

A RESERVOIR OF SILENCE

There are silences so deep
you can hear
the journeys of the soul,
enormous footsteps
downward in a freezing earth.

—John Haines

In his remarkable book, *The Tuning of the World,* R. Murray Schafer uses the term "keynote" to mean the sonic ground of a particular place; the sound against which all others are perceived. Rarely do we listen to these keynotes. Often, they are most conspicuous in their absence. On the coast, the keynote is the roar of surf; on city streets and highways, the roar of the automobile; inside most modern homes and buildings, the sixty-cycle electrical hum.

The keynote of the northern interior is silence. The rivers are frozen much of the year. Snow mutes the land. Even the wind is still, more often than not. With human and animal life spread sparsely over sprawling distances, sound is the exception. This pervasive stillness can attune the ear in extraordinary ways. As Schafer observes: "In the special darkness of the northern winter . . . the ear is super-sensitized and the air stands poised to beat with the subtle vibrations of a strange tale or ethereal music."

I listen for that music; in the growl of bootsteps on fresh snow at forty-below zero; in the haunted cry of a boreal owl and the luminous dance of the aurora borealis . . .

Listening carefully, we realize that silence does not literally exist. Still, silence is a deep and mysterious sound-image. In a world going deaf amid a technological din, it is a powerful spiritual metaphor. Much of Alaska is still filled with silence, and one of the most persuasive arguments for preservation of the original landscape here may well lie in its intangible value as a vast reservoir of silence.

To be immersed in that silence is to be near the heart of this place. As each sound passes, the silence returns. A vast and ancient silence that has covered this place like a deep, still ocean, since before Time began. Straining, you can almost hear the reverberations of the earth, stirring in sleep, centuries past; the movements of mountains, the passing of a cosmic storm; resonances so enormous that we hear them not with our ears, but from the oldest, darkest core of our being. And other sounds, unspeakably faint and so high you can almost *see* them, floating on the air, like the sunlight of a summer afternoon, ten thousand years ago.

SONIC GEOGRAPHY

The words of Barry Lopez quoted at the beginning of this essay have the undeniable ring of truth. Deep within the human imagination, we sense that nature itself is our ultimate source of creative forms and energy. And most of us tend to think of landscape as the ultimate ground of nature. To be sure, the ideal of the sublime landscape has inspired many great works of human culture. Yet there is another sense in which the notion of landscape limits our understanding and experience of place.

When Lopez speaks of landscape, the word is full of rich connotations derived from intimate personal experience of the natural world. But for many of us, landscape is something we view from a distance, within the frame of a painting, on the screen of a television set, or through the window of a speeding automobile. Such encounters with place are at best thought-provoking and inspiring. All too often, they are superficial.

In whatever sense we understand the concept, landscape alone is no substitute for authentic personal experience of *being* in a place. As with any true intimacy, this takes time. We can view a landscape in a matter of seconds. But it can take a lifetime to truly know a place.

In my recent work, I aspire to move beyond simple landscape painting with sound to explore the larger territory I call "sonic geography"—that region between environment and culture, between place and imagination.

MUSIC AND THE WILD SOUNDSCAPE

Listening attentively to the music of the natural world, we encounter a different sense of time than that of most human music. The rhythms are often more subtle and complex. Tempos can be extreme—very much faster or slower than those to which we are accustomed. But ultimately, the music of the natural soundscape leads us away from any notions of tempo and rhythm (which imply the temporal "grid" of a regular "beat") to a broader experience of the organic flow of Time.

Deep listening to wild sounds not only expands our perceptions of the relationships between sounds in time and space. It can also expand our understanding of musical meaning.

Wild sounds, as they occur in the world, are not symbols, subjects, or objects. Inherently, they do not represent or evoke anything. They simply *sound*. Their greatest power and mystery lie in their direct, immediate, and non-referential nature. If we listen deeply enough, occasionally we may simply *hear* them, just as they are. Even if we listen metaphorically, each individual sound reverberates with its own unique resonance.

Music, on the other hand, is generally quite a different matter. It is inherently a symbolic and referential phenomenon, the significance of which usually rests in the making and hearing of sounds within a specific cultural context. In most musical compositions, the relationships *between* the sounds mean as much or more than the sounds themselves.

The primal music of bird songs, animal cries, the voices of wind and water, remind us of the strange power of pre-symbolic voices and non-metaphoric listening. By integrating something of the flow of the wild soundscape into human music, we may expand our awareness to encompass not only the symbolic strictures of musical semantics, but also those profound and ancient connections between us and the larger, older world.

WORLD MUSICS AND INTERNATIONALISM

Properly speaking, global thinking is not possible.

—Wendell Berry

In the past fifty years, with the advent of widespread sound recordings, our awareness of the musics of the world has broadened dramatically. Composers of Western "art" music have begun to integrate sounds, forms, and instruments from all over the world into their work, at an unprecedented rate and to an unprecedented extent.

The influence of non-Western musics on recent music in the West has been remarkably healthy in many ways. But, ironically, our passion for the ethnic musical traditions of the world has coincided with the decay of many of those same traditions.

Mass communications and marketing are insidious for the ways in which they can transform authentic voices into mere fashions and commodities. As little-known ethnic musics become widely popularized, they may also become homogenized. The new "world beat" may contain within it the seeds of a kind of cultural colonialism, through which the unique idioms of specific places are devoured by the voracious machinery of the "music industry." Implicit in much of the currently fashionable cultural-crossover is an attitude that views the world as a storehouse of raw materials for our convenience and amusement. Whether the product is automobiles, hamburgers, or compact discs, the arrogance is the same.

Cultural exchange is as old as humanity and a natural process of cultural evolution. But I believe that any new "global" vision of culture should be based on an unwavering commitment to cherish and sustain the diversity of local cultures. Artistic pluralism is not only necessary to cultural vitality. It is also, quite literally, a matter of cultural survival.

Diversity is an essential characteristic of healthy biological systems. This is an incontrovertible law of nature. And the same may be said of human culture. The extent to which we realize the imperative for diversity in art and culture will inevitably shape our consciousness, our fundamental attitudes toward the earth itself, and, ultimately, our own survival as a species.

THE INDIGENOUS CONTEXT

We are here on this earth,
a tribe,
anybody.

—Pawnee song

Like the first photographs of the Earth taken from space, recordings of music from other cultures have given us in the West a radically new perspective on the world of music. But, as Wendell Berry observes: "Look at one of those photographs of half the earth, taken from outer space, and see if you recognize your neighborhood. If you want to *see* where you are, you will have to get out of your space vehicle, out of your car, off your horse, and walk over the ground." The same can be said for truly *hearing* where you are.

The longer I live in Alaska, the more I am drawn to the musics of its indigenous Eskimo and Indian peoples, and the more I find my work influenced by those musics, which sound so fully the sympathetic resonances of thousands of years of living and listening in this place. The sheer survival of those peoples and their musics, in light of the physical adversities presented by their homeland and the incredible social upheavals confronting their cultures, is also a continuing source of inspiration.

I hope something of the energy and spirit of indigenous Alaskan musics may eventually find its way into my own music. But I am unavoidably someone else, of another history and another culture. What I hear in other musical traditions (as in nature) will be filtered through my own contemporary perspective and experience. So my search must be to find the resonances of this place within myself.

TOWARD NEW INDIGENOUS MUSICS

> *I will build a new culture, fresh as a young animal.*
> *It will take time . . . It will take time . . . There will be time.*

—R. Murray Schafer

Composers and sound artists all over the world are turning their ears to the music of the earth, in the places they call home. Conversant with the broadest range of musics from other times and places, these artists have consciously chosen to listen to and work with the sources most closely at hand. In doing so, they are helping create genuine, viable alternatives to a dominant, cosmopolitan monoculture.

This is not self-conscious primitivism or simplistic regionalism. It is an essential part of a vital current in the flow of human culture and consciousness. The musical explorations and discoveries of the twentieth century have given us a wealth of new tools—musical and technical—with which to work. But in order to fulfill that most basic creative need—to perceive and re-create order between ourselves and the world around us—we must continually renew our connections with older, deeper sources.

There is perhaps a certain naivete in this attitude. But in such a jaded and cynical age, a little naivete may be salutary. Much of the music we make from this beginning may sound rough or tentative, especially compared with the facile gloss and technical brilliance of more cosmopolitan styles. But in time, more complete and mature statements will follow.

Writing about a festival of indigenous Hispanic music in his home, New Mexico, Peter Garland expresses his amazement at "the integrity and survival of this music," and observes that "this kind of regionalism is now no longer an isolated one, but one that embraces its own values—in the face of everything else in the world."

For those of us who have lost a sense of our own, in the face of the mass media, pop culture, and "everything else in the word," such musics remind us that we can still rediscover and reclaim our own and, along with it, a deeper sense of who and where we are. While maintaining appreciation and respect for musics from all other times and places, we can begin to make new indigenous musics, here and now.

A Tall White Pine:
Thinking about Prophecy

LEWIS HYDE

WHEN I WAS YOUNG and longed to write, I was much in love with Emerson and Thoreau. I loved the plain declarative sentences and flat statements of belief from which these men built their work. Nature's "laws are the laws of [the scholar's] mind . . . ," said Emerson. "So much of nature as he is ignorant of, so much of his own mind does he not yet possess."

Thoreau has the same confident cadence: "I believe that there is a subtle magnetism in Nature, which, if we unconsciously yield to it, will direct us aright. It is not indifferent to us which way we walk. There is a right way. . . . "

I liked that Emerson and Thoreau sort life into the sacred and profane, the important and the unimportant, the living and the dead. Take the first paragraphs of Thoreau's essay "Walking":

> I wish to speak a word for Nature, for absolute freedom and wildness, as contrasted with a freedom and culture merely civil. . . . There are enough champions of civilization: the minister and the school committee and every one of you will take care of that.
>
> I have met with but one or two persons in the course of my life who understood the art of Walking, that is, of taking walks—who had a genius, so to speak, for *sauntering*, which word is beautifully derived "from idle people who roved about the country, in the Middle Ages, and asked charity, under pretense of going *à la Sainte Terre*," to the Holy Land, till the children exclaimed, "There goes a *Sainte-Terrer*," a Saunterer, a Holy-Lander.

They who never go to the Holy Land in their walks, as they pretend, are indeed mere idlers and vagabonds; but they who do go there are saunterers in the good sense, such as I mean.

Emerson and Thoreau draw the line and make a choice. The "merely civil," the "mere idler" lowlife surrounds us, but we needn't be a part of it. That elevated tone I loved, and I loved the demands that followed on it:

We should go forth on the shortest walk . . . In the spirit of undying adventure, never to return—prepared to send back our embalmed hearts only as relics to our desolate kingdoms. If you are ready to leave father and mother, and brother and sister, and wife and child and friends, and never see them again—If you have paid your debts, and made your will, and settled all your affairs, and are a free man, then you are ready for a walk.

I was in my early twenties when I read these essays, and I longed for someone to tell me what to do. My life was not what I wanted. I had quit graduate school in a late adolescent huff. I wished to be a writer, but I wasn't a writer. The country was at war; my best friend in jail. I was stuck in a bad marriage, having neither the wisdom to improve it nor the wit to leave. I was terrified of death, convinced my heart might stop at any minute. I lay in bed unable to sleep, rebuilding in fantasy a stone wall I had once built in childhood.

And I loitered near the tables where old men were saying, "I believe . . ." and "There is a right way," and "Each age must write its own books." "Believe," "is," "must"—what beautiful, simple verbs! I wanted to talk like that; I wanted a heroic voice.

I didn't know it then, but the voice that attracted me to these essays is rightly called "prophetic." We have a tradition of prophetic literature that goes back to the Old Testament, of course, and, though it is hardly the popular style in the modern age, one sometimes still finds prophetic poems, even prophetic novels. Whitman has this voice: he makes us feel we may be one of the immortals, large-mannered, spanning continents.

As for novels, E. M. Forster once gave a lecture on prophetic fiction, and his examples were Dostoevsky, Melville, Emily Brontë, and D. H. Lawrence. I would add Flannery O'Connor: prophets offer revelation, and so would O'Connor; she designed her tales to induce in us that second sight by which we see the workings of an invisible world.

Poems and novels are not what concern me here, however. I want here to reflect on the prophetic essay, the kind that Emerson and Thoreau wrote, and others after them (among the essayists who work in this tradition—or try to—I would name Whitman in *Democratic Vistas,* W. B. Yeats, Simone Weil, D. H. Lawrence, James Baldwin, Czeslaw Milosz, Norman Mailer and Barry Lopez). I'm not here going to try to cover this whole field (let alone go back to the Old Testament). I'm going to look at Thoreau and "Walking" as a first stab at a more general description of the prophetic voice in modern prose.

Before I begin, I should say that by "prophetic" I do not mean "telling the future." The prophetic voice has an odd relation to time, but telling the future is the least of it. The prophet does not say that the price of soy-beans will go up in October or that Jackie Kennedy will soon remarry. Rather, *the prophet speaks of things that will be true in the future because they are true in all time.* In 1963, when Martin Luther King, Jr. said that if the "repressed emotions [of American Blacks] are not released in nonviolent ways, they will seek expression through violence," he was not predicting the race riots of the later sixties, he was describing the nature of things no matter the decade. Sometimes a prophet's words do come true, of course, but that has more to do with whether or not we've paid attention than it does with any prescience on the prophet's part.

Several things mark the prophetic essay. To begin with, it always has a person in it. The mock-modest demand that Thoreau makes at the beginning of *Walden* states the case well:

> In most books, the *I,* or first person, is omitted; in this it will be retained. . . . It is, after all, always the first person that is speaking. I should not talk so much about myself if there were anybody else whom I knew as

well. Unfortunately, I am confined to this theme by the narrowness of my experience. Moreover, I, on my side, require of every writer, first or last, a simple and sincere account of his own life...some such account as he would send to his kindred from a distant land.

In the prophetic essay, a person comes forward and addresses us. This person is not, however, the proud or glum or obsessed and confined first person who carries on in the journals we keep or the letters we address to estranged lovers. The prophetic first person speaks at the point where the personal touches what is in no way personal. When Dante says, "In the middle of the journey of our life, I found myself in a dark wood," the shift in pronoun lets us know, if we needed the hint, that he is talking both about himself and about every human being. "In Dostoevsky," says Forster, "the characters and situations always stand for more than themselves; infinity attends them. . . . Mitya is—all of us. So is Alyosha, so is Smerdyakov." Similarly, in *Walden* Thoreau implicitly claims he's not writing about *his* life but about *the* life, the life each of us would lead were we communicants in the church of Nature. The prophetic voice may give a "simple and sincere account" of its story, but it does so in a way that makes us feel we are reading the story of the race, not the story of one man or woman.

The second thing to say about the prophetic voice is that it asks us to imagine being free of the usual bonds of time and space. In regard to time, the rhetoric of prophecy typically invokes daily and seasonal cycles rather than the straight arrow of chronology. "We had a remarkable sunset one day last November," Thoreau tells us toward the end of "Walking":

> It was such a light as we could not have imagined a moment before, and...when we reflected that this was not a solitary phenomenon, never to happen again, but that it would happen forever and ever, an infinite number of evenings...it was more glorious still.

The conceit is typical: the prophet pushes off with a particular day and a particular year, only to swamp them both in eternity, wiping out large sections of history; one November is all Novembers, each evening all evenings.

The prophetic voice alters space as well, though here the technique is slightly different. An unobtrusive description at the beginning of Isak Dinesen's *Out of Africa* sets a tone for the whole book: "The farm lay at an altitude of over six thousand feet. In the day-time you felt that you had got high up, near to the sun...." Dinesen has a touch of the prophet, and these phrases should alert us to that fact, for the prophetic voice is spoken from high ground. Nothing in Concord stands at six thousand feet, but in "Walking" we find Thoreau climbing up whenever he can. He climbs a tall white pine and finds a flower his townsmen never saw. He climbs a hill and looks down on civilization in miniature:

> The farmers and their works are scarcely more obvious than wood-chucks and their burrows. Man and his affairs, church and state and school, trade and commerce, and manufactures and agriculture, even politics.... I am pleased to see how little space they occupy in the landscape. Politics is but a narrow field... I pass from it as from a beanfield into the forest, and it is forgotten. In one half-hour I can walk off to some portion of the earth's surface where a man does not stand from one year's end to another, and there, consequently, politics are not, for they are but as the cigar smoke of a man.

Spoken from on high, the prophetic voice strips the lowlands of their detail. Republican and Democrat, Sunday and Monday, New York and Concord—distinctions that preoccupy us in the valley are flattened out as if drawn on a commemorative plate. From Thoreau's hill the wood-chuck and the first selectman may as well occupy the same burrow.

This does not mean, however, that the prophet is above it all. He may not be constrained by the place of his birth, but the high altitudes have their own, subtler constraints. At one point in "Walking," Thoreau imagines himself higher even than that hill: "The outline which would bound my walks," he says, "would be... one of those cometary orbits which have been thought to be non-returning curves... in which my house occupies the place of the sun." We are so high up now that earth's gravity itself has been cancelled. And yet the sun's remains. Solar gravity may be (what?) thinner or more expansive, but it still exerts its pull. "There is a subtle magnetism in Nature," remember, and we cannot feel it until we get up high. There we drop the accidents of time and place and feel only the constraints of what it is to be human. High up, those constraints seem less personal, and therefore less of a burden. At six thousand feet, Denys Finch-Hatton's grave is the grave of all lost lovers. Set in space, Thoreau's house is the temporary dwelling of all of us who will one day die.

Extended thus in space and time, the prophetic voice speaks in declarative sentences. It does not debate or analyze. It does not say "several options face us," or "only time will tell," or "maybe yes, maybe no," or "studies should be done." The prophetic voice dwells in the verb "to be," from which it draws the simple syntax of belief. "This is the case," it declares, or "I am I," or "I am the Way." Thoreau's sentences are long and shapely but they are grounded in such simplicity: "The sun is but a morning star." "Every walk is a sort of crusade." "In wildness is the preservation of the world."

In the prophetic essay, declarations of belief appear in the foreground, and this alone makes it different from most essays we now read in magazines. The television show *Dragnet* used to feature a cop named Joe Friday whose interrogations were punctuated with the phrase, "Just the facts, ma'am; just the facts." Joe Friday is the ghost writer of most of the essays written in my lifetime. Michael Arlen's masterful *New Yorker* series on the making of a television commercial (later published as a book, *Thirty Seconds*) is a good example. Arlen is a genius of photorealist prose. In this case, he took a topic that cries out for ethical reflection and forswore to engage in it. Such reticence gives the "fact essay" a feel of manliness and sobriety. Like Humphrey Bogart refusing to kiss, there's nothing mushy about the fact essay.

The prophetic essay isn't exactly mushy, but it would never make it through the *New Yorker*'s fact-checking department. "In wildness is the preservation of the world." There is no way to check that fact. It certainly does not follow from evidence the way conclusions in an analytical essay follow. And yet that does not mean it is not true. Students are often disappointed to discover that Thoreau used to go into town to eat his meals with the Emersons. It's a fact: Thoreau was not a hermit. But the facts of the case are not the spirit of the case, and sometimes the spirit is primary. Thoreau didn't need to be wholly isolated to describe the solitude of our lives.

The prophet stoops neither to argue nor to cede belief to the facts, and these refusals bring us to the dangers, or at least the limitations, of the prophetic voice. Most of the vices of prophecy follow from its virtues. In particular its appeal to our desire for a unified self and a unified world. All the marks of prophecy that I have touched on so far—the "extended first person" speaking for all humanity, the rise of the particular into the eternal, the declarations of simple belief—imply that the divisions, confusions, and ambiguities marking our lives are illusory. Under the spell of the prophetic voice, we are led to believe that there is a simple unity toward which each of us might travel.

But there are times we cannot or should not make the move toward unity, either in the self or in society.

To begin with a social example, to the degree that the prophetic voice flattens out diversity, it is at odds with pluralism. If democracy begins with the call to "come and reason together," then we will have a problem with prophets, for they are not reasonable. They are particularly dangerous, therefore, when they manage to get political power—witness the prophet Khomeini and the fate of the Baha'i in Iran. The voice of fascism borrows from the voice of prophecy, and in a mass society we are right to be suspicious of it. (I suspect that the proper politics of prophecy will be, therefore, decentralized and nonviolent. Thoreau, at least, made that connection, as did both Gandhi and Martin Luther King, Jr.)

Politics is not the only realm in which the mythology of wholeness may simplify or even repress. Not all scientists or philosophers, for example, assume the great underlying harmony that Emerson and Thoreau impute to Nature and to mind. Things now seem more fragmentary, more ambiguous, than they did a hundred years ago. There are those in this century for whom even the laws of physics are only local laws, not constant over time and space. "The real [may be] sporadic, spaces and times with straits and passes . . . ," says Michel Serres, a French historian of science. To know the truth in such a world is to navigate, he says, among "fluctuating tatters," and where that is the case, the prophetic voice will not speak the truth.

Confined to the mountaintop, the prophetic voice says nothing of life in the caves and shady valleys. Down in the lowlands, the world is messier than the prophet allows. The valley is, by definition, a "long depression." There we find not death but the shadow of death, and there we find the vale of tears. When we're down in the dumps we're down in the valley, and the dumps are a jumble of all we have cast off, denied, or abandoned. Our failed relatives live in the valley and invite us to visit.

But the valley is also Keats's "vale of soul-making," and, as the phrase implies, gloom is not without its fruit. The prophetic essay leads us on a redemptive journey—about which I shall say more in a minute—but there is a redemption of the valley as well, a redemption that comes from abandoning all hope of getting it together. If you need to come apart you do not need to listen to the prophetic voice. Stop trying to be a hero. There is a time to fall to pieces, to identify with the mess of your life as it is, confined inexorably to your present age and your present apartment. Not the ever-returning sunset but this particular one with its stringy clouds and its number on the calendar.

D. H. Lawrence had the prophetic voice, but he also had the voice of the valley:

> I know I am nothing.
> Life has gone away, below my
>   low-water mark.
> I am aware I feel nothing, even
>   at dawn . . .

My whole consciousness is cliche
and I am null;
I exist as an organism
and a nullus . . .

Thoreau never says "I am nothing." He associates the boggy fens with the Prince of Darkness, and he does no work there. Death is elevated in Thoreau; we know he was depressed by his brother's death, but he wrote no essay about that. His journals fill volumes, but they contain no record of his dreams and their confusion. The prophet has risen above confusion; he cannot therefore lead us to the redemption of giving up, of not gathering one's wits but letting them scatter.

Things in the valley may be messier than prophecy allows, but they are also funnier. E. M. Forster contrasts prophecy with fantasy, and the novel that is his prime example, *Tristram Shandy,* reminds us that the comedy of the valley includes digression, coincidence, and muddle. Hermes rules these lowlands, farting, inventing silly puns, and telling lies that make his father laugh. The prophetic voice has none of the Hermes spirit, of course. Thoreau sometimes makes us smile, to be sure—the line about writing your will before you take a walk is funny, for example—but his humor always has an upward thrust. We laugh at the mundane so as to move toward the eternal. We're not talking Richard Pryor here. Thoreau never jokes about his penis, or about race relations, or about Christians and Jews. He lacks, in short, the humor of pluralism, of the particular, of fluctuating tatters—all those jokes that help us live our inexorable divisions in this body, time, and place.

Be this as it may, I listen up sharply when I hear the prophetic voice, for it offers something we cannot get from humor or analysis or public debate.

I spoke above about a sort of redemptive journey in Thoreau's essay. It has several stages. At the beginning, as in fairy tales that open with a wicked king and a famine in the land, all is not well in Concord. "Every walk is a sort of crusade," Thoreau says, ". . . to go forth and reconquer this Holy Land from the hands of the infidels." The evil days are apparently upon us. A saunterer's requisite leisure "comes only by the grace of God," and few now have such grace. "Some of my townsmen . . . have described to me . . . walks which they took ten years ago, in which they were so blessed as to lose themselves for half an hour in the woods; but I know very well that they have confined themselves to the highway ever since. . . ." Thoreau himself sometimes "walk[s] a mile into the woods bodily, without getting there in spirit . . . the thought of some work" running constantly through his head.

The essay begins, then, reminding us of our "quiet desperation" in the fallen present. Thoreau wakes our dissatisfaction and uses it to lever us out of the present and into the heights, the second stage of this journey. Here, we see the world below with new eyes. Mircea Eliade once suggested that when evil days are upon us, the sacred survives by camouflaging itself within the profane. To recover it we must develop the eyes—some sort of night vision or hunter's attentiveness—that can discover the shapes of the sacred despite its camouflage. Prophets speak to us at the intersection of time and eternity and, if we join them there, we are given that vision, those eyes. The prophetic voice is apocalyptic: It uncovers what was covered and reveals what was hidden. As we walk, we see common flowers we never saw before.

I suggested at the outset that the prophetic voice is spoken in the extended first person. When we identify with such a speaker, we are led to imagine our lives differently. We have, for a moment, two lives, the one we actually lead and a concurrent imaginary one. The second is not imaginary in the sense of "invented," however. If the prophet is speaking of things that will be true tomorrow because they are true in all time, then that second life is real even if it isn't realized. The prophetic voice juxtaposes today and eternity to make it clear that the latter may inform the former. It sets the mundane against the imaginary so that we might see whether or not they match up. Where they are congruent, we discover the true value hidden in the everyday; where they are incongruent, we discover what we may abandon. In either case there is a reevaluation, a redemption. You look at your work, your loves, your children, parents, politicians, and, as at a funeral or birth, you see what matters and what doesn't.

In the final stage of his essay, Thoreau returns to home ground. He claims at the outset that the walker must be ready to leave home never to return but, nonetheless, in his final pages we find him sauntering home with the sun "like a gentle herdsman" at his back. A true walk changes the walker, not the walker's hometown. We read in books of some distant past when there were giants on the earth, or of some future when they will return. The prophetic voice seeks to have us see that the golden age is not in the past or the future. It is here. We who have been "saunterers in the good sense" return to find the Holy Land in the Concord we left behind. Where before we and all our townspeople looked like infidels, now we see that each might be a hero. "This [is] the heroic age itself, though we know it not."

There is yet another stage to the prophetic journey, though it takes place after the prophet falls silent. The prophetic voice doesn't necessarily push us into action. It is more declarative than imperative, more revelatory than moralizing. In *Moby Dick,* Melville is fascinated by the whiteness of the whale; he doesn't tell us what to do, he sings about the mystery of evil. And yet where revelation succeeds, we suddenly see paths that were obscure before. "It is not indifferent to us which way we walk. There is a right way . . . " Most of us live in a world of almost paralyzing free choice. In America, at least, it's difficult to buy the right couch, let alone find the right way. But under the spell of the prophetic voice we can, sometimes, sort the true from the false and begin to move.

You quit graduate school, rent a room somewhere, and start to read in earnest. You hunker down in your pointless job and paint at night. You go back to the family farm and begin the fifty-year job of reclaiming the spent land. You leave a hopeless marriage or rededicate yourself to a good one. You resist an immoral war and go to jail. The heroic age will not be with us unless we will be its heroes. Great cold air masses gather on the Canadian shield and slide slowly south. Sometimes in a city at night you get an unexpected whiff of that northern air. You had forgotten that you live in a city on the great plains, and now you remember.

Contributors

JOHN LUTHER ADAMS is a composer whose works have been heard internationally through concerts, records, radio, television, and films. He has received awards and fellowships from the National Endowment for the Arts, Meet the Composer, the Lila Wallace Trust, and the Rockefeller Foundation. Adams has served as executive director for public radio station KUAC-FM, and as composer-in-residence with the Fairbanks Symphony, the Arctic Chamber Orchestra, and the University of Alaska-Fairbanks. He now devotes himself entirely to composing and to recording natural sounds for his Alaska Soundscape Project.

JENNIFER BRICE is finishing a Master of Fine Arts degree in creative nonfiction at the University of Alaska-Fairbanks and working on a book about wilderness homesteaders. She is the recipient of a Jacob K. Javits Fellowship in the Humanities.

HUGH BRODY is a British anthropologist who has worked extensively among indigenous peoples to assess the effects of social and economic change, most recently in India. Educated at Oxford, he has taught at the Scott Polar Research Institute, Queen's University-Belfast, and McGill University. His research into hunting, fishing, and trapping practices of Canadian Inuit and Athabaskans resulted in two books, *Maps and Dreams* and *Living Arctic*. His recent book, *Means of Escape*, is a collection of short stories. He has also produced and directed a number of films, among them *On Indian Land, Hunters and Bombers,* and *Time Immemorial*.

JERAH CHADWICK has lived for the past twelve years on Unalaska Island, one of the most beautiful places on the planet. Having first moved there to raise goats, he now heads the University of Alaska rural program for the Aleutian Region. His work has appeared in numerous journals and anthologies, and his third chapbook, *From the Cradle of Storms,* was published by State Street Press in 1990. Currently, he is completing his first full-length collection, *Story Hunger.*

NORA MARKS DAUENHAUER is a native speaker of Tlingit and recognized internationally as an editor and translator of Tlingit oral literature. She is author of *The Droning Shaman,* a collection of poems. With her husband, Richard Dauenhauer, she has translated and edited *Haa Shuká, Our Ancestors: Tlingit Oral Narratives,* which won the American Book Award in 1991, and *Haa Tuwunáagu Yís, For Healing Our Spirit: Tlingit Oratory.* She continues work on this series, published by the University of Washington Press, and on her poetry at her home in Juneau, Alaska.

LAUREN DAVIS lives near Mono Lake in eastern California. She is the former editor for the Mono Lake Committee, a grassroots citizens group dedicated to preserving the lake from excessive water diversions. Currently, she works as a naturalist/writer for the Forest Service in the Mono Basin. Between caring for an elderly house, a young family, and a neurotic cowdog, she's completing a book of essays on women writers and the natural world.

MARTHA DEMIENTIEFF is an Aleut who has lived most of her life in Athabaskan country. Her home is Holy Cross, Alaska, in winter and, in summer, Nenana, where she and her husband have operated a barge service on the Yukon River for thirty-two years. She is the mother of four and grandmother of ten and a high school social studies teacher with a master's in education from Harvard. A village elder, she is a tradition bearer in her storytelling as well as the activities of berry picking, gathering and preserving wild food, cooking, and sewing.

JIM DODGE has produced three books of fiction—*Fup, Not Fade Away,* and *Stone Junction.* He is also the author of several poetry chapbooks including *Palms to the Moon* and *Bait and Ice.* Other articles, poems, and short fiction have appeared in various small magazines and anthologies. He has worked at a variety of jobs, including environmental consulting and restoration, gambling, and teaching at Humboldt State College in California.

KEN DOLA, a graduate of the University of Virginia, has lived much of the last ten years in Alaska, Oregon, and Colorado. He makes his living working in the woods. His poems have appeared in *Poetry East* and the *Virginia Quarterly Review.*

DAVID GRIMES grew up on the northern edge of the Ozarks in Daniel Boone County, Missouri, not far from the formerly glacial Missouri River. In Alaska for the past fifteen years, he has lived in Prince William Sound, fishing for salmon and herring, with occasional stints as an alpinist and a wildlife filmmaker and a river guide. He currently divides his time between his old wooden boat in Cordova, Alaska, and Santa Cruz, California. He considers himself a musician but will call himself anything, even a writer, for a piece of watermelon or chocolate.

JOHN HAINES homesteaded in Alaska from 1947 until 1969. He studied painting and sculpture before turning to poetry and writing. His first book, *Winter News,* was published in 1966. Since then, several volumes of poetry and five collections of essays have appeared. *New Poems, 1980–88,* won the Western States Arts Federation Award for poetry in 1990, and the Lenore Marshall/*Nation* Award for 1991. *The Owl in the Mask of the Dreamer,* his collected poems, was published by Graywolf Press in 1993. He has taught at George Washington University, Ohio University, and the University of Cincinnati, among others.

LEWIS HYDE is the author of *The Gift,* a meditation on the situation of creative artists in a commercial society. He teaches at Kenyon College in

Ohio. His next book will deal with trickster figures (such as Raven on the Pacific coast), and will have something more to say about the prophetic voice—this time the voice of "prophetic tricksters."

WES JACKSON is founder and co-director of the Land Institute in Salina, Kansas, an education and research organization devoted to looking for sustainable alternatives in agriculture and earth stewardship. He holds advanced degrees in botany and genetics, has taught both high school and college, and has published widely in regional and national journals and magazines. His books include *Altars of Unhewn Stone, New Roots for Agriculture, Man and the Environment,* and *Becoming Native to This Place.* He is a recent recipient of a MacArthur fellowship award.

ELIZA JONES is a Koyukon Athabaskan who grew up in the village of Huslia, Alaska, where she heard some of the traditional stories told by a notable Koyukon storyteller. Later, she became involved in Native language preservation at the Alaska Native Language Center, University of Alaska-Fairbanks. There, for many years, she taught and published books in her native language. She now lives in Koyukuk, where she continues work on a comprehensive Koyukon verb dictionary, teaches her language in the local school, and, through a university teleconference course, reaches students elsewhere in the state.

MARY KANCEWICK was born and raised in Chicago and holds degrees from Northwestern University and the University of Chicago Law School. She has lived in Alaska for twelve years, working with Native communities throughout the state on tribal government issues, as well as teaching at the University of Alaska. She has won a number of writing awards and published poetry and personal essays in various journals, including *Saturday Night* and *Northward Journal.* Her essay here is the introduction to a book manuscript supported by grants from the National Endowment for the Humanities and the Alaska Humanities Forum.

SETH KANTNER was born in a remote area of northern Alaska. He was educated by his parents at night, while during the day he mushed dogs, trapped, and hunted. He received scholarships to attend the University of Alaska, and later transferred to the University of Montana where he earned a B.A. in journalism. He currently lives alone at his family's home in the Brooks Range, and is working on a novel and other writing.

JOHN KEEBLE is the author of five books, including the novels *Yellow-fish* and *Broken Ground* and a work of nonfiction, *Out of the Channel: The Exxon Valdez Oil Spill in Prince William Sound*. He recently wrote the script for a PBS documentary on Raymond Carver, *To Write and Keep Kind*. At present he is completing a work on petroleum and culture in North America.

WILLIAM KITTREDGE teaches creative writing at the University of Montana in Missoula. He is author of two collections of stories—*The Van Gogh Fields* and *We Are Not in This Together*. He also has written a collection of essays entitled *Owning It All* and, most recently, a memoir, *Hole in the Sky*. Other writing has appeared in numerous magazines and journals, and he was co-editor of *The Last Best Place: A Montana Anthology*.

JANE LEER came to Alaska in 1962 as a child, living mostly in Anchorage, Kenai, and Fairbanks. *Keeping Watch* was written during the three years of her husband's illness. She finished an M.F.A. in creative writing at the University of Alaska-Fairbanks in 1990.

BARRY LOPEZ has written *Arctic Dreams,* for which he received the National Book Award, an illustrated fable called *Crow and Weasel,* and *Crossing Open Ground,* a collection of essays. His work appears often in *Harper's,* the *Paris Review, American Short Fiction, North American Review, Orion,* and elsewhere. He has collaborated several times with the composer John Luther Adams, also represented in this collection. He lives on the McKenzie River in Oregon with his wife, Sandra, an artist.

NANCY LORD is the author of two short-story collections—*The Compass Inside Ourselves* (Fireweed Press, 1984) and *Survival* (Coffee House

Press, 1991). She received an M.F.A. from Vermont College, and lives in Homer, Alaska.

ELSIE MATHER is an interpreter and translator of her native Yup'ik Eskimo language who lives in Bethel, Alaska. She has worked as an educator in bilingual/bi-cultural programs, and has collected, translated, and transcribed Yup'ik folklore for a National Public Radio series. Among her other publications is *A Survey of Yup'ik Eskimo Grammar* and *CAUYARNARIUQ: It is Time for Drumming*. She has served on the State Committee of the Alaska Humanities Forum, as a consultant for oral history projects, as official translator at the Inuit Circumpolar Conference, and as a lecturer on Yup'ik ceremonial history.

STEPHANIE MILLS is a bioregionalist living on Michigan's Leelanau Peninsula. She is the author of *Whatever Happened to Ecology?* (Sierra Club Books, 1989) and edited and wrote essays for *In Praise of Nature* (Island Press, 1990). Her forthcoming book on ecological restoration will be published by Beacon Press. Mills's articles and book reviews have appeared in *Utne Reader* and *Whole Earth Review*. She is also a public speaker and forest aficionado.

MELINDA MUELLER grew up in western Montana and eastern Washington. She studied with Nelson Bentley at the University of Washington, and earned a master of science in biology at Central Washington University. She is a teacher of high school biology in Seattle, Washington.

GARY PAUL NABHAN has been involved in nature writing, conservation biology, and ethnobotanical fieldwork since 1975. He is research director of Native Seeds/SEARCH based in Tucson, where he also serves as writer-in-residence at the Arizona-Sonora Desert Museum. His recent books include *Songbirds, Truffles and Wolves* (Pantheon), *Counting Sheep* (University of Arizona Press), and a collaboration with Stephen Trimble, *The Geography of Childhood* (Beacon Press, 1994).

JAMES M. NAGEAK is an instructor of his native Inupiaq language at the University of Alaska-Fairbanks. He collaborated in the recording, translation, and editing of the oral history of Walter Bodfish, Sr.—*Kusiq: An Eskimo Life History from the Arctic Coast of Alaska,* published by the University of Alaska Press. He holds a bachelor's degree in sociology and a master's in divinity, and has served as liaison officer for history, language, and culture for the North Slope Borough. He has taught arctic survival classes, and is a knifemaker and hunter.

RICHARD K. NELSON is a cultural anthropologist who has spent many years studying the relationship between Alaska Native peoples and their environments. Published works include *Shadow of the Hunter, Hunters of the Northern Forest, Hunters of the Northern Ice,* and *Make Prayers to the Raven,* which was developed into an award-winning PBS series narrated by Barry Lopez. He is a contributor to the book *Alaska: Reflections on Land and Spirit,* and has written for *Antaeus, Orion, LIFE, Outside, Parabola,* and the *Los Angeles Times.* He makes his home in Sitka, Alaska, where he has been writing a book on deer.

SHEILA NICKERSON has lived in Juneau, Alaska, since 1971. She has served there as Alaska Poet Laureate; writer-in-residence to the Alaska State Library; arts director of a statewide prison education program, University Within Walls; and, most recently, editor of the state's conservation magazine, *Alaska's Wildlife.* She retired from working for the State of Alaska in 1992. Her most recent books include *Feast of the Animals: An Alaska Bestiary,* Volumes I and II; *In the Compass of Unrest;* and *On Why the Quilt-maker Became a Dragon.* She was a member of the first and tenth faculties of the Sitka Symposium.

CHET RAYMO is a professor of physics and astronomy at Stonehill College in Massachusetts. He is also a writer, illustrator, and naturalist, exploring relationships between science, nature, and the humanities. He has written seven books on science including *365 Starry Nights, The Soul of the Night,* and *Honey from Stone.* He has also published two novels—*In the Falcon's Claw* and *The Dork from Cork*. He writes a weekly column for the *Boston Globe* in which he reflects on the human side of science.

PATTIANN ROGERS authored four books of poetry before *Geocentric* was published by Gibbs Smith in the spring of 1993. *Firekeepers: New and Selected Poems* was published by Milkweed Editions in the fall of 1994. She is the recipient of two NEA grants, a Guggenheim Fellowship, and a Lannan Fellowship in Poetry, and has been a visiting writer at the University of Texas, the University of Arkansas, and the University of Montana. Her poems have appeared recently in the *Paris Review*, the *Hudson Review*, the *Gettysburg Review*, *TriQuarterly*, the *Iowa Review*, *The Georgia Review*, and *American Poetry Review*.

WILLIAM PITT ROOT lives in Durango, Colorado, when not teaching at Hunter College in Manhattan. *Faultdancing* (1986) is his latest book; forthcoming are *Trace Elements from the Lost Kingdom: The First Five Books of William Pitt Root* and *The Selected Odes of Pablo Neruda*. "Seekers, Eye-jugglers, and Seers: Ways of Viewing Wilderness," the talk Root delivered at the Third World Wilderness Congress at Findhorn, has been published in *Wilderness: The Way Ahead* (Lorian/Findhorn Press).

NANAO SAKAKI was born to a poor family in Japan in 1923. He graduated from elementary school and began to live by himself at the age of fourteen. Following his service in the Japanese Navy during World War II, he studied art, music, anthropology, and astronomy, and began to write in English. His travels have taken him to the United States, Holland, England, Czechoslovakia, Australia, China, and Indonesia. For many years, he has worked to save the coral reefs, forests, and rivers of Japan.

PAUL SHEPARD is a conservationist and teacher, active in environmental affairs for five decades, author of several books on human ecology, including *The Tender Carnivore and the Sacred Game, Nature and Mad-*

ness, and, forthcoming, *The Others: Animals and Human Being*. He and his wife, Florence Krall, are converting their property in Bondurant, Wyoming, into wetlands.

GARY SNYDER is the author of several volumes of essays and seven collections of poetry, including the Pulitzer Prize–winning *Turtle Island*, *Axe Handles, Left out in the Rain,* and *Practice of the Wild*. A member of the American Academy of Arts and Letters, he teaches literature at the University of California–Davis, and lives with his family on San Juan Ridge in the Sierra foothills.

WILLIAM STAFFORD, a longtime resident of Oregon, taught poetry and literature over many years in many places. His work appeared in the *Atlantic*, the *Nation, Poetry, Harper's*, the *Hudson Review*, the *New Yorker*, and *Northwest Review*, among others. He served as poetry consultant for the Library of Congress. His collections of poetry include *Stories That Could Be True, A Glass Face in the Rain, An Oregon Message, Passwords*, published by Harper & Row (Harper-Collins); and *Smoke's Way* from Graywolf Press. His prose books on writing from the University of Michigan Press are *You Must Revise Your Life* and *Writing the Australian Crawl*.

TERRY TEMPEST WILLIAMS is naturalist-in-residence at the Utah Museum of Natural History in Salt Lake City. Her most recent book is She is also the author of *An Unspoken Hunger: Stories from the Field, Refuge: An Unnatural History of Family and Place, Coyote's Canyon* and *Pieces of White Shell: A Journey to Navajo Land,* which received the 1984 Southwest Book Award. Her work has appeared in numerous magazines and anthologies, and she has lectured and led workshops on the female voice in writing.

ABOUT THE EDITOR

CAROLYN SERVID is the director of The Island Institute and a founder of the Sitka Symposium on Human Values and the Written Word in Sitka, Alaska, where she has lived since 1980. Her essays and poetry have been published in *Alaska Quarterly Review, North Dakota Quarterly, Petroglyph: A Creative Journal of Natural History Writing, Loonlark: Orca Anthology of Poems and Prose, World Order,* and *Western American Literature.* She holds an M.A. in English from Claremont Graduate School.

This book was designed by
Jonathan Greene in Galliard type
by the Typeworks and manufactured by
BookCrafters
on acid-free paper.